THE BEST OFFICIAL
MANCHESTER
UNITED
Quiz Book Ever!

COMPILED BY IVAN PONTING

First published in 2001

10 9 8 7 6 5 4 3 2 1

Copyright © Manchester United Plc
Text and design copyright © 2001 Carlton Books Limited

Manufactured and distributed by
Manchester United Books
an imprint of
Carlton Books Limited
20 Mortimer Street
London W1T 3JW

A CIP catalogue record for this book is available from the British Library

ISBN 0 233 99962 0

Printed and bound in Great Britain

CONTENTS

FIRST HALF

Answers - see page 11

Who said the following:

1   When the seagulls follow the trawler it is because they think sardines will be thrown into the sea.
2   My choice of challenge has sometimes left something to be desired.
3   Winning isn't everything. There should be no conceit in victory and no despair in defeat.
4   Loyalty has been the anchor of my life and it's something I learned in Govan.
5   He came a stranger and he left a stranger.
6   I always like to give value for money.
7   I think I've found a genius.
8   Whatever happened afterwards, I still had half of me at United wherever I went.
9   I have no time for longevity. Living fast and hard, that's what interests me.
10 Bloody hell, this United team could win the Boat Race.
11 I'm a footballer. But I'm also a company.
12 What time is the kick-off on Saturday, Jimmy? I can't miss the Wolves match.
13 He has a fire in his belly that burns at just the right temperature.
14 I've still got an inverted 'Mitre' stamped on my chest.
15 I never understood why the manager persevered with me.
16 I see myself as a fan who plays for the team.
17 Just because we have beaten United does not mean we are at their level.
18 I have a prawn sandwich every now and then myself.
19 Keep the flag flying. Keep things going till I get back.
20 I don't know about professional referees. They love themselves enough as it is now.

ANSWERS

Pot Luck - 2 *(see page 11)*
1 Sir Matt Busby Way. 2 Jesper Blomqvist. 3 Nick Culkin. 4 Billy Garton. 5 Chris Turner. 6 Charlie Roberts. 7 Joe Spence. 8 Eric Cantona. 9 Cliff Butler. 10 George Best, aged 21 in 1968. 11 8-0 v Yeovil Town in 1949. 12 Pat McGibbon, against York City in the League Cup. 13 Denis Law. 14 Leicester City. 15 QPR. 16 John O'Shea. 17 Richard Wellens. 18 Andy Ritchie. 19 Carlo Sartori. 20 Paul Scholes.

Answers – see page 12

1 Who described David Beckham as the finest 11-year-old footballer he had seen since opening his football school?

2 Apart from United, which other club made an approach to sign the schoolboy Beckham?

3 Where was David born?

4 Which winner's medal did Beckham pick up in 1992?

5 With which club did David spend a brief loan spell in 1994/95?

6 What was unusual about one of the two goals he scored in the Third Division?

7 David made his senior debut for United in September 1992 in a League Cup clash with which opponents?

8 That day he rose from the bench as a substitute for which player?

9 In what competition did David score his first senior goal for United?

10 Against which opponents did he score that night in December 1994?

11 In what season did David earn a regular place in United's starting line-up?

12 What was the first senior honour he secured?

13 How long after that did he have to wait for his second?

14 Against which opponents did he score famously from his own half in August 1996?

15 Who was the goalkeeper who saw the ball soar over his head that day?

16 Which England boss called David into the full squad for the first time?

17 Who were the opponents when Beckham made his full England entrance, in a World Cup qualifier in September 1996?

18 Who made his full England debut in the same match?

19 Who were the victims as David scored a goal spectacular even by his standards, a sizzling 35-yarder, in London in January 1997?

20 Beckham supplied two pinpoint corners for which big fellow to head crucial goals at Anfield in the 1996/97 title run-in?

Answers - see page 9

1   What is the name of the road which runs past the front entrance of Old Trafford?
2   Which Swede did Alex Ferguson sign from Parma in the summer of 1998?
3   Which goalkeeper did United loan to Bristol Rovers throughout 2000/2001?
4   Which versatile United defender was forced out of the professional game through ill-health in 1990?
5   Which former United goalkeeper went on to manage Leyton Orient and Hartlepool United?
6   Which star centre-half captained United to their first League title?
7   Who was the club's most prolific scorer between the wars?
8   Who was the first man to win English title medals in successive seasons with different clubs?
9   Who is the long-serving editor of the Manchester United matchday programme?
10 Who is the youngest man to be elected Footballer of the Year?
11 What is United's record victory in the FA Cup?
12 Who was sent off during his only senior appearance for United in 1995?
13 Who missed three United penalties during 1968/69?
14 From which club did United recruit new manager Frank O'Farrell in June 1971?
15 Of which club was Dave Sexton the boss before he joined United in July 1977?
16 Which young Irish central defender had a successful loan period with Bournemouth during 1999/2000 before returning to Old Trafford?
17 Which midfielder left Old Trafford for Bloomfield Road in March 2000?
18 Who scored 13 goals and made 26 starts for United before being sold by Dave Sexton?
19 Which Italian-born redhead broke into the United side towards the end of Sir Matt Busby's managerial reign?
20 Decipher the anagram: ULAP CHOSSLE

Answers - see page 10

1   The tag has been employed for various players, but to Stretford Enders of a certain age, there is only one 'King'. Name him.

2   Which wing-half who perished at Munich was dubbed 'Snakehips'?

3   'The Black Pearl of Inchicore' was which world-class central defender?

4   Who was the first Red Devil to be known widely as 'Pancho'?

5   Upon whom was conferred the identical nickname some two decades later?

6   Who was dubbed 'El Beatle' after destroying Benfica in 1966?

7   Which winger signed by Tommy Docherty delighted in the nickname of 'Merlin'?

8   In December 1972, United signed a full-back from Partick Thistle and the fans knew him as 'Bruce'. What was his real name?

9   No one was sure which was 'Daisy' and which was 'Dolly', but one was Steve Bruce. Who was the other one?

10 There's only one 'Sparky', also known as . . .

11 Which dreadnought centre-forward of the immediate post-war years was dubbed 'The Gunner'?

12 Which ex-coalminer who scored freely for United between 1910 and 1915 was popularly known as 'Knocker'?

13 To fans of both Manchester United and England, he was 'Captain Marvel'. How else was he known?

14 In his Chelsea days he was known as 'Butch' but after joining United he dropped the tag. What was his real name?

15 'The Black Prince' was a prolific centre-forward who was unlucky not to claim a regular United berth after the Munich tragedy. Who was he?

16 Which United midfielder aspired to the title of 'The Guv'nor'?

17 Which little fellow from north of the border was known as 'The Judge'?

18 Because of his bandy legs, one of the greatest defenders in United's history was known as 'Cowboy'. Name him.

19 United fielded a footballing graduate dubbed 'Bamber'. What was he really called?

20 Because his name rhymed with something edible, a versatile Scot was known as 'Choccy', but what was the name on his passport?

Answers - see page 15

1   Where was Bobby Charlton born?
2   What was the main industry in his local area?
3   Which Newcastle United star was his mother's cousin?
4   Who is Bobby's older brother?
5   Bobby was born the second of how many Charlton sons?
6   How many FA Youth Cup Finals did United win with Bobby in the side?
7   Against which appropriately named opposition did Bobby Charlton play his first senior match?
8   How many goals did he score that day?
9   Bobby pocketed his first League Championship medal in 1955/56. True or false?
10 Did Bobby play in the 1957 FA Cup Final against Aston Villa?
11 Against which home country did Bobby make his full international debut in April 1958?
12 Bobby scored that afternoon, converting a cross from which all-time great winger?
13 Bobby Charlton was a survivor of the Munich air crash. True or false?
14 How many League Championship medals did Bobby win?
15 How many FA Cup winner's medals adorn his trophy cabinet?
16 Against which club did Bobby play his first FA Cup tie?
17 Bobby Charlton was England's second cap centurion. Who was the first?
18 In how many full England internationals did Bobby play?
19 Which Bobby reached 100 caps first: Charlton or Moore?
20 Who were England's opponents when Bobby Charlton reached the three-figure mark?

Answers - see page 16

1   Who was the first black footballer to play a senior game for Manchester United?
2   For which successful club was Jordi Cruyff playing in the spring of 2001?
3   Decipher the anagram: PAJA MAST.
4   Which United player was centre-forward for Wales in their 1958 World Cup quarter-final?
5   Who were the Welshmen's opponents in that match?
6   Which Red Devil scored two goals on his debut for Northern Ireland in February 2000?
7   How many senior appearances had the young Ulsterman made for United before making his full international entrance?
8   For which promotion-seeking Lancastrians was that same young man scoring goals in the spring of 2001?
9   Which Norwegian forward failed to make the grade at Old Trafford in the late 1990s?
10 Which striker joined United from Nottingham Forest for £1.25 million in October 1980?
11 That player waited 30 matches for his first League goal for his new club. True or false?
12 For which club did he sign when he left Old Trafford in September 1982?
13 Which manager recruited right-back Alex Forsyth in December 1972?
14 From which club was the Scottish full-back signed for £100,000?
15 Which Red Devil netted four times against Southampton in February 1971?
16 Who was the next man to score that many times for United in a League match?
17 Which manager recruited Ted MacDougall for United in September 1972?
18 Prior to his arrival at Old Trafford, Ted had netted 103 times in 146 games for which club?
19 Which United boss sold him in March 1973?
20 Which club bought him?

ANSWERS

Title Trail 1995/96 (see page 16)
1 Steve Bruce. **2** Aston Villa. **3** Grey. **4** David Beckham. **5** Dwight Yorke. **6** 'You win nothing with kids.' **7** True. **8** Eric Cantona. **9** Dave Beasant of Southampton. **10** Gordon Strachan. **11** Andrew Cole v Newcastle. **12** William Prunier. **13** Lee Sharpe. **14** David May. **15** Bolton Wanderers. **16** Faustino Asprilla. **17** Coventry defender David Busst. **18** Away to Southampton. **19** Middlesbrough. **20** David May.

Answers - see page 13

1 Against whom did the Red Devils start the defence of their European crown?
2 Who was in charge of the visitors to Old Trafford that night?
3 Which Austrian opponents did United meet on their first continental journey of the campaign?
4 At home to Marseille, a former Evertonian opened the scoring for the visitors. Name him.
5 Who equalised against the Frenchmen with a spectacular overhead kick?
6 Whose persistence resulted in United's late winner?
7 By what score were the Reds beaten in the return match in the South of France?
8 Which Italians inflicted United's second reverse of that term's competition?
9 Who signed a lucrative new contract with the Reds before facing Valencia at Old Trafford, then celebrated by hitting the opening goal?
10 Which future Gunner faced United when they entertained Bordeaux in March?
11 Whose sumptuous control and clinical finish scuppered Bordeaux late in the game at Stade Lescure?
12 Who opened the scoring for Fiorentina with one of the most spectacular goals seen all season at Old Trafford?
13 Who responded four minutes later with the sweetest of half-volleys?
14 Whose header against the bar set up Keane to put the Reds ahead?
15 Whose measured nod tied up an enthralling 3-1 triumph over the Florentines?
16 Which oft-criticised goalkeeper starred in keeping Valencia at bay in the goalless encounter at Mestalla Stadium?
17 Which former Liverpool star excelled in United's goalless quarter-final meeting with Real Madrid in Spain?
18 Whose own goal gave Real Madrid a shock lead at Old Trafford?
19 Who netted twice in three second-half minutes to give Real an unassailable advantage?
20 Who responded with a sensational solo goal for United which made nonsense of criticisms that he 'couldn't dribble past opponents'?

Answers - see page 14

1 Who rose from the bench to receive the Premiership Trophy?
2 Against which opponents did United begin their Premiership campaign?
3 What colour shirts were they wearing on that opening day?
4 Who scored United's only goal on that occasion?
5 Which future United star netted for the opposition?
6 What advice did BBC pundit Alan Hansen have for Fergie?
7 The Reds won their next five League games to go top of the League. True or false?
8 Who returned to the United fold in October?
9 Which keeper conceded three goals in the first nine minutes at Old Trafford?
10 Which former United star was wearing number 26 for the opposition when the Reds visited Highfield Road?
11 Which Red Devil netted a brilliant goal against his former club two days after Christmas?
12 Which Frenchman made his debut at home to Queen's Park Rangers?
13 Who scored the only goal of the game as United beat the reigning champs in February?
14 Who was playing against his former club as the Reds secured those three vital points?
15 Which Lancashire neighbours were humbled 6-0 on their own turf in February?
16 Who made his home debut for League-leaders Newcastle against the Reds in March?
17 Who suffered a horrendous injury when United entertained Coventry in April?
18 In which game did United change their strip at half-time?
19 Where did Fergie's men clinch the crown on the final afternoon of the season?
20 Who scored United's opening goal on that joyous occasion?

QUIZ 9

FIRST HALF

Pot Luck - 3

see page 19

Answers - see page 19

1 United sold young Scottish striker Alex Notman to which club?
2 Where did goalkeeper Nick Culkin spend the whole of 2000/2001 on loan?
3 Which former Luton Town boss was a high-ranking United coach at the turn of this century?
4 From which club did Manchester United sign Johnny Giles?
5 Who paid £37,500 for him when he left Old Trafford in August 1963?
6 Where did Giles become player-boss in June 1975?
7 Which was Neil Webb's first club in League football?
8 How much did a transfer tribunal decree that the Reds should pay for Webb in the summer of 1989?
9 Who was the selling manager?
10 Neil was playing for England when he ruptured an achilles tendon in 1989, against which country?
11 For which club did Neil Webb play his final League game?
12 Of which side was Webb made the skipper in December 1991?
13 Which title-winning inside-forward did Matt Busby sell to Leicester City in October 1957?
14 Which Red Devil of the 1950s played county cricket for Lancashire, then finished his football career as a manager in the USA?
15 Which title-winning United keeper later managed Shelbourne?
16 United paid Chelsea £35,000 for which international inside-forward in November 1963?
17 With which club did that tall, blond maker and taker of goals first make his reputation?
18 Who scored nine penalties for the Reds during 1984/85?
19 Who added six from the spot in 1987/88?
20 Decipher the anagram: BRATEL NOSCLAN.

United v Liverpool - 1 *(see page 19)*

1 In October 1895. **2** Anfield. **3** They lost 7-1. **4** Newton Heath won 5-2. **5** February 1898.
6 Liverpool. **7** No. **8** United won 2-1. **9** Liverpool won 7-4. **10** Lost 5-0. **11** Joe Spence.
12 United won 4-1. **13** John Hanlon. **14** Jack Rowley. **15** Matt Busby. **16** One point.
17 George Kay. **18** United won 5-0. **19** Stan Pearson. **20** Maine Road.

ANSWERS

1 How many times did Duncan Edwards help United to lift the League title?
2 In how many FA Cup Finals did Duncan appear?
3 Duncan went in goal when Ray Wood was injured in the 1957 FA Cup Final. True or false?
4 In which Worcestershire town was Duncan born?
5 Which Midlands giants were upset when he signed on at Old Trafford?
6 How many times did Duncan win an FA Youth Cup winner's medal?
7 How old was Duncan when he made his debut in the Football League First Division?
8 Who provided the opposition at Old Trafford that day in April 1953?
9 What was the result?
10 How old was Duncan when he lost his life at Munich?
11 How many England caps did he win?
12 How old was he when he made the first of those full international appearances?
13 Who succeeded Duncan as the youngest England player of the 20th century?
14 What number did Duncan usually wear?
15 When Duncan emerged, which United left-half was Matt Busby looking to replace in the long term?
16 Who were the opponents in Duncan's last match for United?
17 On what ground did he make his final League appearance?
18 How many times did Duncan score in that match?
19 Which club did Duncan face in the last FA Cup match of his all-too-short life?
20 How many senior games did he play as a Red Devil?

Answers - see page 17

1 When did United (as Newton Heath) first meet Liverpool in senior competition?
2 What was the venue of that first encounter between the two north-western rivals?
3 What was the mortifying outcome for Newton Heath?
4 Three weeks later the clubs met again with a contrasting outcome. What was the score?
5 When did the two first meet in the FA Cup?
6 After a draw in Manchester, who won the replay?
7 Did the clubs ever meet again before the Mancunians adopted their modern name?
8 In their first term as United, Liverpool provided first-round opposition. Who won?
9 In United's first title season of 1907/98, they suffered a spectacular reverse at Anfield. What was the score?
10 On regaining their top-flight status in 1925/26, United went to Anfield in early autumn. What happened?
11 Whose hat-trick helped United thump the Merseysiders 6-1 in 1927/28?
12 When already doomed to relegation in 1930/31, United met Liverpool at Old Trafford. What was the result?
13 Who netted twice in a 2-0 win over Liverpool on the last day of 1938/39?
14 Which United hero scored a total of nine times for the club against Liverpool during various wartime meetings?
15 Which former Liverpool player was manager of United when peace resumed?
16 What was the margin when Liverpool beat United to the first post-war title in 1946/47?
17 Who was the successful Liverpool manager?
18 The first clash between the clubs since the war was also the most one-sided. What was the score?
19 Who grabbed a hat-trick in that opening post-war encounter?
20 Where was that game played?

Answers - see page 18

1   Which United midfielder was sent off in the Manchester derby in April 2001?
2   Who was the victim of the foul which led to that dismissal?
3   How many times previously had Keane been ordered off since joining United?
4   This was the third time Keane had been dismissed by the same referee, David Elleray. True or false?
5   Decipher the anagram: LEWSEY WORNB.
6   Who scored a hat-trick for United at home to Millwall in August 1974?
7   Which Irish winger scored on his senior United debut in an FA Cup tie with Bury in January 1993?
8   At the time of writing, only one man had scored a hat-trick on his senior United debut. Name him.
9   Who was the last man to hit the target twice on his Reds debut?
10 Bobby Charlton was United's top League scorer in 1972/73, his last term as a United player, with how many goals?
11 From which club did United sign Reg Allen, the keeper who helped to lift the League title in 1951/52?
12 From which Irish club did the Red Devils sign Trevor Anderson in October 1972?
13 To which club was Trevor sold just over two years later?
14 What unusual feat did he perform for that club in April 1976?
15 Which Urmston-born utility man did United sell to Charlton Athletic in January 1976?
16 Which richly promising rookie forward was forced out of the game with a back injury in 1989?
17 Which pre-war United half-back became England's first and longest-serving manager?
18 Which of the so-called 'Fergie's Fledglings' finished his English League career with a brief stint at Bristol Rovers in the early 1990s?
19 Alex Ferguson signed Viv Anderson from which club in July 1987?
20 Which club did Viv help to lift the European Cup in consecutive seasons?

ANSWERS

Duncan Edwards - 1 *(see page 18)*

1 Twice. 2 One. 3 False. 4 Dudley. 5 Wolverhampton Wanderers. 6 Three.
7 Sixteen years old. 8 Cardiff City. 9 United lost 1-4. 10 He was 21. 11 Eighteen caps.
12 Eighteen years old. 13 Michael Owen. 14 Number six. 15 Henry Cockburn. 16 Red Star Belgrade. 17 Highbury. 18 Once. 19 Ipswich Town. 20 175

Answers - see page 23

1 Estudiantes de la Plata were United's 1968 opponents in the World Club Championship, of which country?

2 What was the result of the first leg in South America?

3 Which Red Devil was sent off near the end for an innocuous gesture?

4 Which United man had a first-leg goal disallowed outrageously for offside?

5 Who was dismissed in the stormy second leg at Old Trafford?

6 Who netted United's equaliser in a 1-1 draw on the night?

7 Who thought he had levelled the aggregate scores, only to discover that the referee already had blown for full-time?

8 When the Reds next contested the World Club Championship, 31 years later, who scored the only goal of their clash with Palmeiras?

9 In which country do Palmeiras play their domestic football?

10 In which city did the one-off match take place?

11 Who received a new car as his man-of-the-match award?

12 Which United keeper gave one of the finest displays of his brief but turbulent career as a Red Devil?

13 In which famous stadium did United play all three games in the FIFA Club World Championship in January 2000?

14 In what city is that stadium situated?

15 Who grabbed the Reds' late equaliser in their opening game against Necaxa?

16 Who committed two horrendous errors within two minutes to concede an insuperable advantage to Vasco de Gama?

17 Who profited from the mistakes by scoring two goals?

18 Who added a sublime third goal for the Brazilians before half-time?

19 Which South African struck twice for United in their 2-0 victory over South Melbourne?

20 Which California-born goalkeeper made his senior Reds debut as a late substitute for Raimond van der Gouw?

Answers - see page 24

1 Where was Ryan Giggs born?
2 What was Ryan's surname before he changed it to Giggs?
3 For which Rugby League club in Lancashire did Ryan's dad, Danny, play?
4 At which club's School of Excellence did Ryan play between the ages of nine and 14?
5 Who turned up on the Giggs doorstep on his 14th birthday?
6 Of which international schoolboys team was Ryan Giggs the skipper?
7 Against which opponents did Ryan get his first taste of senior action in March 1991?
8 That day he went on as a substitute to replace which team-mate?
9 How old was Ryan on that momentous occasion?
10 Who were the opposition when he was given his first senior start?
11 That day Giggs scored the only goal in a 1-0 victory. True or false?
12 The young Welshman finished the season by joining the action for a late cameo role in the European Cup Winners' Cup Final. True or false?
13 Which nation did Ryan face when he made his full international entrance, as a substitute, in October 1991?
14 Who was the boss who gave Giggs his international debut?
15 Giggs scored with a fabulous free-kick on his first full international start. Who were his victims?
16 What medal did Ryan collect at the end of his first season as a United regular?
17 Earlier that season, Ryan supplied a semi-final winner against which opponents?
18 On his first senior Wembley outing for United, Giggs laid on the only goal for which team-mate?
19 How many FA Cup winner's gongs adorn the Giggs collection?
20 Ryan helped the Reds lift the FA Youth Cup in 1992. Who were the beaten finalists?

ANSWERS

George Best - 1 (see page 22)

1 Belfast. 2 1946. 3 Eric McMordie. 4 1961. 5 1963. 6 West Bromwich Albion. 7 Ian Moir.
8 No. 9 Burnley. 10 1964. 11 Wales. 12 Two. 13 None. 14 The second. 15 1968. 16 Yes,
in 1968. 17 Northampton Town. 18 Kim Book. 19 Four. 20 37.

Answers - see page 21

1 Which Brazilian gave Bayern Munich an early lead against the Reds in the Olympic Stadium in April 2001?

2 Who scored United's consolation goal that night as they were eliminated from the Champions League?

3 Injury forced which former United keeper to retire after only a handful of senior outings for Crewe Alexandra in the mid 1990s?

4 Which 17-year-old defender did United recruit from Wigan for £45,000 in June 1990?

5 To which Scottish club was that sandy-haired youngster sold for £265,000 in September 1994 after making only one League appearance as a Red Devil?

6 Which Mancunian had only one League outing for United before being transferred to Chesterfield in November 1956?

7 For which club did Viv Anderson leave Old Trafford in January 1991?

8 Later Viv became player-boss of which Yorkshire outfit?

9 Later still, he became number-two to which former Old Trafford hero at another club?

10 Who was United's right winger as they lifted the FA Youth Cup in 1964?

11 That winger never made the grade as a Red, but later he played more than 200 League games for which Midlands club?

12 In which Dorset town was Colin Gibson born?

13 With which club did Colin earn a League Championship medal?

14 Which former Busby Babe helped Nottingham Forest lift the FA Cup in 1959?

15 Which club had that gifted wing-half joined on leaving Old Trafford in November 1957?

16 Which former United team-mate was the manager who took him from United?

17 Decipher the anagram: CAKJ WRYLEO.

18 The father of which United keeper won a League Championship medal in 1962?

19 For which club was that title-winner playing?

20 How many times did his Red Devil son play for England?

Answers - see page 22

1 Where was George Best born?
2 In what year?
3 Who was the future Middlesbrough player with whom George first travelled to Old Trafford, then returned to Ireland homesick?
4 When did Best join the Old Trafford groundstaff?
5 When did George turn professional with United?
6 Against which club did George make his League debut in September 1963?
7 Which Scot wore the number seven shirt in the matches immediately before and after Best's debut?
8 Did George score on his first senior outing as a Red Devil?
9 George's second game saw United win 5-1, just two days after losing 6-1 to the same opponents. Who were the opposition?
10 In what year did George become a full international?
11 Who were the opponents as Best won his first full cap?
12 How many times did George help the Reds to win the title?
13 How many times did he appear in an FA Cup Final?
14 Which of United's four goals in the 1968 European Cup Final did George score?
15 In which year was George voted Footballer of the Year?
16 Did he ever receive the European Footballer of the Year accolade?
17 Against which club did George net six times in an FA Cup tie in 1970?
18 Who was the unfortunate goalkeeper on that muddy afternoon?
19 Under how many managers did Best play while with United?
20 How many full caps did George win for Northern Ireland?

ANSWERS

Ryan Giggs - 1 *(see page 22)*

1 Cardiff. 2 Wilson. 3 Swinton. 4 Manchester City's. 5 Alex Ferguson. 6 England. 7 Everton. 8 Denis Irwin. 9 17 years old. 10 Manchester City. 11 True. 12 False. 13 West Germany. 14 Terry Yorath. 15 Belgium. 16 League Cup winner's medal. 17 Middlesbrough. 18 Brian McClair. 19 Three. 20 Crystal Palace.

Answers - see page 27

1 With what sea-going vessel is Eric indelibly associated?

2 From which club did United sign Cantona?

3 That club's chairman was inquiring about the availability of which United defender when the Cantona deal was mooted?

4 Which manager sanctioned Eric's move from his club to Old Trafford?

5 During the previous season, which English club had seemed to be on the verge of securing Cantona?

6 Who was the boss of that club, whose request to stay for a trial period was refused by Eric?

7 How many league-title medals did Eric accumulate during his career in English football?

8 How many goals did he score in FA Cup finals?

9 How many times was Eric capped by his country?

10 During which season did Manchester United sign Eric Cantona?

11 How much did they pay to secure his signature?

12 For how many clubs did Eric make appearances in the French League?

13 For which of those clubs did he score the most goals?

14 Did Eric ever miss a penalty for United?

15 Where was Eric born?

16 In the words of the Nike advertisement, which year was a good one for English football because Eric was born?

17 After signing for the Red Devils, Cantona watched his new team-mates for the first time from a seat in the stand of which stadium?

18 Against which club did Eric make his United debut?

19 In that game he substituted which player?

20 What was the result of the match?

United v Arsenal - 1 *(see page 27)*

ANSWERS

1 The 1999 semi-final replay. 2 Newton Heath in 1892, Woolwich Arsenal following a year later. 3 Highbury. 4 Nine. 5 5-4 to United. 6 Roy Keane's. 7 October 1894. 8 A 3-3 draw. 9 1982/83. 10 1897/98. 11 Viv Anderson. 12 March 1906. 13 Sandy Turnbull. 14 David Platt. 15 Teddy Sheringham. 16 George Graham. 17 Arsenal had been relegated. 18 Once, in 1979. 19 David Herd. 20 False.

Answers - see page 28

1 Which former United wing-half became a coach at Old Trafford, then lost his life at Munich?

2 What was the name of the United trainer who also died in the tragedy?

3 Who was the footballing father of Peter Barnes?

4 With which club did Barnes senior enjoy an illustrious career?

5 What is United's biggest FA Cup victory?

6 What is their heaviest defeat in the same competition?

7 With which club did former Reds goalkeeper Jimmy Rimmer earn his second European Cup winner's medal?

8 Jimmy pocketed his first after being called on as a substitute against Benfica in 1968. True or false?

9 Which club did Jimmy join on leaving Old Trafford?

10 Since changing their name to Manchester United, what is the Reds' record League victory?

11 Only once since the war have the club run up double figures in one match. Who were the opponents?

12 At the time of writing, who was the youngest man to play League football for the Reds?

13 What was United's longest sequence without a League win?

14 In what year did they set that unenviable record?

15 Who was the first black England captain?

16 Who scored on his senior debut for United in a League Cup encounter with Portsmouth in September 1989?

17 Who was the United chairman from 1951 to 1965?

18 He had played for United, but also had helped which club to win the FA Cup in 1906?

19 Decipher the anagram: TREEP CHILMSECHE.

20 In eight Manchester derbies during the reign of Ron Atkinson, how many times did United lose?

Johnny Carey *(see page 28)*

1 Dublin. **2** 1936/37. **3** Scott Duncan. **4** Gentleman John. **5** Promotion to the First Division. **6** Inside-forward. **7** Outside-left. **8** Right-back. **9** Matt Busby. **10** The FA Cup. **11** 1948. **12** 1949. **13** Stanley Matthews. **14** 21 for the Republic of Ireland and seven for Northern Ireland. **15** Right-half. **16** 1951/52. **17** The Rest of Europe. **18** 1953. **19** Blackburn Rovers. **20** Nottingham Forest.

Answers - see page 25

1 What was the final FA Cup meeting of the two teams during the 20th century?
2 Who entered the Football League first; Newton Heath (United) or Woolwich Arsenal?
3 Where did United face the Gunners in their last domestic game before Munich?
4 How many goals did the teams share on that dank February afternoon in 1958?
5 What was the result of that memorable confrontation?
6 Whose Highbury brace gave United victory in August 1999?
7 When did the clubs first meet in senior competition?
8 What was the result of that Division Two encounter?
9 In which season did Arsenal and United clash in the semi-finals of both domestic cup competitions?
10 In which season did both clubs win their home fixture by five goals to one?
11 Which England international full-back left Highbury for Old Trafford in July 1987?
12 When did United and Arsenal first meet in the FA Cup?
13 Who scored all four goals as the Gunners were beaten 4-2 in November 1907?
14 Who headed the winner against United at Highbury in November 1997?
15 Who struck twice for the Red Devils in that same match?
16 Which former player of both clubs achieved massive success as Arsenal boss?
17 Why did the two clubs not meet in 1913/14?
18 How many times have United and Arsenal contested an FA Cup Final?
19 What former Arsenal sharpshooter starred for United throughout the 1960s?
20 Arsenal defeated United on their road to FA Cup glory in 1950. True or false?

ANSWERS

Eric Cantona - 1 *(see page 25)*
1 A trawler. **2** Leeds United. **3** Denis Irwin. **4** Howard Wilkinson. **5** Sheffield Wednesday. **6** Trevor Francis. **7** Five, including one with Leeds. **8** Three. **9** 45 times. **10** 1992/93. **11** £1.2 million. **12** Five. **13** Auxerre. **14** Yes. **15** Caillols, near Marseille. **16** 1966. **17** Highbury. **18** Manchester City. **19** Ryan Giggs. **20** 2-1 to United.

Answers - see page 26

1 In which fair City in the Republic of Ireland was Johnny Carey born?
2 During which season did he cross the Irish Sea to join the Red Devils?
3 Which manager enlisted Johnny to the Old Trafford cause?
4 By what nickname was Carey widely known?
5 What success did Johnny help United to achieve in 1937/38?
6 In what role was he specialising at that time?
7 Eventually he was to play for the Reds in every position except one. Name it.
8 In what berth did Johnny settle eventually to become a world-class performer?
9 Who made Carey captain of the Reds in 1945?
10 What was the first trophy Carey held aloft as United skipper?
11 In what year did he experience that glorious feeling?
12 When was Johnny voted Footballer of the Year?
13 Who was the only winner of that accolade?
14 How many caps did Johnny win?
15 To what position did Carey switch midway through his sole title-winning campaign?
16 In what season was he captain of the champions?
17 Which side did Johnny lead against Great Britain in 1947?
18 In what year did Johnny retire as a player?
19 Which club gave him his first management job a few weeks after he had hung up his boots?
20 Which club did Johnny guide to the runners-up spot behind United in the 1966/67 title race?

Answers - see page 31

1 Who was voted Footballer of the Year by the game's writers in 2001?
2 Who was only two votes behind the winner in second place?
3 Who nudged home City's late equaliser in the Manchester derby at Old Trafford in April 2001?
4 In what country did Gary Bailey grow up?
5 Which former United player discovered Gary playing abroad and sent him to Old Trafford?
6 Gary was offered his first-team debut in November 1978 when a deal for which Scottish international keeper fell through at the last moment?
7 How old was Gary when a knee injury halted his United career?
8 Tommy Baldwin played two matches for United on loan from which club during 1974/75?
9 With which club had Baldwin kicked off his senior career?
10 Which former United full-back joined Bolton and appeared in the famous 1953 FA Cup Final against Blackpool?
11 Which Manchester-born full-back left United for Preston in 1948, going on to make more than 400 League appearances for the Deepdale club?
12 Which Salford-born ex-Red Devil was playing for Port Vale in 2000/2001?
13 Who is the oldest man to play senior football for United since the war?
14 Decipher this anagram: DWRANE OCEL.
15 What is United's most emphatic victory in the League Cup?
16 What was the last season in which United remained unbeaten at home in all senior competitions?
17 How many games did that involve?
18 With which future club boss was Brian Kidd sent off in an FA Cup tie with Spurs at White Hart Lane in January 1968?
19 Paddy Crerand was given his marching orders against which opponents on Boxing Day 1963?
20 On which ground did Paddy make that unscheduled exit?

Answers - see page 32

1   By which system, now discarded, was the margin of United's title triumph calculated?

2   Presuming United didn't score, how many goals would Aston Villa have needed in the season's last game to prevent the Reds becoming champions?

3   Who was the manager of the 1964/65 runners-up?

4   Which club topped the table in September, then again in March, but finished third?

5   How many home League defeats did United suffer during 1964/65?

6   The Reds began the campaign with a 2-2 draw against which opponents?

7   United won only once in their first six League games. Who were their victims?

8   Which wing-half lost his place and was sold to Stoke City in November?

9   How many of United's forward line managed double figures in goals?

10 Which goalkeeper made his debut against Everton, the club who had rejected him as a youngster?

11 Against which club did United score a magnificent seven?

12 Which future European Cup hero made his senior debut in April?

13 Which gifted but mercurial Scottish winger played his last game for the Reds against Blackpool, the club he then joined?

14 Who kept goal for the opening five games, then didn't get another chance all season?

15 An Aberdonian half-back made his debut as deputy for Nobby Stiles in February. Name him.

16 Who scored United's final goal of the season, at Villa Park?

17 United's 89 League goals were equalled by which other club?

18 Only two visiting clubs scored twice at Old Trafford. One was West Bromwich Albion; who was the other?

19 Over how many opponents did United complete League doubles?

20 Denis Law broke United's goalscoring record in 1964/65. True or false?

Answers - see page 29

1 Which city in Greater Manchester was the birthplace of Paul Scholes?
2 How many goals did Paul score in the 1992 FA Youth Cup Final victory over Crystal Palace?
3 On which ground did Paul make his senior level debut in November 1994?
4 In what competition was he playing?
5 How many times did he score that evening in United's 2-1 victory?
6 During the following season Paul netted more senior goals than all but one team-mate. Who outscored him?
7 What was the first senior honour Paul pocketed as a Red Devil?
8 Who did Scholes replace during the 1996 FA Cup Final triumph over Liverpool?
9 Three years later in the Wembley final, Paul made a goal for a colleague, then that team-mate created one for him. Who was his collaborator?
10 Why did Paul miss the 1999 European Cup Final?
11 Scholes' goal in Milan cemented the Reds' place in that term's semi-final. But did he find the net against Internazionale or AC Milan?
12 In March 2000 Paul netted with a volley, direct from a Beckham corner. What was the venue for this masterpiece?
13 Who were England's opponents when Scholes won his first full cap in May 1997?
14 On which ground did Paul become a full international?
15 The following month, Paul scored on his first start for England against which leading European power?
16 Again, Paul set up a goal for a colleague who then laid on one for him. With whom did he enjoy that productive partnership?
17 Paul scored an international hat-trick in a European Championships qualifier at Wembley against which opponents in March 1999?
18 Scholes poached a late winner as United came from behind against which French opponents at Old Trafford in September 1999?
19 Paul's first senior hat-trick for the Red Devils came in the 7-1 annihilation of which United at Old Trafford in April 2000?
20 Paul was sent off for two bookable offenses in which FA Cup quarter-final?

Pot Luck - 7 *(see page 29)*

ANSWERS

1 Teddy Sheringham. 2 David Beckham. 3 Steve Howey. 4 South Africa. 5 Eddie Lewis. 6 Jim Blyth of Coventry. 7 29 years old. 8 Chelsea. 9 Arsenal. 10 John Ball. 11 Joe Walton. 12 Michael Twiss. 13 Jack Warner at 38 years and 213 days. 14 Andrew Cole. 15 7-2 against Newcastle United in October 1976. 16 1982/83. 17 29 games. 18 Joe Kinnear. 19 Burnley. 20 Turf Moor.

Answers - see page 30

1 Who scored a Boxing Day hat-trick for United at home to Nottingham Forest in 1961?

2 Decipher the anagram: LIBL KOFUSLE.

3 With which Scottish club did goalkeeper Gary Walsh spend a period on loan during 1988/89?

4 Which former United player made a successful £250,000 bid to take Gary to The Riverside?

5 Which opponents made United the first team from the top division to be knocked out of the FA Cup by penalty shoot-out in 1992?

6 Which was Peter Barnes's second League club?

7 And his third?

8 Which England star made his only appearance for United in a League Cup encounter with Bournemouth?

9 Who was United's star left-winger during their successful era before the First World War?

10 Which blond central defender, who won a Second Division title medal with Burnley, did Tommy Docherty sign for the second time in May 1976?

11 With which club did Ian Ure reach the semi-finals of the European Cup in 1963?

12 From which club did United recruit Ure in August 1969?

13 Who was the first player to be sent off in a Manchester derby?

14 How many times have United won the League and FA Cup double?

15 The Reds have won that double more times than any other club. True or false?

16 Who is the only player to captain clubs to victory in both the Scottish Cup and the FA Cup?

17 Which United man has made most League Cup appearances (51)?

18 Who inflicted on the Red Devils their heaviest League Cup defeat?

19 Which goalkeeper has made most senior appearances for United?

20 How many England caps did Viv Anderson claim?

ANSWERS

Title Trail 1964/65 *(see page 30)*
1 Goal average. 2 Nineteen. 3 Don Revie of Leeds United. 4 Chelsea. 5 One. 6 West Bromwich Albion. 7 West Ham. 8 Maurice Setters. 9 All five. 10 Pat Dunne. 11 Aston Villa. 12 John Aston Jnr. 13 Ian Moir. 14 David Gaskell. 15 John Fitzpatrick. 16 Bobby Charlton. 17 Chelsea. 18 Burnley. 19 Six. 20 False.

Answers - see page 35

1 By what tag, borrowed from an ex-Old Trafford namesake, was the swashbuckling Pearson known to his fans?

2 From which club was Stuart signed during the summer of 1974?

3 Name the player who went the other way in the £200,000 deal.

4 Pearson was out on his own at the top of United's League scoring charts in his first two seasons, but with whom did he share that honour in his third?

5 Stuart scored 22 League goals during the Red Devils' Second Division campaign of 1974/75. True or false?

6 Who were the victims as Stuart grabbed his only senior hat-trick for the club in November 1974?

7 How many times did Stuart play for England at full international level?

8 How many goals did he score for his country?

9 Who first picked Stuart for England in May 1976?

10 Who was the England boss when Pearson's international career ended two years later?

11 How many FA Cup Final goals did Stuart score for the Red Devils?

12 A knee injury sidelined Pearson for virtually the whole of which season?

13 Stuart's final game for United was an FA Cup draw against which Londoners?

14 Which Old Trafford manager sold Pearson in August 1979?

15 Stuart's new employers were . . ?

16 What were United paid for his services?

17 For which England star did Stuart set up the only goal of the FA Cup Final in his first term at his new club?

18 In 1985 Stuart played Rugby Union for which club?

19 With which non-League club did Pearson enter management?

20 Of which Midlands club was he caretaker manager for a brief spell in 1991?

---

1 Against which Irish side did United kick off the campaign with a 6-0 away victory?
2 Who netted twice that day in his home city of Dublin?
3 Which Red Devil deputised for the injured Eddie Colman?
4 The Old Trafford return was a much tighter affair. What was the score?
5 Whose goal set United on the victory path in their next tie, at home to Dukla Prague?
6 The Reds lost the return in Czechoslovakia. By what score?
7 Who scored a rare goal in the home quarter-final victory over Red Star Belgrade?
8 Which Welsh youngster made his European debut in that match?
9 Who was the expensive new goalkeeper United fielded against Red Star?
10 By what aggregate score did United defeat the Yugoslavian champions?
11 Who netted twice for United in the second leg?
12 Who was the only man to play in every match for the Reds during their first two European Cup campaigns?
13 How many players lost their lives in the Munich air crash, on the way home from Belgrade?
14 What was the date of the disaster?
15 Two players survived the crash but never played again, including an England winger. Name him.
16 The other was a Northern Irish international centre-half who had played also at inside-forward and wing-half. Who was he?
17 Who took over team affairs while Matt Busby recovered from his injuries?
18 Among those who perished was a reserve full-back. What was his name?
19 Only two of the survivors played in United's next match, an FA Cup tie. One was Harry Gregg; who was the other?
20 It was less than three months after the crash when the Reds played their semi-final. True or false?

Answers - see page 33

1 Which international keeper made his senior debut for United on the day they lifted the Premiership title in April 2001?

2 Which teenage centre-half made his only League appearance for the Reds at Upton Park in March 1964?

3 A tackle by which Blackburn player left young winger Ben Thornley with a chronic knee injury in the spring of 1994?

4 What is the highest number of players United have used in senior competition in a single season?

5 To which club was the recovered Ben transferred in the summer of 1998?

6 Who was Thornley's first boss away from Old Trafford?

7 How many goals did Ben score in his 14 senior outings for United?

8 Which manager recruited Mickey Thomas to the United cause?

9 From which club was the workaholic Welsh international midfielder signed?

10 When Mickey left Old Trafford, he joined Everton in a deal involving which England international?

11 Decipher the anagram: OGRER NERBY.

12 With which club did Ernie Taylor pick up his first FA Cup winner's medal?

13 He played inside-right to which great right winger when he pocketed his second two years later?

14 For which club was Ernie appearing on that memorable occasion?

15 In what season did Ernie seek to make it a hat-trick of winners' medals with United?

16 Gordon Strachan was awarded the CBE in 1993. True or false?

17 Which was Strachan's first senior club?

18 With which club did he thrive under Alex Ferguson before joining United?

19 Which club did he help to pip the Red Devils for the League title?

20 With which club did Strachan enter management?

Answers - see page 34

1 Where was Matt Busby born?
2 Which was Matt's first professional club as a footballer?
3 What was his playing position?
4 How many full Scottish international caps did Matt win?
5 For which club was Matt playing when he hung up his boots?
6 In what year did he become manager of Manchester United?
7 Who was his predecessor as Old Trafford boss?
8 What was Matt's first senior match in charge?
9 What League position did the Red Devils occupy at the end of each of Matt's first three seasons at the helm?
10 What was United's first trophy of the Busby era?
11 What was Matt's view of the 'Busby Babes' tag for his young team of the 1950s?
12 How many times did Busby's sides claim the League title during the 1950s?
13 How many championship crowns did he lift during the 1960s?
14 In what year did he become Sir Matt?
15 What was the name of his son, who signed for Blackburn but never made the grade?
16 Which United player of the 1950s became Busby's son-in-law?
17 Who took over team affairs from Sir Matt in April 1969?
18 For what period did Busby resume control temporarily?
19 In what year did Sir Matt Busby die?
20 How old was he?

Answers - see page 39

1 Who did Alex Ferguson succeed as manager of Manchester United?
2 When did Fergie take the reins at Old Trafford?
3 What was the full name of England's top division at the time?
4 Which of Fergie's former Aberdeen stars did he find already at Old Trafford?
5 Which goalkeeper was to follow Ferguson from Aberdeen to Manchester?
6 What was Alex's first match with United?
7 Where in the table did United finish in Fergie's first full season south of the border?
8 Which England full-back became Alex's first buy, from Arsenal in July 1987?
9 Which Scottish international marksman arrived from Celtic in the same month?
10 What name did the press coin for the young players Alex blooded early in his reign?
11 Which former hero did Fergie restore to Old Trafford in the summer of 1988?
12 Which striker did pundits credit with saving Ferguson's job thanks to a goal against Nottingham Forest in January 1990?
13 What was United's first major trophy success under Alex?
14 Who succeeded Archie Knox as Alex Ferguson's number two?
15 Which many-capped Irish defender did Fergie recruit from Luton in autumn 1988?
16 Alex plucked a tall, shaven-headed marksman from the comparative obscurity of Cambridge United in 1992. Who was he?
17 Which versatile Welshman did Alex employ at left-back throughout most of 1990/91?
18 Which member of the Ferguson family earned a Premier League medal in 1992/93?
19 Which Watford star, much admired by Alex, chose to join Liverpool rather than United in 1987?
20 In the 1988 close-season, which midfielder assured Fergie that he would join United, but later changed his mind?

Give the nicknames of the following opponents faced by Manchester United during season 2000/2001:

1 Sunderland
2 Leicester City
3 West Ham United
4 Arsenal
5 Coventry City
6 Watford
7 Bradford City
8 Everton
9 Fulham
10 Leeds United
11 Chelsea
12 Newcastle United
13 Ipswich Town
14 Charlton Athletic
15 Derby County
16 Southampton
17 Liverpool
18 Tottenham Hotspur
19 Manchester City
20 Middlesbrough

Answers - see page 37

1 What is Andrew Cole's biggest haul of goals in a single match for the Red Devils?
2 Who were Andrew's victims on that record-breaking day in March 1995?
3 Who was the goalkeeper who suffered?
4 What was the result of the match?
5 From which club did Alex Ferguson sign Andrew Cole in January 1995?
6 Which United winger travelled in the opposite direction as part of the deal?
7 Who did Andrew succeed as United's highest scorer in Europe's premier competition?
8 Against which opposition did Cole grab a hat-trick as he established that new record at Old Trafford in September 2000?
9 Which has been Andrew's most prolific League season since arriving at Old Trafford?
10 What was his tally in that glorious Premiership campaign?
11 Who were the opponents when Cole made his United debut at Old Trafford in January 1995?
12 Andrew scored the only goal of the match that day. True or false?
13 Cole netted on both occasions that United lifted the title on the season's last day. He did it against Spurs in 1999; who were his other victims?
14 Against which Dutchmen did Andrew score his first European hat-trick?
15 What is Andrew's highest tally in one match against his former employers, Newcastle?
16 Against which nation did Cole make his full England debut, at Wembley in March 1994?
17 Who were the opponents when Andrew broke his international scoring duck in a World Cup qualifier in March 2001?
18 After that match, Cole had a collection of how many full caps?
19 With which club did Andrew begin his senior football career?
20 For which West Country club did Andrew shine in the early 1990s?

Fergie at United - 1 (see page 37)

ANSWERS

1 Ron Atkinson. 2 November 1986. 3 The Today League Division One. 4 Gordon Strachan. 5 Jim Leighton. 6 Away to Oxford United. 7 Runners-up. 8 Viv Anderson. 9 Brian McClair. 10 Fergie's Fledglings. 11 Mark Hughes. 12 Mark Robins. 13 The FA Cup in 1990. 14 Brian Kidd. 15 Mal Donaghy. 16 Dion Dublin. 17 Clayton Blackmore. 18 Darren Ferguson. 19 John Barnes. 20 Paul Gascoigne.

Answers - see page 38

1 Including replays, United featured in 33 FA Cup semi-final matches in the ninety years between 1909 and 1999. True or false?

2 The Red Devils faced one club six times (replays included), more than any other, at that stage of the competition. Was it Leeds or Liverpool?

3 Who were United's semi-final opponents on the way to FA Cup glory in 1909?

4 What was the venue for that single-goal triumph in 1909?

5 Who beat the Reds 3-0 in the last four in 1926?

6 Who scored a hat-trick as United defeated Derby County on the way to Wembley in 1948?

7 Who netted for the Reds in their 1-1 draw against Wolves in 1949?

8 Which ground hosted the 1949 replay against the Molineux club?

9 By what margin did Wolves triumph?

10 Who were United's last-four opponents in 1957?

11 Who scored against his former club in that 1957 encounter at Hillsborough?

12 Who played at centre-forward and scored the first FA Cup goal of his career in that same semi-final?

13 Who netted twice as the Reds drew 2-2 with Fulham in 1958?

14 Which future TV pundit supplied a goal for the Cottagers?

15 Whose hat-trick was crucial to the Reds' replay triumph?

16 Which Welsh international wore United's number-seven shirt during both meetings with Fulham?

17 On which ground did the Reds' book their passage to Wembley in 1958?

18 Which England star was Fulham's creative fulcrum?

19 Which veteran newcomer from Blackpool pulled the midfield strings for a United side recently ravaged by the Munich crash?

20 How many goals did Fulham concede over the two matches against the Reds in 1958?

Pot Luck - 10 (see page 38)

ANSWERS

1 Black Cats. 2 Foxes. 3 Hammers. 4 Gunners. 5 Sky Blues. 6 Hornets. 7 Bantams. 8 Toffees. 9 Cottagers. 10 United. 11 Blues (formerly Pensioners). 12 Magpies. 13 Blues, Town or (unofficially) Tractor Boys. 14 Addicks. 15 Rams. 16 Saints. 17 Reds. 18 Spurs. 19 Blues or Citizens. 20 Boro.

Answers - see page 43

1 Which star striker did Manchester United sign in April 2001?
2 From what club?
3 How tall is the new man?
4 Which United favourite had been recruited from the same source three seasons earlier?
5 How much did the new marksman cost?
6 The fee was a world record. True or false?
7 Which European giants made a late enquiry about the player, only to be spurned?
8 Why had United not completed the deal a year earlier?
9 From which club did Ron Atkinson sign Terry Gibson in January 1986?
10 With which club had the player made his First Division debut?
11 Who did Terry help to beat Liverpool in the 1988 FA Cup Final?
12 Which United keeper of the 1970s and early 1980s finished his League career with a lengthy spell at Halifax?
13 How many Republican of Ireland caps did he collect?
14 To which club was he transferred by the Red Devils?
15 Decipher the anagram: REGOGE STEB.
16 Which United boss recruited Nikola Jovanovic in January 1980?
17 For what country was the newcomer an experienced international?
18 From which club was Nikola signed?
19 Who were United's opponents when Jovanovic scored twice in September 1980 at Old Trafford?
20 With which club did post-Munich emergency buy Stan Crowther finish his League career?

Answers - see page 44

1 What is Mark Hughes's first name?
2 How many times did Mark sign for the Red Devils?
3 What is the main nickname of the Welsh centre-forward?
4 Against which club did Mark make his senior debut for United?
5 To whom was Hughes transferred in the summer of 1986?
6 Who were Mark's German employers during 1987/88?
7 In which years was Hughes voted the PFA Player of the Year?
8 During his entire career, how many times did Mark pocket an FA Cup winners' medal?
9 Who were United's opponents when Mark scored with a dramatic late volley in the 1994 FA Cup semi-final at Wembley?
10 Against whom did Mark grab his first senior hat-trick for United?
11 What was special about his full international debut, apart from scoring a goal?
12 How many full caps did Mark win for Wales?
13 In what year did he make his final appearance for his country?
14 What was the occasion of his farewell outing for the Reds?
15 Whose arrival at Old Trafford in January 1995 led to Mark's departure a few months later?
16 Which manager signed Mark for Chelsea in the summer of 1995?
17 Who were Mark's next two employers after leaving Stamford Bridge?
18 For which First Division club was Mark playing in season 2000/2001?
19 How was Hughes honoured in January 1998?
20 Of which team did Mark take charge when he entered management?

ANSWERS

Pot Luck - 12 (see page 40)

1 Huddersfield Town. 2 Oldham Athletic. 3 Alex Dawson. 4 Preston North End. 5 Nobby Lawton. 6 Ashley Grimes. 7 Barnsley. 8 Blackburn Rovers. 9 Philip Mulryne. 10 Norwich City. 11 £500,000. 12 David Beckham. 13 True. 14 Oxford United. 15 Djurgardens. 16 Mark Hughes. 17 Les Sealey. 18 Albert Quixall, who cost £45,000 from Sheffield Wednesday in 1958. 19 Alan Gowling. 20 Huddersfield Town.

Answers - see page 41

1 Who managed United to the Second Division Championship?
2 Who was the skipper?
3 At what ground was promotion secured?
4 How many points clear were United after 42 games?
5 Who were runners-up?
6 Who were promoted in third place?
7 Who was the Reds' leading scorer in the Second Division?
8 Who were the only club to complete the double over United?
9 This was the Reds' first Second Division campaign since which season?
10 There were no ever-presents, but two men missed only one game, Martin Buchan and who else?
11 Which cricketing centre-half made a dozen League appearances?
12 Alex Stepney made 40 appearances between the posts. Who made the other two?
13 Which Chelsea forward was borrowed for two games but never signed a full contract?
14 A great Welsh centre-forward made eight substitute appearances. Name him.
15 At what ground did United start their promotion campaign?
16 Who was the Bristol Rovers battler who contributed an own goal at Old Trafford?
17 How many times were United beaten during their season in the Second?
18 A midfielder destined for success in management rose from the bench for his sole League contribution of the season. Who is he?
19 Who was the United chairman during 1974/75?
20 The Reds started the season without losing for nine games. Who beat them in the tenth?

Pot Luck - 11 *(see page 41)*
1 Ruud van Nistelrooy. 2 PSV Eindhoven. 3 6ft 3ins. 4 Jaap Stam. 5 £19 million.
6 False. 7 Real Madrid. 8 Because Ruud suffered a serious knee injury. 9 Coventry City.
10 Tottenham Hotspur. 11 Wimbledon. 12 Paddy Roche. 13 Eight caps. 14 Brentford.
15 George Best. 16 Dave Sexton. 17 Yugoslavia. 18 Red Star Belgrade. 19 Leicester City. 20 Brighton.

ANSWERS

QUIZ 36

Pot Luck - 12

FIRST HALF

Answers - see page 42

1 Of which club did title-winning full-back Ian Greaves become manager in 1968?
2 Ian signed off his playing days with a spell at his hometown club. Which one?
3 Which centre-forward scored 54 goals in 93 starts for United, but was found surplus to Matt Busby's requirements in October 1961?
4 In 1964 that same spearhead scored an FA Cup Final goal for which club?
5 Which former United colleague was the losing captain that day at Wembley?
6 Who is the least famous of the former United players depicted in an eye-catching mural outside a food outlet on Sir Matt Busby Way?
7 Utility defender John Curtis was loaned out to which club during 1999/2000?
8 To which club was he subsequently sold?
9 Which Northern Ireland international scored a hat-trick against Birmingham City in a friendly before the 1998/99 campaign?
10 The following March he left to join which club?
11 What fee did United receive for the promising youngster?
12 Decipher the anagram: ADDIV CHABMEK.
13 Manchester United won the first five FA Youth Cup Finals from 1953 to 1957. True or false?
14 Who were the hosts in May 1988 when United attracted an attendance of 8,966 fans, their lowest League gate since the war?
15 Who were the Reds visiting in September 1964 when only 6,537 people made up their smallest crowd for a European fixture?
16 Who was the only non-goalkeeping post-war footballer to have two playing spells as a Red Devil?
17 Mark Bosnich was one of two goalkeepers to share that distinction. Who was the other?
18 Who was the first footballer for whom Matt Busby broke the British transfer record?
19 United made a club record sale of £60,000 in June 1972. Who was the player to leave Old Trafford?
20 Which was the buying club?

ANSWERS

Mark Hughes - 1 *(see page 42)*

1 Leslie. 2 Two. 3 Sparky. 4 Port Vale in the Milk Cup, October 1983. 5 Barcelona. 6 Bayern Munich. 7 1989 and 1991. 8 Four. 9 Oldham Athletic. 10 Aston Villa in March 1985. 11 It was played in his hometown of Wrexham. 12 72. 13 1999. 14 The 1995 FA Cup Final against Everton. 15 Andrew Cole's. 16 Glenn Hoddle. 17 Southampton and Everton. 18 Blackburn Rovers. 19 He became an MBE. 20 Wales.

1 Alex Ferguson managed Scotland at the same time as being a club boss. Who had taken that same part-time role when he was United manager?

2 During 2000/2001, who was voted the best Scottish player of all time?

3 Who is the most recent United player to win a full Scotland cap?

4 Who was the Scottish international winger signed by Matt Busby from Celtic in 1946?

5 Did Ralph Milne ever win a full cap?

6 Which international keeper followed Alex Ferguson from Pittodrie to United?

7 Which Scottish international who had served Alex Ferguson at Aberdeen was already at Old Trafford when the manager arrived?

8 Which Scottish international winger joined the Reds from Leeds in 1983?

9 Which Arsenal and Scotland marksman arrived at Old Trafford in 1961?

10 An expensive Scottish international striker struggled as a Red following his purchase in June 1984. Name him.

11 Which Scotland international full-back made nearly 500 senior appearances for United between 1974 and 1988?

12 Which fiery Scot with an Irish first name was recruited from Celtic in 1963?

13 Which towering Scottish stopper crossed the Pennines to Old Trafford in 1978?

14 Frank O'Farrell recruited which classy 23-year-old defender from Aberdeen in 1972?

15 Which costly, diminutive Scot netted on his United debut in January 1973?

16 Which young full-back was signed from Partick Thistle in December 1972 by the man who had given him his Scotland debut?

17 Which rugged United centre-half and folk hero figured in the 1974 World Cup Finals?

18 He was a Leeds player at the time, but a future United star whose goal clinched Scotland's place in the 1974 World Cup Finals. Name him.

19 Which blond Scottish stopper arrived from Highbury in August 1969?

20 Which United and Scotland defender went on to become manager of Queen's Park Rangers?

ANSWERS

Pot Luck - 13 (see page 47)
1 Maurice. 2 Wigan. 3 Barclays' Young Eagle of the Month. 4 Blackburn Rovers.
5 Bournemouth. 6 Paul Bielby. 7 Hartlepool United. 8 Clayton Blackmore. 9 Tommy
Bogan. 10 Bishop Auckland. 11 Three. 12 Teaching. 13 Bristol Rovers. 14 Eastville.
15 Geoff Bradford. 16 Peter Davenport. 17 Nottingham Forest. 18 Macclesfield Town.
19 Steve Bruce. 20 Tony Dunne.

1 After their 2-0 triumph over Newcastle, how many times had United lifted the FA Cup?

2 Who had won it more often?

3 Who collected the trophy despite playing for only nine minutes?

4 Who netted the opening goal some 96 seconds after leaving the bench?

5 Who scored the second with a low left-footer?

6 Complete the chant which echoed around Wembley: 'David May, superstar, got more medals than . . .'

7 Who was the Newcastle manager?

8 Which Scottish spearhead did the Magpies introduce for the second half?

9 Who was the bald Georgian who shot against a United post towards the end?

10 Which Croatian squandered a golden opportunity to set up a grandstand finish?

11 Who had conquered Newcastle at Wembley a year earlier?

12 Who partnered David May in the centre of United's defence?

13 Who boosted the Reds' rearguard for the last quarter of an hour?

14 Who was minding the Geordies' net?

15 Who received the trophy from Prince Charles?

16 By whom was the FA Cup sponsored for the first time in 1998/99?

17 This was the last FA Cup Final at the original Wembley stadium. True or false?

18 Raimond van der Gouw was one of United's non-playing substitutes. Who was the other?

19 Which Peruvian international occupied Newcastle's right flank?

20 Who did the Magpies defeat in their semi-final?

Answers - see page 45

1 What is Roy Keane's middle name?
2 In what Rugby League stronghold was Russell Beardsmore born?
3 For what honour was he chosen by Bob Paisley in January 1989?
4 To what club was Russell loaned in December 1991?
5 When Russell left Old Trafford in June 1993, who were his new employers?
6 Which young forward made his United debut in the Manchester derby in the spring of the Reds' 1973/74 relegation season?
7 After only four senior outings, he was allowed to join which club in his native north-east?
8 Who won his first cap for Wales in 1985 after making only two senior appearances for United?
9 Which Scotland international forward did Matt Busby sign from Preston North End in August 1949?
10 From which famous amateur club was winger Warren Bradley recruited in the wake of the Munich air disaster?
11 Warren did well in the First Division, going on to win how many England caps?
12 In what profession outside the game did Warren Bradley flourish?
13 Which underdogs dumped United out of the FA Cup in January 1956?
14 On which ground did the Red Devils suffer that 4-0 thrashing?
15 Which recently capped England international scored against United that day?
16 Who was United's leading scorer in senior competitions during 1986/87?
17 From which club had United signed him?
18 Which club was he managing in 2000/2001?
19 Who tied with Brian McClair as United's top scorer in League games during 1990/91?
20 Decipher the anagram: YONT NUDEN.

Answers - see page 46

1 What was the name of the club which would later change its name to Manchester United?
2 In what year was that club formed?
3 In what industry did its members work?
4 On what ground did that founder club play?
5 In which year did the club first apply to join the newly-formed Football League?
6 When was the club accepted into the League?
7 In what competition had they played previously?
8 What was the nickname of the club before it became United?
9 Who beat the newcomers in their first League encounter?
10 Who was the first man to score a League goal for the club?
11 What position in the table did the future United occupy at the end of their first campaign?
12 In what year did they move from their first home to their second?
13 Where was the club's new headquarters?
14 At the end of 1893/94, the club finished bottom of the First Division and lost a play-off clash with which Second Division champions?
15 In March 1895 the club beat Walsall Town Swifts 14-0 but the result was nullified because of complaints about the pitch. How did the replay end?
16 When did the future United win the Manchester Cup for the first time?
17 In what year did the club go bankrupt, then re-form under the current name?
18 What possible title for the reborn club was dismissed as being too Scottish?
19 Who suggested the name of Manchester United?
20 Who was the new United's first president and major benefactor?

ANSWERS

FA Cup Final 1999 (see page 46)

1 Ten. 2 Nobody. 3 Roy Keane. 4 Teddy Sheringham. 5 Paul Scholes. 6 She-ee-rar.
7 Ruud Gullit. 8 Duncan Ferguson. 9 Temuri Ketsbaia. 10 The substitute Silvio Maric.
11 Arsenal. 12 Ronny Johnsen. 13 Jaap Stam. 14 Steve Harper. 15 Peter Schmeichel.
16 AXA. 17 False. 18 Jesper Blomqvist. 19 Nolberto Solano. 20 Chelsea.

48

Answers - see page 51

1 When United faced Aston Villa, what unique achievement did they have in their sights?
2 Which former Old Trafford boss guided a club to a second victory over United in a major final?
3 Which namesake of the Villa boss opened the scoring for the Midlanders?
4 What colour shirts did the Red Devils wear at Wembley?
5 Who sponsored the League Cup in 1994?
6 Who was a tower of strength at the heart of the Villa defence?
7 Which Welsh international doubled the Midlanders' lead?
8 Whose goal gave United renewed hope as time was running out?
9 Who was sent off for handball in the 89th minute?
10 What was the immediate consequence for the offender?
11 Who netted from the spot to clinch Villa's victory?
12 Who was Villa's in-form goalkeeper?
13 Who retired from the action when Brian McClair went on as a late substitute?
14 Which substitute was not used by United?
15 Which Villa man had won League titles with two different clubs?
16 Who played in goal for United in place of the suspended Peter Schmeichel?
17 Which Yorkshire club did the Reds beat 5-2 on aggregate to reach Wembley?
18 Who were Villa's semi-final opponents?
19 Who was the Villa captain who held aloft the trophy?
20 How many years had it been since Villa had faced United in a Wembley final?

Answers - see page 52

1   What was United's lowest post-war points total, compiled when they were relegated in 1973/74?

2   From what club did the Red Devils sign Ashley Grimes?

3   Decipher the anagram: RECI NANTACO.

4   In what campaign did the Reds run up 92 points, their highest total?

5   How many Premiership goals did Sir Alex Ferguson's men total in 1999/2000?

6   United lost ten successive League games to which club between 1914 and 1931?

7   Which club have lost on all ten League visits to United?

8   Which blond midfielder did Dave Sexton recruit from Ballymena in August 1978?

9   Which full-back played 449 League and FA Cup games for the Red Devils between 1919 and 1934?

10 With which club did Maurice Setters finish his playing days?

11 Which former United and Northern Ireland winger died in an accident on a building site in 1978?

12 To which club did United sell Jim Ryan in April 1970?

13 Which United full-back went on to become chairman of Aberdeen?

14 Against which club did he excel in Bobby Charlton's testimonial game?

15 After Tommy O'Neil left Old Trafford, for which club did he have more than 200 senior outings?

16 Of which creative Dutchman did Martin Buchan once exclaim: 'He's the only man in English football I would pay to watch'?

17 Many United fans were upset by the sale of which young striker to Brighton for £500,000 in October 1980?

18 Which young defender won three England under-23 caps but then lost his United place before being sold to Oldham Athletic in March 1973?

19 Albert Kinsey scored twice in an FA Cup tie against Chester in January 1965, his only senior outing for United. True or false?

20 For which club did Albert top the Fourth Division scoring chart as they were promoted in 1969/70?

Denis Law - 1 *(see page 52)*

ANSWERS

1 False. **2** Huddersfield Town. **3** Bill Shankly. **4** Manchester City. **5** £55,000. **6** Luton Town. **7** Rest of the World. **8** Manchester City. **9** Torino. **10** Joe Baker. **11** £115,000. **12** Wales. **13** One. **14** West Bromwich Albion. **15** Yes, one. **16** True. **17** Four. **18** 46. **19** 1963/64. **20** Two.

1 Who scored twice as United began their 1994/95 Champions League campaign with a 4-2 home win against Gothenburg?

2 Which summer signing from Blackburn made his European debut for United at right-back?

3 Which red-haired United midfielder was making his first European start against the Swedes?

4 What was the outcome of the Reds' away clash with Galatasaray in September 1994?

5 Who replaced Steve Bruce as United skipper for the home meeting with Barcelona in October 1994?

6 Who opened the scoring in that exhilarating 2-2 draw with the Spaniards?

7 Which Brazilian nipped in with Barca's equaliser?

8 Who squared the match with a cheeky flick ten minutes from time?

9 Which future Red made a second-half appearance for the Spanish club?

10 What colours did United wear for the return encounter at the Nou Camp?

11 Who replaced Peter Schmeichel in goal because of the 'foreigners' rule which then prevailed?

12 Which Bulgarian starred as the Red Devils were crushed 4-0?

13 A United player gave the hosts a flying start with an early own goal. Who was the culprit?

14 Which future Chelsea defender contributed Barca's fourth goal?

15 Which winger, who was destined to help United to lift the Treble, tormented David May as the Reds were whipped 3-1 by Gothenburg in November 1994?

16 Who opened the scoring as United thrashed Galatasaray 4-0 at Old Trafford two weeks later?

17 Which future England captain contributed the Reds' second goal that night?

18 Who ejected United from the 1995/96 UEFA Cup in the first round?

19 By what rule did the Reds lose?

20 Whose goal preserved United's unbeaten home record in Europe with only a minute to spare?

Answers - see page 50

1   Denis Law entered senior football with Aberdeen, his hometown club. True or false.

2   Which club was the young Scot's first in England?

3   Who was his manager when he made his League debut for that club?

4   In 1960, Denis became the costliest player to move between two British clubs. Who signed him?

5   What was that record fee?

6   Law once scored six times in an FA Cup tie, only for the game to be abandoned. Who were the lucky opponents?

7   Denis faced England at Wembley in October 1963. But for whom?

8   With which English club did Law enjoy two stints?

9   Which Italian club signed Denis Law for £110,000 in 1961?

10 Which England centre-forward shared the same Italian employers?

11 Matt Busby broke the British transfer record when he brought Denis back to England in 1962. How much did he pay?

12 Who were the opponents when Law made his full international debut in October 1958?

13 How many goals did he score that day?

14 Who provided the opposition when Denis made his League entrance for the Red Devils at Old Trafford in August 1962?

15 Did Law manage a debut goal in that 2-2 draw?

16 Denis pocketed an FA Cup winner's medal at the end of his first season with United. True or false?

17 In how many seasons did the Scot top 20 League goals for the Reds?

18 In 1963/64 Denis made 41 League and Cup appearances for United. How many times did he score?

19 In which season did the Lawman average a goal a game in 30 League appearances?

20 How Championship medals did Denis Law earn with United?

Pot Luck - 14 *(see page 50)*

ANSWERS

1 32 points. 2 Bohemians. 3 Eric Cantona. 4 1993/94. 5 97 goals. 6 Newcastle United.
7 Chesterfield. 8 Tom Sloan. 9 Jack Silcock. 10 Charlton Athletic. 11 Jackie Scott.
12 Luton Town. 13 Ian Donald. 14 Celtic. 15 Southport. 16 Arnold Muhren. 17 Andy
Ritchie. 18 Paul Edwards. 19 False, he scored once. Geroge Best scored the other.
20 Wrexham.

Answers - see page 55

1   In August 1982 Ron Atkinson signed a schemer whose forenames were Arnoldus Johannes Hyacinthus. What was that creative midfielder's surname?

2   From which club did he come?

3   Which major European honour had he helped that club to lift?

4   Which of United's four goals in the 1983 FA Cup Final replay did he score from the spot?

5   How old was he when he played for Holland in the final of the European Championships against the USSR in 1988?

6   To which club did United transfer Mark Robins in August 1992?

7   Which German club did he snub to make that move?

8   For which club was Mark scoring prolifically in 2000/2001?

9   Which United captain of the Edwardian era was dubbed 'The Ghost In Boots' because of his pale complexion?

10   From which club did that inspirational skipper join United in 1904?

11   With which club did he enjoy an Indian summer?

12   Decipher the anagram: RONDOG CRASHANT.

13   Which former United marksman was managing Oldham Athletic in 2000/2001?

14   For which Yorkshiremen had Andy played between 1983 and 1987?

15   Which Salford-born half-back made his only senior appearance for United in a League Cup tie at Valley Parade in November 1960?

16   Which Scottish international striker did United sign from Spurs in June 1984?

17   For which club was that marksman playing when he won the bulk of his caps?

18   Who were his final Football League employers?

19   Which young centre-half who shared the same surname made two substitute appearances for the Reds in 1989 and 1990?

20   Of which club was former United keeper Jimmy Rimmer the caretaker manager for a brief period during the mid 1990s?

Answers - see page 56

1 Who scored the first goal of United's League campaign, against Newcastle?
2 A statue of which former England manager was unveiled before the Red Devils' fixture at Portman Road?
3 Who was the first player to score a Premiership goal past Fabien Barthez?
4 Against who did United squander a two-goal lead, late in an August encounter?
5 In that dramatic contest, which Red Devil struck two shots against the woodwork with the score at 2-2?
6 Who skippered United in their home clash with Bradford City?
7 In that meeting, who netted in his third consecutive League outing?
8 Who scored two great goals when Sunderland came a-calling in September?
9 Which giant Czech mustered Anderlecht's sole reply when United slammed five past the Belgians?
10 Who made his first senior appearance for more than a year when United visited Goodison Park in September?
11 Who rifled a spectacular opener for Chelsea at Old Trafford?
12 Whose penalty gave United the lead against PSV in Eindhoven before the Reds slumped to a 3-1 defeat?
13 Who scored a wonder goal for Arsenal at Highbury to inflict on United their first League defeat of the season?
14 Which table-toppers did United beat with a 3-0 away victory in October?
15 Which keeper was beaten more times on that one afternoon than he had been in all his previous games that season?
16 Who scored United's crucial second goal with a sweet volley at home to PSV Eindhoven in October?
17 Who scored his first goal of 2000/2001 to seal the result against the Dutchmen?
18 Which rookie Leeds goalkeeper prevented a rout at Old Trafford?
19 Which United sub was named man of that particular match?
20 Whose scuffed penalty reduced the arrears but was not enough to avert defeat by Anderlecht in Belgium?

ANSWERS

Pot Luck - 16 *(see page 56)*

1 His 25th. **2** Patrick Kluivert. **3** Den Bosch. **4** Midfielder. **5** Heerenveen. **6** One. **7** Bobby Robson. **8** 1998/99. **9** Rio Ferdinand's £18 million move from West Ham to Leeds. **10** Dwight Yorke from Aston Villa for £ **12** 6 million. **11** Frank Barson. **12** Aston Villa. **13** Alex Bell. **14** Dick Duckworth. **15** Francis Burns. **16** Bobby Charlton. **17** Shamrock Rovers. **18** Bohemians. **19** Coventry City. **20** Telford United.

54

1 What was the reported fee when United signed Teddy Sheringham from Spurs in the summer of 1997?

2 Teddy took a penalty on his United debut – against Spurs. What happened?

3 When did United first face Spurs in League competition?

4 In which season did Spurs and United last share Second Division status?

5 Who scored United's winner against Spurs at Old Trafford in May 1999, clinching the Premiership title in the process?

6 Who had stunned the United faithful into silence with the first goal of that match?

7 Which grandson of a Spurs fan had supplied the Reds' equaliser on that day?

8 Which former United player was managing Spurs at the time?

9 In which season did United and Spurs record 5-1 home victories over each other?

10 In the first of those matches, at White Hart Lane, which Spurs star beat five United defenders before scoring?

11 In the Old Trafford return, a United icon scored with a thunderbolt which was savage even by his standards. Name him.

12 In that same encounter, which Spur contributed an own goal?

13 In May 2000 United were presented with the Premiership trophy after beating Spurs 3-1 at Old Trafford. Who opened the scoring for the Reds?

14 Who equalised for Spurs?

15 Who contributed a glorious 20-yard curler for his eighth senior goal of the season?

16 Whose two goals at White Hart Lane sunk Spurs on the last day of August 1955?

17 Which Spurs and England centre-forward notched a hat-trick as United lost 4-3 at the Lane in November 1957?

18 Who nodded an own goal as United nosedived 3-1 at Tottenham in October 1999?

19 Who sealed the Londoners' victory that day with a 30-yard scorcher from the right flank?

20 Spurs have faced United in two major finals. True or false?

Answers - see page 54

1. What birthday did Ruud Van Nistelrooy celebrate on 1 July 2001?
2. Which other Dutch international striker, once linked with a move to United, was born on the same day?
3. What was Ruud's first professional club?
4. In what position was he specialising when he joined that club?
5. What was the Dutchman's second professional club?
6. How many goals did Van Nistelrooy score in his first ten games for Holland?
7. Which English boss nurtured Ruud's skills at his final Dutch club?
8. In what season was Van Nistelrooy voted Dutch player of the year by his fellow footballers?
9. United's purchase of Ruud outstripped which transaction as the British record deal?
10. Who was United's previous record signing?
11. Which former blacksmith lived up to his iron-man reputation as United's centre-half in the 1920s?
12. Which club did he help to win the FA Cup in 1920?
13. Which wing-half, born in South Africa of Scottish parents, made more than 300 League and FA Cup appearances for United between 1903 and 1913?
14. He operated in tandem with which other magnificent wing-half?
15. Which Scottish international full-back left United for Southampton in June 1972?
16. Under the management of which former Old Trafford colleague did he serve Preston?
17. After playing more than 400 Football League games, with which Irish club did he continue his career?
18. From which Irish club did United recruit Gerry Daly?
19. Which was Gerry's third English club?
20. At which non-League club did Daly become manager in 1990?

ANSWERS

Season 2000/2001 - 1 (see page 54)

1 Ronny Johnsen. **2** Sir Alf Ramsey. **3** Fabian Wilnis. **4** West Ham United. **5** David Beckham. **6** Teddy Sheringham. **7** David Beckham. **8** Paul Scholes. **9** Jan Koller. **10** Wes Brown. **11** Jimmy Floyd Hasselbaink. **12** Paul Scholes'. **13** Thierry Henry. **14** Leicester City. **15** Tim Flowers. **16** Paul Scholes. **17** Dwight Yorke. **18** Paul Robinson. **19** David Beckham. **20** Denis Irwin's.

Answers – see page 59

1 United's victory over Liverpool scuppered what unique achievement?
2 Which of the two famous Reds changed to white shirts for the final?
3 After losing, who said to Margaret Thatcher: 'To tell you the truth, love, I'm absolutely knackered!'
4 What pair of brothers turned out for United?
5 The game's three goals were scored in the space of ten minutes. True or false?
6 Who netted United's opener?
7 Which born-and-bred Scouser supplied a spectacular equaliser for Liverpool?
8 Off whose chest did the ball bounce for United's winner?
9 Who took the original shot from which that fateful deflection occurred?
10 Which Liverpool and England midfielder struck the woodwork towards the end of each half?
11 Why was rookie Arthur Albiston playing at left-back for the Red Devils?
12 What magnanimous gesture did Albiston make after the match?
13 Who were United's semi-final opponents?
14 Who was the Liverpool keeper too dejected to applaud his own fans at the end?
15 How many previous visits to Wembley as a player or manager had United boss Tommy Docherty made without a victory?
16 Why was Docherty sacked later that summer?
17 In what city, a few days later, did Liverpool claim ample compensation for their Wembley reverse?
18 Which United's star's fitness to play in the final had been in serious doubt?
19 Which future England manager was playing for the Merseysiders?
20 Which Liverpudlian was United's assistant manager at the time of the final?

Answers - see page 60

1   How many years had it been since United had last lifted the title?
2   They kicked off their League campaign with defeat on which ground?
3   United were swamped 3-0 at Old Trafford by which club in their second match?
4   Whose goal enabled them to scrape a home draw with Ipswich in their third League outing?
5   Who supplied the only goal as the Reds claimed their first victory in their fourth game, at Southampton?
6   Whose arrival coincided with a dramatic upsurge in United's fortunes?
7   Against whom did the Reds recover from a three-goal deficit on Boxing Day?
8   Who scored two late goals in a minute to rescue three points at home to Southampton in February?
9   Which Latic's goal halted United, albeit temporarily, in their title-chasing tracks?
10 Which former Red Devil offered Norwich's lone reply to a three-goal United salvo at Carrow Road?
11 During the title run-in, against whom did United claim victory in the seventh minute of added time?
12 The last match United played before being confirmed as champions was at which ground?
13 Mark Hughes scored one goal during that game, a 2-0 victory. Who grabbed the second?
14 Which result meant that Manchester United were champions?
15 Who scored the only goal of that contest?
16 Who did the Reds defeat the following night to celebrate their triumph?
17 United's only regular outfielder who had not scored a League goal that term set the record straight in that game. Name him.
18 How many players made 40 or more League appearances?
19 Who topped United's League scoring chart with 15 goals?
20 Who accompanied team skipper Steve Bruce to collect the trophy?

Answers - see page 57

1   Paul Scholes has a brother who has played for Stockport County. True or false?
2   Mike Duxbury was one of the most versatile players in the country, but in which position did he make the majority of his United appearances?
3   How many full England caps did Mike earn?
4   At the end of which season was Duxbury given a free transfer?
5   How many FA Cup winner's medals did Mike earn as a Red Devil?
6   In his first season at senior level, how many different numbers did Duxbury wear for United?
7   Who was United manager during that campaign?
8   Which club did Duxbury join after leaving United?
9   Under which former Red Devil did he serve later at Bradford City?
10 Decipher the anagram: VESTE PLOPCLE.
11 In what season did John Fitzpatrick make his League entrance for the Red Devils?
12 In which campaign did the abrasive Aberdonian make 43 senior appearances for United?
13 What ended his career at the premature age of 26?
14 Which top English club had rejected Alex Forsyth as a teenager?
15 Which major honour did Alex win with Partick Thistle in 1972?
16 What became Forsyth's home ground after he left Old Trafford?
17 With which club did the full-back finish his senior career?
18 What caused the accident in which John Gidman once nearly lost an eye?
19 With which club did John pick up a League Cup winner's medal in 1977?
20 Which club did Gidman join on leaving United?

Answers - see page 58

1 Which Manchester United manager signed Brian McClair?

2 What was Brian's previous club?

3 How much did a tribunal order the Reds to pay for his services?

4 How many League goals did he score in his first campaign as a Red Devil?

5 Who was the previous United man to contribute 20 or more League goals in one term?

6 Which season was McClair's first at Old Trafford?

7 With which Midlands club was Brian a teenage apprentice?

8 With which club, based at Fir Park, did he make his first senior appearances?

9 In what season had Brian been voted Scottish Footballer of the Year?

10 What Wembley final was decided by a single McClair goal?

11 How many FA Cup Final goals did Brian score for the Red Devils?

12 How many title medals did Choccy collect during his glorious stay at Old Trafford?

13 How many times was Brian capped by Scotland at full international level?

14 Who were the victims of Brian's first hat-trick for United in April 1988?

15 Eventually McClair was switched from front-man to which other position?

16 Whose arrival in the summer of 1993 cost Brian a regular place during the following campaign?

17 Against which side did Brian open United's account in the semi-final of the 1991 European Cup Winners' Cup?

18 After leaving United in 1998, with which club did McClair complete his playing days?

19 Which Lancashire club made Brian assistant manager?

20 Who was his boss?

Answers - see page 63

1   At the start of which season did Peter Schmeichel arrive at Old Trafford?
2   From which club was he signed?
3   His fee was a world record for a goalkeeper. True or false?
4   When he retired from international football in 2001, how many times had Peter played for Denmark?
5   How many goals had he scored in international football?
6   Peter scored once for the Red Devils. Who were the opponents?
7   What was the club competition in which he headed home?
8   Who was chosen mysteriously (with all due respect) ahead of Peter as the players' goalkeeper of the year in both 1997/98 and 1998/99?
9   Who were United playing in December 1996 when Peter made a save that has been likened to Gordon Banks' World Cup classic tip-over from Pele?
10 Who delivered that header which Schmeichel managed somehow to repel?
11 Peter captained United to one major trophy during his eight there. What was it?
12 During those eight terms with the Dane between the posts, what was United's lowest League finish?
13 Against which First Division opposition did Peter make his senior United debut in August 1991?
14 Following his arrival at Old Trafford, how many consecutive clean sheets did Schmeichel keep before being beaten?
15 What was Peter's first domestic honour in English football?
16 From which Dutch star did Peter make a crucial penalty save for Denmark in the semi-final of the 1992 European Championships?
17 With Schmeichel in imperious form. who did Denmark beat in the final?
18 Against which FA Cup quarter-final opponents was Peter Schmeichel sent off in 1994?
19 Which major game did the giant keeper miss as a result of the suspension which followed?
20 In what year did Peter become a full international?

Bill Foulkes *(see page 63)*
ANSWERS
1 Bobby Charlton. 2 St Helens. 3 Liverpool. 4 Billy Liddell. 5 Four. 6 True. 7 In a coal mine. 8 1954/55. 9 Northern Ireland. 10 Sheffield Wednesday. 11 Ronnie Cope. 12 Three. 13 One. 14 Real Madrid, in the European Cup semi-final. 15 36 years old. 16 1969/70. 17 Tommy Docherty. 18 Bob Paisley. 19 Japan. 20 Golf.

Answers - see page 64

1 Who was Manchester United's chief scout in 2000/2001?
2 Some years earlier, the same man served which Old Trafford boss as his number two?
3 What is the official title of the United matchday programme?
4 What is the traditional emblem which appears on the cover?
5 United youngster George Clegg and occasional first-teamer Michael Clegg are brothers. True or false?
6 Which youth coach nurtured the class of '92 which featured the likes of Beckham, Scholes, Butt and the Nevilles?
7 Which former Norwich City manager was a United coach in 2000/2001?
8 Whose autobiography is the book 'Soccer My Battlefield'?
9 Who was the subject of Eamon Dunphy's controversial tome 'A Strange Kind Of Glory'?
10 Who came one hundredth when United magazine staged a poll to determine the club's 100 greatest players of all time?
11 With which club did Freddie Goodwin first become a manager?
12 Which Midlanders did Freddie boss from 1970 to 1975?
13 Decipher the anagram: RUTSAT OARSPEN.
14 Which rookie centre-half made his debut in front of 53,000 fans at Anfield in October 1968?
15 From which club did Alex Ferguson sign Jim Leighton in May 1988?
16 What fee was involved?
17 For which League club did Leighton make eight appearances on loan while still a United player in 1991/92?
18 Jim put in a stint as understudy to David Seaman at Arsenal. True or false?
19 To which club did United sell Leighton for £150,000 in February 1992?
20 How old was Jim Leighton when he retired from senior football in the summer of 1998?

ANSWERS

League Cup Final 1983 *(see page 64)*

1 False, it was only the third time in succession. 2 Norman Whiteside. 3 Alan Hansen. 4 Alan Kennedy. 5 Ronnie Whelan. 6 Arsenal. 7 Burnley. 8 Lou Macari. 9 Frank Stapleton. 10 Mike Duxbury. 11 Milk Cup. 12 Bruce Grobbelaar. 13 Gary Bailey. 14 They won the FA Cup. 15 David Fairclough. 16 Craig Johnston. 17 Arnold Muhren. 18 Graeme Souness. 19 Bob Paisley. 20 League Championship.

Answers - see page 61

1   Only one man has played more senior games for United than Bill Foulkes. Name him.

2   Bill was born in which Lancashire rugby league stronghold?

3   Against which north-western rivals did he make his First Division debut in December 1952?

4   Which magnificent Scottish winger was the rookie right-back's direct opponent that day?

5   How many Championship medals did Foulkes collect?

6   Bill helped to win more League titles than any other Red Devil of his era. True or false?

7   Incredibly, when Bill was awarded his sole England cap, he was a part-time footballer. Where had he been working on the day before the game?

8   During which season was Foulkes honoured by his country?

9   Who were the opponents on his one day out with England?

10   Bill captained United in their first game after he had survived the Munich crash. Which side did he face in that FA Cup tie?

11   During 1960/61 Bill switched to his preferred position of centre-half. Who did he replace as the Red Devils' regular number-five?

12   How many times did Foulkes feature in FA Cup Finals?

13   How many times did he finish on the winning side in those finals?

14   The most important goal of his life put United into the 1968 European Cup Final. Who did it eliminate?

15   How old was Bill at the time of that European final at Wembley?

16   During what season did Bill play his last senior game for the Reds?

17   After that he coached at Old Trafford for four years. Who was manager when he left?

18   When he left Manchester, which Liverpool legend recommended him for a coaching job in the USA?

19   Bill has also coached successfully in Norway and what other country?

20   In which sport has Bill Foulkes represented Cheshire?

Answers - see page 62

1 When Liverpool beat United at Wembley in 1983, the Merseysiders were claiming the League Cup for the fourth time in succession. True or false?
2 United led for most of the match through an early goal by which marksman?
3 Which Liverpool defender had been gulled in the creation of that goal?
4 Whose dipping drive produced the Merseysiders' late equaliser?
5 Whose sublime extra-time curler took the trophy back to Anfield?
6 Who had United defeated in at the semi-final stage?
7 Who had been Liverpool's last-four opponents?
8 Who was United's 70th-minute substitute for the injured Kevin Moran?
9 Who subsequently moved to centre-half when Gordon McQueen took a knock?
10 Which United and England full-back finished the game as the other central defender?
11 What was the sponsored name of the League Cup in 1983?
12 Who was the Liverpool keeper who escaped with a booking after body-checking the crippled McQueen near the end of normal time?
13 Who was minding the net for United?
14 What consolation did the Red Devils claim six weeks later?
15 Who appeared as an 83rd-minute substitute for Liverpool?
16 Which South-African born attacking midfielder made way for him?
17 Who was the Dutchman at the heart of United's midfield?
18 Two future Liverpool managers were on the pitch. One was Kenny Dalglish; who was the other?
19 Who was bossing the Merseysiders at the time of the final?
20 What other trophy did the Anfielders claim at season's end?

Answers - see page 67

1 When United clinched the title in 2000/2001, how many consecutive seasons had they finished in the top two?

2 That title was the Reds' third in succession. Arsenal, Liverpool and which other club had previously attained this feat?

3 Who was the first manager to preside over three Championships in a row?

4 How many major domestic honours (thus discounting the Charity Shield) had Sir Alex Ferguson garnered for United by the spring of 2001?

5 Who was United's principal goalkeeper during their hugely successful first decade of the 20th century?

6 In what city was Kevin Moran born?

7 How many times was he capped by the Republic of Ireland?

8 Which United manager decided to dispense with the services of the 32-year-old Moran?

9 Which club did he join on leaving United?

10 Which manager brought him back into the English League?

11 Which was Kevin's final League club?

12 Did Kevin Moran ever add a League title medal to his collection of honours?

13 How many FA Cup winner's gongs did the Irishman earn?

14 Decipher the anagram: MYASM CRYMIOL.

15 At what price was Remi Moses valued in the package deal which took him to Old Trafford in September 1981?

16 What was his previous club?

17 Where was Remi born?

18 For how many clubs did Moses play under Ron Atkinson?

19 How many England caps did Remi Moses accumulate?

20 How many FA Cup winner's medals adorn Remi's trophy cabinet?

Lee Sharpe (see page 67)

ANSWERS

1 Torquay United. 2 Cyril Knowles. 3 17 years old. 4 West Ham United. 5 Left-back. 6 Left wing/left midfield. 7 Arsenal. 8 Highbury. 9 Leeds United. 10 1990/91. 11 19 years old. 12 Graham Taylor. 13 Eight caps. 14 A European Cup Winners' Cup medal in 1990/91. 15 Sheffield Wednesday. 16 Three. 17 Against Liverpool in 1996. 18 Leeds United. 19 Sampdoria. 20 Portsmouth on loan.

Answers - see page 68

1 Who was the United manager as the Reds set about defending their European crown?

2 Who netted seven times as the Red Devils outclassed Waterford 10-2 on aggregate in the first round?

3 Who was called on as a substitute keeper for Alex Stepney in Ireland?

4 Which full-back hit the target in the 7-1 Old Trafford victory?

5 For the home tie with Anderlecht, United were missing their two first-choice wingers. One was George Best; who was the other?

6 This was United's first encounter with Belgian opposition in senior competition since the opening game of their European history. True or false?

7 Who scored twice as the Red Devils triumphed 3-0 at Old Trafford?

8 United fell 3-1 in Brussels. Who scored the crucial goal which gave them a 4-3 aggregate victory?

9 Which full-back who failed to carve a niche in Manchester, but would later excel in Scottish football, faced Anderlecht on their own soil?

10 Which defender, in his 37th year, returned to help the defence in Begium?

11 Who made his European debut at centre-half in the home leg of the quarter-final against Rapid Vienna?

12 What Irish imp struck twice in the 3-0 victory?

13 What was the result of the second leg of the quarter-final in Vienna?

14 Who was sent off as United lost 2-0 to AC Milan in the semi-final in Italy?

15 What is name of Milan's stadium?

16 Which famous Swede scored the Italians' second goal?

17 Who hammered home the only goal of the second leg?

18 What missile from the Stretford End hit Milan keeper Cudicini after United had a goal disallowed?

19 Which England defender was dropped by United for the Milan games?

20 How many years would elapse before United played once more in Europe's premier club competition?

Answers – see page 65

1 From what club did United recruit Lee Sharpe in 1988?
2 Who was the manager who struck the deal with Alex Ferguson?
3 How old was Lee when he made his senior United debut?
4 Who were the opponents on that Old Trafford afternoon in September 1988?
5 In what position did Lee play that day?
6 Later, in what role did he settle?
7 Who were the victims of a fabulous Sharpe hat-trick in the League Cup in November 1990?
8 Where was it scored?
9 That season Lee scored in both legs of a League Cup semi-final against which opponents?
10 In what season was Sharpe named Barclays Young Eagle of the Year?
11 How old was Lee when he made his full England debut?
12 Which England boss gave him his first chance at the top level?
13 How many England caps had Lee won by the end of 2000/2001?
14 What was Sharpe's first major club honour?
15 Against which club did Lee provide three crosses for goals which saw United recover from a 3-0 deficit on Boxing Day 1992?
16 How many times did Sharpe help United to championship glory?
17 For which FA Cup Final was Lee a non-playing substitute?
18 To which club was Sharpe transferred in August 1996?
19 With which leading Italian outfit did Lee complete a loan stint during 1998/99?
20 For whom was Lee Sharpe playing his foootball in the spring of 2001?

Pot Luck - 19 (see page 65)
1 Ten seasons. 2 Huddersfield Town. 3 Sir Alex Ferguson. 4 Twelve. 5 Harry Moger.
6 Dublin. 7 71 times. 8 Alex Ferguson. 9 Sporting Gijon of Spain. 10 Don Mackay.
11 Blackburn Rovers. 12 No. 13 Two. 14 Sammy McIlroy. 15 £650,000. 16 West
Bromwich Albion. 17 Manchester. 18 Two clubs. 19 None. 20 None.

Answers - see page 66

As season 2000/2001 ended, who was managing the following clubs against the Red Devils during another enthralling campaign?

1 Bayern Munich
2 Coventry City
3 Ipswich Town
4 Fulham
5 Tottenham Hotspur
6 Southampton
7 Liverpool
8 Aston Villa
9 Leicester City
10 Valencia
11 Sunderland
12 West Ham United
13 Arsenal
14 Chelsea
15 Leeds United
16 Newcastle United
17 Manchester City
18 Bradford City
19 Charlton Athletic
20 Derby County

ANSWERS

Reds in Europe 1968/69 *(see page 66)*
1 Sir Matt Busby. 2 Denis Law. 3 Jimmy Rimmer. 4 Francis Burns. 5 Willie Morgan.
6 True. 7 Denis Law. 8 Carlo Sartori. 9 Frank Kopel. 10 Bill Foulkes. 11 Steve James.
12 George Best. 13 0-0. 14 John Fitzpatrick. 15 San Siro. 16 Kurt Hamrin. 17 Bobby
Charlton. 18 A brick. 19 David Sadler. 20 Twenty four.

Answers - see page 71

1   Jack Crompton minded the net in all six of United's FA Cup ties in 1948. How many clean sheets did he keep?

2   Jack was a player at Old Trafford during two title-winning campaigns, but did he qualify for a medal on either occasion?

3   In how many seasons was Jack a regular in a United side which finished runners-up in the top flight?

4   Which club did Jack join as a coach when he left United in October 1956?

5   What precipitated his return to Old Trafford as trainer in 1958?

6   Jack managed which club briefly in the early 1970s?

7   During 1973/74 Jack was Preston North End's trainer. Under which boss did he serve?

8   Where was granite-hard stopper Allenby Chilton born?

9   How old was Allenby when he won his first England cap?

10   Chilton was United's only ever-present when they lifted the title in 1951/52. True or false?

11   Allenby completed his United League service with 166 consecutive outings. What age was he when he played the last of those games?

12   Which club did Chilton guide to the Third Division (North) title as player-boss in 1955/56?

13   Which north-eastern club finished bottom of the Fourth Division under his management in 1962/63?

14   What number shirt did Henry Cockburn wear in the 1948 FA Cup Final?

15   In how many League matches had Henry played when he won his first full England cap in September 1946?

16   How many times did the tiny Cockburn play for his country?

17   Did Henry earn a medal when United won the League Championship in 1951/52?

18   Henry Cockburn played League football with one club after United. Name it.

19   Who played at right-half when United won the FA Cup in 1948?

20   To which Midlands club was that Cup-winner transferred in October 1949?

Answers - see page 72

1 Which Anfield marksman tipped the title scales in Liverpool's favour with the only goal against United at Anfield in May 1947?

2 Which wing-half, who would go on to become the most successful of all Liverpool managers, faced United in 14 consecutive meetings after the war?

3 In 1947/48 United were drawn at home to Liverpool in the FA Cup, but where was the game played?

4 United won the game 3-0. Who scored the third goal?

5 When was the last time United faced Liverpool on Christmas Day?

6 Was the match a Christmas cracker?

7 Had the pair met in League competition on December 25 before?

8 Official cautions were rare at the time but a future Liverpool boss was booked during the 2-1 victory over United in August 1950. Name him.

9 Which Mancunian took over as manager of Liverpool in 1951?

10 The brother of which Northern Ireland manager made his United debut against Liverpool in November 1951?

11 Which future England star and United skipper also made his First Division entrance that day?

12 Which defender played his first senior game for United at Anfield in December 1952?

13 Which Merseyside hero was the youngster's direct opponent on his debut?

14 Who scored twice for the Red Devils as they thrashed Liverpool 4-0 on their run-in to the title in the spring of 1952?

15 Who grabbed a hat-trick for the Merseysiders at Anfield in August 1953?

16 Two first-half goals from which costly centre-forward set United on their way to a 5-1 triumph at Old Trafford in December 1953?

17 Which Liverpool defender broke a leg attempting to prevent one of those goals?

18 Why did United-Liverpool fixtures fall into abeyance after 1954?

19 Which friend of Matt Busby took over as Liverpool boss in December 1959?

20 Matt dissuaded his chum from resigning during difficult early days at Anfield? True or false.

Answers - see page 69

1 Which former United defender was managing Inverness Caledonian Thistle at the turn of the century?

2 Which club bought Danny Higginbotham from Manchester United in the year 2000?

3 Who became Danny's new manager?

4 With which club had Higginbotham spent 1998/99 on loan?

5 Did Ronnie Wallwork play enough times for a Premiership medal in 2000/2001?

6 From which club did the Red Devils recruit Jonathan Greening in March 1998?

7 With which top Swedish club did Jesper Blomqvist first forge an international reputation?

8 Against which club did Terry Cooke perform a piece of magic on his debut to set up a goal for Ryan Giggs in September 1995?

9 Who signed Terry from United in April 1999?

10 To which club was he loaned during 2000/2001?

11 How much did the Red Devils pay to sign Karel Poborsky in the summer of 1996?

12 In what country was the long-haired winger-cum-midfielder born?

13 Which other English club had wanted to acquire Karel before he opted for Old Trafford?

14 To which cash-strapped Portuguese club was he sold in December 1997?

15 Also in the summer of 1996, the Reds enlisted Jordi Cruyff from which famous club?

16 Jordi's dad is quite famous! Name him.

17 Jordi played in how many successive Charity Shields for United?

18 To which club was he loaned in January 1999?

19 Jordi scored the final goal of which title-winning campaign?

20 Decipher the anagram: MYOTM YOLTAR

Answers - see page 70

1 Where was Roy Keane born in August 1971?
2 Which Irish club did he serve before arriving in English football?
3 His first English employers were . . . .
4 Who was his first manager in the Football League?
5 How old was Keane when he won his first full cap, against Chile in Dublin?
6 Robbie Keane of Leeds is his younger brother. True or false?
7 At the end of his first season in England, Roy faced which opponents in the FA Cup Final?
8 A fellow midfielder hogged most of the headlines that day. Name him.
9 His second major Wembley final ended in League Cup defeat by which club?
10 In what summer did Roy Keane sign for Manchester United?
11 What was the British record transfer fee which changed hands in the transaction?
12 During Roy's first term as a Red, who was the man most frequently sidelined by the presence of the vigorous newcomer?
13 How many major gongs did Keane pocket at the end of that first campaign?
14 Roy netted twice in his second League outing for the Red Devils. Who were his victims?
15 Where did the Irishman score his first FA Cup goal for United?
16 Roy has been dismissed in two FA Cup semi-final replays. Who were the Reds playing on the first occasion?
17 Who also received his marching orders during that game?
18 What was the second FA Cup semi-final rematch in which Keane was dismissed?
19 That time, who was ordered off along with Roy?
20 What shirt number has become synonymous with Roy Keane?

Answers - see page 75

1 Who was Jackie Blanchflower's older brother?
2 At which ground did Jackie make his senior United debut in November 1951?
3 Which future captain of United made his First Division entrance in the same match?
4 What was Blanchflower's nickname among team-mates?
5 In what position did the stylish Irishman play most of his games when he earned a title medal in 1955/56?
6 In what role did he start the 1957 FA Cup Final?
7 What job did he take on for much of that controversial match?
8 An injury to which team-mate prompted the switch?
9 Having seemingly settled on his favoured position before Munich, Jackie faced fierce rivalry for the shirt from which colleague?
10 Jackie lived through the crash, but did he ever play football again?
11 How many full caps did the versatile Ulsterman win?
12 Shortly before Munich, Jackie helped Northern Ireland qualify for the 1958 World Cup Finals by beating which top European nation?
13 Which United comrade, a keeper, missed that triumph through injury?
14 How old was Jackie at the time of the accident?
15 During which season did Jackie win his first international cap?
16 Which club did his brother captain to the League and FA Cup double in 1960/61?
17 In what year did Jackie enlist at Old Trafford as a 16-year-old amateur?
18 Jackie scored an FA Cup hat-trick at Burnley in January 1954. True or false?
19 At what did the eloquent Irishman experience huge success in later life?
20 How old was Jackie Blanchflower when he died in 1998?

Answers - see page 76

1 Chris Casper is the son of which former Burnley player and manager?
2 In which position did Chris play on his rare outings for United?
3 To which club was he sold in 1998?
4 Against which opposition did Simon Davies score his sole senior goal for the Red Devils?
5 How many full caps did Simon earn as a Red Devil?
6 For which country did he play?
7 Who paid £150,000 for Davies in the summer of 1997?
8 Simon was on the books of which Lancashire club in 2000/2001?
9 Who signed goalkeeper Kevin Pilkington from the Red Devils?
10 Decipher the anagram: OYR ANEEK.
11 Which club did Graeme Tomlinson serve before joining United?
12 For whom was Graeme playing in 2000/2001?
13 Keith Gillespie was enjoying a renaissance with which promotion-hunting Lancashire club in the spring of 2001?
14 Who was his manager at that time?
15 To which club had the Ulsterman been loaned earlier in the season?
16 How many times did Francis Burns play for Scotland?
17 How many full Scottish caps did John Fitzpatrick receive?
18 Jim Leighton was capped 101 times by Scotland. True or false?
19 What was Jim's penulitmate club before retirement?
20 With which club did Alex Dawson close his League career?

United Ulstermen *(see page 76)*

ANSWERS

1 Belfast. 2 Sammy McIlroy. 3 David Healy. 4 Preston North End. 5 Jackie Blanchflower. 6 Harry Gregg. 7 Phil Mulryne. 8 Keith Gillespie. 9 Pat McGibbon. 10 Wigan Athletic. 11 Mal Donaghy. 12 Jackie Scott. 13 Ronnie Briggs. 14 Jimmy Nicholson. 15 Norman Whiteside. 16 Tom Sloan. 17 Jimmy Nicholl. 18 David McCreery. 19 Trevor Anderson. 20 Tommy Jackson.

Answers - see page 73

1 Which famous Frenchman made his United debut against City as a substitute at Old Trafford in December 1992?

2 Whose spectacular long-range effort answered critics who predicted he would be the man to make way for the newcomer?

3 Which Manchester derby has Sir Alex Ferguson referred to as his lowest moment as manager of United?

4 Whose fabulous volley offered the Reds their only crumb of consolation on that desolate occasion?

5 Whose 77th-minute winner settled the final Manchester derby of the 20th century in April 1996?

6 Who scored the second of City's two equalisers in that match?

7 That season ended with United as champions and City relegated. True or false?

8 Who was City's manager during that traumatic campaign?

9 Whose fourth-minute header was the only goal at Old Trafford in October 1995?

10 What did fans and video-makers dub the clash between City and United at Old Trafford in November 1994?

11 Who bagged a hat-trick in that one-sided affair?

12 During 1994/95, what was the goals aggregate for the two meetings between United and City?

13 Who returned from a five-match suspension to score the two goals in five minutes which sunk City at Old Trafford in April 1994?

14 Which man with two title medals was facing United that day?

15 Who scored twice in the first half to put City in charge against United at Maine Road in November 1993?

16 Whose second-half double redressed the balance in that compelling contest?

17 Whose left-wing surge paved the way for United's dramatic late winner?

18 Who arrived late in the box to snatch the 87th-minute winner?

19 Which future United coach was between City's posts as they suffered that debilitating reverse?

20 Which ex-Anfielder was wearing the light blue of City that day?

ANSWERS

Jackie Blanchflower (see page 73)
1 Danny Blanchflower. 2 Anfield. 3 Roger Byrne. 4 Twiggy. 5 Inside-forward. 6 Centre-half. 7 Goalkeeper. 8 Ray Wood. 9 Mark Jones. 10 No. 11 Twelve. 12 Italy. 13 Harry Gregg. 14 24 years old. 15 1953/54. 16 Tottenham Hotspur. 17 1949. 18 False. 19 After-dinner speaking. 20 65 years old.

1   In which Northern Irish city was George Best born?
2   Which former United star became Northern Ireland's national manager in 2000?
3   Which rookie striker scored twice on his full debut for Northern Ireland?
4   To which Lancashire club did Sir Alex Ferguson sell him during 2000/2001?
5   Which Ulsterman suffered severe injuries at Munich and never played again?
6   What United star was voted the top goalkeeper in the 1958 World Cup Finals?
7   United sold a Northern Ireland international to Norwich in March 1999. Name him.
8   Which winger joined Newcastle in the deal which took Andrew Cole to United?
9   Which centre-back earned his first full cap for Northern Ireland during 1995/96?
10 To what club was he sold in March 1997?
11 A Belfast-born utility man won 89 caps for Northern Ireland between 1980 and 1994, not all of them while a Red Devil. Who is he?
12 Another boy from Belfast won two full caps after leaving United for Grimsby Town in the summer of 1996. Name him.
13 Which keeper conceded seven goals against Sheffield Wednesday in an FA Cup tie, but went on to play for Northern Ireland?
14 Who made his United entrance as a 17-year-old in 1960/61, then played for Northern Ireland before his next birthday?
15 In 1982, which Ulsterman became the youngest player every to appear in the World Cup Finals?
16 Which blond, Ballymena-born midfielder made a dozen senior appearances for the Reds before serving Chester during 1982/83?
17 Which red-headed Northern Ireland international started his career with United, then later had two stints with Glasgow Rangers?
18 Which United 'supersub' earned 67 full caps for the Ulstermen?
19 Which former Portadown youngster helped United escape relegation in 1972/73?
20 Which experienced Northern Ireland performer bolstered the United midfield on their return to the top flight in 1975/76?

ANSWERS

Pot Luck - 22 *(see page 74)*
1 Frank Casper. 2 Central defender. 3 Reading. 4 Galatasaray. 5 One. 6 Wales. 7 Luton Town. 8 Rochdale. 9 Port Vale. 10 Roy Keane. 11 Bradford City. 12 Exeter City. 13 Blackburn Rovers 14 Graeme Souness. 15 Wigan Athletic. 16 Once. 17 None. 18 False, he had 91 caps. 19 Hibernian. 20 Brentford.

Answers - see page 79

1 Who was guarding the United net when the Reds lost 2-7 at home to Sheffield Wednesday in an FA Cup tie in February 1961?

2 How many goals did that same 'keeper concede on his League debut at Leicester less than two weeks earlier?

3 That same keeper went on to earn two full international caps for which country?

4 With which club did he play his last League game in 1967/68?

5 Which keeper with more than 50 England amateur international caps to his credit made four League appearances for United in 1960/61?

6 With which club did that player finish his League career?

7 Which promising United marksman of the 1950s went on to become a distinguished defender with Leyton Orient?

8 The arrival at Old Trafford of which fellow countryman cost Eire international left-back Joe Carolan his long-term place?

9 Genial Joe joined which club after leaving United?

10 With which Yorkshire side did Mark Pearson end his League playing days?

11 At which ground was Mark dismissed in March 1958?

12 On what emotional occasion did Mark made his senior United entrance?

13 Which London club did Pearson serve in the mid 1960s?

14 How has Johnny Giles made his living since giving up soccer management?

15 Which Northern Ireland international scored the goal by which United beat Juventus in a friendly in Turin in May 1963?

16 To which Welsh club was the Ulsterman sold on the following Christmas Eve?

17 Decipher the anagram: THWIGD KYREO.

18 After leaving United, Jimmy Nicholson made more than 300 appearances for which club?

19 Where did Jimmy end his League days?

20 How many times did Jimmy Nicholson play for Northern Ireland?

Answers - see page 80

1 From which club did Matt Busby sign Albert Quixall in September 1958?
2 How many Second Division title medals had Albert won with his first employers?
3 United paid a British record fee for the inside-forward's services. What was it?
4 What role did Albert play in United's first game after the Munich crash?
5 How many times had Quixall played for England by the time he arrived at Old Trafford?
6 How many caps did he add to that total as a United man?
7 For what item of his kit was Albert famed in the 1950s?
8 How many games did Albert have to wait before enjoying his first League win as a Red Devil?
9 In what League position did United finish in his first season at the club?
10 In what year's FA Cup Final did Albert win his sole honour as a Red?
11 Quixall scored one of United's three goals that day. True or false?
12 In how many of that season's FA Cup ties did Albert hit the target?
13 He scored a fourth-round winner against which Midlands opponents?
14 In which season, his most prolific as a Red Devil, did Albert weigh in with 15 senior goals?
15 Against which Lancashire rivals did Quixall contribute a hat-trick in April 1961?
16 Which other United star also plundered three goals in the same game?
17 Who did Albert join when he left United in September 1964?
18 What was the fee?
19 Which was Albert's final League club?
20 For which non-League club did Quixall perform subsequently while running a scrap metal business?

Answers - see page 77

1   Was Bryan Robson wearing a bubble-curled perm or a crew-cut when he checked in at Old Trafford in October 1981?

2   From which club was he signed?

3   Which team-mate from his old club arrived a little earlier but was seen as part of the same package deal?

4   What was Robbo's British record fee?

5   With what manager was he reunited in Manchester?

6   Who advised the United boss to 'pay whatever it took' to sign Bryan?

7   From what part of the country does Robson hail?

8   His leadership qualities inspired what nickname?

9   How many times did Bryan skipper the Red Devils to FA Cup triumph?

10   He waited a long time for a title medal, but how many did he collect in the end?

11   Bryan never won a major European club competition medal. True or false?

12   How many times did Robbo take the field for his country at full international level?

13   In how many of those games was he England captain?

14   How many goals did Bryan score for England?

15   In how many World Cup Final tournaments did Robbo take part?

16   How long did it take him to find the net against France in the 1982 competition?

17   With whom did Bryan jointly accept the Premier League trophy for United in 1992/93?

18   Bryan left Old Trafford in 1994 to become player-boss of which club?

19   At his first League club, Bryan broke a leg three times in the space of 12 months. True or false?

20   Who was the manager who sold Bryan Robson to Manchester United?

Answers - see page 78

1   Who scored Bayern Munich's second goal in the second leg of the 2001 Champions League quarter-final?

2   Which muscular marksman scored 22 League and FA Cup goals in a mere 22 appearances for United in the late 1940s?

3   Which Manchester teacher and United centre-forward had only four first-team outings but set an impeccable example to the reserves in the 1950s?

4   Which manager bought England under-23 forward Phil Chisnall from United in April 1964?

5   For which club did Phil make the most League appearances?

6   At what ground did Chisnall finish his senior career?

7   Which Aberdonian started the 1963/64 League season in United's number-seven shirt after a Charity Shield defeat, 4-0 by Everton, prompted sweeping changes?

8   To which club was that skilful Scot transferred in February 1965?

9   He ended his playing days with a second stint for which Welsh club?

10   Which promising Welsh midfielder was sold to Derby in 1978 after making only one senior appearance for the Reds, as a substitute?

11   Who was the Derby boss who bought him?

12   Which England youth international keeper was recalled from a loan stint with Torquay to make his senior United entrance in April 1972?

13   Six months later he joined the club he had faced on his Reds debut. Name it.

14   Which Irish left-back, who made his only two League appearances during 1978/79, fetched £37,000 when he was sold to Glentoran in 1982?

15   Who has scored the most senior hat-tricks for Manchester United?

16   How many?

17   How many times have United won the League Cup?

18   Who netted in each of his first four League Cup games for United, in 1987/88?

19   Who played 61 consecutive FA Cup games for United between 1954 and 1967?

20   Decipher the anagram: BONBY SETLIS.

ANSWERS

Albert Quixall (see page 78)
1 Sheffield Wednesday. 2 Two. 3 £45,000. 4 He skippered their opponents, Sheffield Wednesday. 5 Five. 6 None. 7 His short shorts. 8 Seven. 9 Second. 10 1963. 11 False. 12 Four. 13 Aston Villa. 14 1960/61. 15 Burnley. 16 Dennis Viollet. 17 Oldham Athletic. 18 £7,000. 19 Stockport County. 20 Altrincham.

Answers - see page 83

1 What was the score as United beat Blackpool to lift the FA Cup for the second time?

2 What colour shirts did the Reds wear at Wembley?

3 Name the United skipper who was presented with the trophy.

4 Blackpool were known as the Tangerines, but that was not their official nickname. What was?

5 The world's most famous player was on the pitch. Who was he?

6 Who put Blackpool ahead from the penalty spot?

7 Who committed the foul to concede the spot-kick?

8 Who scored twice for United?

9 Which England centre-forward netted for Blackpool?

10 Which feisty inside-forward took a quick free-quick to set up United's second equaliser.

11 Who put United in front for the first time?

12 Who contributed a late, long-range shot to clinch the victory?

13 Who had United defeated in the semi-final to reach Wembley?

14 Who was manager of Blackpool?

15 Why was United keeper Jack Crompton in constant pain?

16 That same season, in what League position did United finish?

17 Which England wing-half was wearing United's number-six shirt?

18 Which United star played despite anxiety about the overdue birth of his second child?

19 United played Blackpool in the League four days later. Who won?

20 What England player was captain of Blackpool?

ANSWERS

Pot Luck - 25 *(see page 83)*
1 10-1. **2** Wolves. **3** John Downie. **4** £20,000. **5** John Connelly. **6** £40,000. **7** Stoke City. **8** 1983/84. **9** Two goals. **10** Charlton Athletic. **11** 1982/83. **12** Real Madrid. **13** West Bromwich Albion. **14** A car crash. **15** Airdrieonians. **16** £570,000. **17** 1986/87. **18** Everton. **19** Nottingham Forest. **20** Alex Ferguson.

Answers - see page 84

1 United's run to the 1996/97 semi-finals of the Champions League opened with a 1-0 away defeat by Juventus. Who scored the goal?

2 What is Juve's nickname?

3 What is the name of the Turin giants' stadium?

4 Which Czech international was making his European entrance for United?

5 Who scored on his first European Cup start, in the 2-0 home victory over Rapid Vienna?

6 Who open the scoring for the Reds in the 2-0 triumph over Fenerbahce in Turkey?

7 Who inflicted on United their first ever home defeat in European competition?

8 Who scored the goal that shattered the Reds' proud 40-year record?

9 Who conceded the penalty against Juventus which cost United a home defeat for the second time in succession?

10 The man who was fouled got up to net from the spot. Name him.

11 Which future World Footballer of the Year lit up Old Trafford with his skills?

12 From whom did Peter Schemichel make the most famous save of his life as the Red Devils won in Vienna in December 1996?

13 Who opened the scoring for United in the 4-0 quarter-final drubbing of Porto at Old Trafford?

14 Who scored his final goal in European competition to put the Reds two up?

15 What was the result of the second leg in Portugal?

16 Which Brazilian marksman was off target with a succession of shots?

17 Which United midfielder struck a post in the 1-0 semi-final defeat by Borussia Dortmund in Germany?

18 Who replaced the injured Peter Schmeichel for the game in Dortmund?

19 By what score did United suffer their third home reverse of the season against continental opposition?

20 Borussia Dortmund went on to lose the final to Juventus. True or false?

Answers - see page 81

1 What was the margin of the first win in the League history of Manchester United, known as Newton Heath at the time of that victory in 1892?

2 Who were the opponents who suffered that day?

3 The signing of which player from Bradford Park Avenue in March 1949 broke United's transfer record?

4 What was the fee involved?

5 United banked their biggest transfer cheque to that point when they sold a winger to Blackburn Rovers in September 1966. Name him.

6 By how much did that transaction swell the Red Devils' coffers?

7. With which club did Garth Crooks start his League career?

8 During which season did he play in seven games on loan with United?

9 How many goals did Garth score for the Reds?

10 With which club was he serving when a back injury forced him to retire in 1990?

11 Lawrie Cunningham had five outings as a Red Devil during which season?

12 From which club did Ron Atkinson take the England winger on loan?

13 With what club had Ron and Lawrie worked together before?

14 What caused Lawrie's untimely death in 1989?

15 Peter Davenport first played Scottish League football for which club?

16 How much did Ron Atkinson pay to sign Davenport in March 1986?

17 In which season was Peter the only United man whose League goals reached double figures?

18 Davenport was an amateur on the books of which major club as a teenager?

19 From which Midlanders did United recruit Peter?

20 Decipher the anagram: XEAL GORSENEFU.

Answers - see page 82

1   Nobody has scored more League goals for United in one season than Dennis Viollet. How many times did he hit the net in 1959/60?

2   Only three players have struck more times than Dennis during their League careers as Red Devils: Bobby Charlton, Denis Law and which other marksman?

3   How many League goals did Dennis contribute to the Old Trafford cause?

4   With which striker did Dennis form such a lethal dual spearhead for the Reds?

5   In what city was the pencil-slim inside-forward born?

6   Who made his senior United debut on the same day as Viollet in April 1953?

7   Who were the opponents that afternoon in the north-east?

8   Dennis shot home the Reds' first goal in European competition. True or false?

9   How many times did Viollet strike in the second leg of United's first European Cup tie, against Anderlecht?

10   Dennis scored in each of his first five European outings. How many goals did he total in that quintet of matches?

11   Who replaced the unfit Viollet in the 1957 FA Cup Final?

12   After suffering injuries but surviving the Munich accident, was Dennis able to play in the 1958 FA Cup Final?

13   How many Championship medals did Viollet win?

14   How many full England caps were awarded to Dennis?

15   At the end of which season did he receive his belated international call-up?

16   Who provided the opposition that day in Eastern Europe?

17   Against which country did Dennis score his sole international goal?

18   Which club did Viollet join when he left Old Trafford in January 1962?

19   What fee secured his unexpected transfer?

20   Which club did Dennis manage briefly in 1971?

Answers - see page 87

1. In 1982, who did Norman Whiteside replace as the youngest player to appear in the World Cup Finals?
2. How many senior appearances had Norman made for United by that time?
3. In what capital city was Norman born?
4. Norman scored when called on as a substitute against Brighton in his first senior outing for United. True or false?
5. How old was he made that appearance?
6. Against what opponents did Whiteside become the youngest scorer in a Wembley final?
7. What was that occasion?
8. How did Norman score the goal which made him the youngest scorer in an FA Cup Final?
9. Who provided the opposition that day?
10. Who were Norman's next FA Cup Final victims?
11. Who was the international keeper who picked the ball out of the net on that May afternoon in 1985?
12. Alongside which Welsh striker did Whiteside play for the United youth team?
13. To what role was front-man Norman later converted?
14. How many full international caps did Norman earn?
15. Norman played his last game for United during what season?
16. How old was Whiteside when Alex Ferguson allowed him to leave Old Trafford?
17. To which club was Norman transferred?
18. How old was Norman when injuries forced his premature retirement?
19. Under which former United star did Whiteside serve briefly as assistant boss of Northwich Victoria?
20. In what field did Norman subsequently become qualified?

Answers - see page 88

1 Which red-headed midfielder made his Premiership debut for United at the Riverside in April 2001?
2 What is that promising young man's nationality?
3 Who was the unlikely opening scorer with a 30-yard thunderbolt that day against Boro?
4 Who netted his first goal of the year to clinch the Reds' victory?
5 Who were the opponents on the day United were presented with the Premiership trophy for 2000/2001?
6 In what subject is Raimond van der Gouw a university graduate?
7 And in which sphere did Alan Gowling obtain a degree?
8 Who was named as United's first League substitute, in August 1965?
9 Who was the first substitute to be brought on by the Red Devils that October?
10 Which fellow Aberdonian did he replace?
11 Who was United's goalkeeping coach in 2000/2001?
12 Did he ever play senior football for the Red Devils?
13 For which club did that coach play the most League matches?
14 Decipher the anagram: EDSIN WIRNI.
15 To which club did the Reds transfer Alan Davies in July 1985?
16 Which club was Alan serving at the time of his tragic death in 1992?
17 Alan Davies was a full international for Wales. True or false?
18 Which club did former United forward Bill Ridding lead to Wembley victory over the Red Devils?
19 Who was the club secretary of Manchester United in 2000/2001?
20 What is the Old Trafford postcode?

Title Trail 1955/56 (see page 88)

ANSWERS

1 Roger Byrne. 2 Mark Jones. 3 Albert Scanlon. 4 David Pegg. 5 Jack Crompton. 6 Tommy Taylor. 7 Jackie Scott. 8 Dennis Viollet. 9 14 matches. 10 Seven. 11 Two. 12 Chelsea. 13 11 points. 14 Blackpool. 15 John Doherty. 16 Ian Greaves. 17 Jeff Whitefoot. 18 Colin Webster. 19 True. 20 Charlton Athletic, 3-0 at The Valley.

1 United faced Benfica at which stadium?
2 In what colours were the Red Devils decked out?
3 Who was United's captain on that glorious night?
4 Which sidelined Old Trafford star watched the game on TV from his hospital bed?
5 Which 36-year-old United stalwart passed a late fitness test and played?
6 Which United winger hit the finest form of his life and was hailed widely as man of the match?
7 Who missed three chances to score, but set up the opening goal?
8 Who was celebrating his nineteenth birthday on the day of the final?
9 What colour were Benfica's shirts?
10 Who skippered the mighty Portuguese?
11 Who hit United's woodwork with a scorching drive early in the game?
12 Did Bobby Charlton net the first goal with his right foot, his left foot or his head?
13 Who was the giant spindly spearhead of Benfica's attack?
14 What was the half-time score?
15 Who equalised for the Portuguese?
16 Who put Matt Busby's men back in front?
17 Whose backpass facilitated the downfield punt which led to United's second goal?
18 What was the score after 90 minutes?
19 Who headed United's third?
20 Who rounded off proceedings with his second goal of the night?

ANSWERS

Norman Whiteside (see page 85)

1 Pele. **2** Two. **3** Belfast. **4** False. **5** Sixteen. **6** Liverpool. **7** The 1983 League Cup Final.
8 With a header. **9** Brighton. **10** Everton. **11** Neville Southall. **12** Mark Hughes.
13 Midfielder. **14** 38 caps. **15** 1988/89. **16** 24 years old. **17** Everton. **18** 26 years old.
19 Sammy McIlroy. **20** Podiatry, the study of foot disorders.

Answers - see page 86

1 Who captained United to Championship glory?
2 Only one man was ever-present as the title was lifted. Name him.
3 Who started the season on the left wing?
4 Who wore the number-11 shirt for most of the season?
5 Who made a single appearance between the posts?
6 Who topped the Red Devils' League scoring charts at season's end?
7 Who was the Irish outside-right who played in one game?
8 Who scored twice as United opened the campaign with a 2-2 draw at Birmingham?
9 How long was the unbeaten run with which the Reds finished the season?
10 How many First Division defeats did they suffer?
11 How many players reached double figures in goals?
12 Who did United replace as champions?
13 By what margin did they top the division?
14 Who were the runners-up?
15 Which Manchester-born inside-right pocketed a title medal on merit?
16 Who replaced Bill Foulkes at right-back for the final third of the season?
17 Which wing-half lost his place to Eddie Colman in November?
18 Which Welsh forward played just enough games to qualify for a medal?
19 United conceded more than half a century of League goals. True or false?
20 Who inflicted the Reds' heaviest defeat of the season?

Answers - see page 91

1 Decipher this anagram: DISNEN TOILEVEL.
2 United are one of only how many clubs to have remained in the top two divisions since entering League football?
3 When was the last time Manchester United won a major honour in the same season as Manchester City lifted one, also?
4 What did City win that term?
5 United were offered a place in the 1958/59 European Cup as a mark of sympathy after the Munich crash. True or false?
6 Who inflicted United's worst single-match defeat in European competition?
7 What was that score?
8 In which competition did the Reds suffer that reverse?
9 Apart from United, which English club has provided the European Player of the Year?
10 Who was the footballer thus honoured?
11 In what year was that award made?
12 From which club did United sign Wyn Davies in September 1972?
13 What was Davies' nickname?
14 What was Wyn's first club?
15 With which Lancastrians did he continue his career?
16 Later Wyn became an idol with which north-easterners?
17 Which seaside club signed Davies when he left United?
18 Which Manchester-born midfielder made his League debut on loan with Swindon during 1984/85 before playing in the First Division for the Reds?
19 Which former Busby Babe was Burnley's chief scout during the early 1980s?
20 In what year will the Reds celebrate the centenary of changing their name to Manchester United?

ANSWERS

United Strips (see page 91)
1 Sharp Electronics. 2 1983. 3 1999/2000. 4 Vodafone. 5 The red Admiral shirt of 1977.
6 Red-and-white quartered shirts, blue shorts. 7 Yellow and green. 8 Blue. 9 1902.
10 White with a deep red 'V'. 11 Maroon with white hoops. 12 Grey shirts and white shorts. 13 Blue and white stripes. 14 1993/94. 15 1998/99. 16 1992. 17 Adidas.
18 1993/94. 19 Nike. 20 Blue.

Answers - see page 92

1 United faced Liverpool for the first time in more than half a decade in January 1960, in which competition?
2 What was the result of the clash, played out in an Anfield quagmire?
3 Who scored two brilliant goals for the visitors?
4 Which future World Cup winner was just beginning to make his mark for Liverpool in 1960?
5 Whose 89th-minute free-kick put Liverpool 3-2 up at Old Trafford in November 1962?
6 Who equalised for the Red Devils with practically the last kick of the match?
7 A Scottish international centre-forward scored in both Liverpool's 1962/63 meetings with United. Name him.
8 Which England under-23 player moved from United to Liverpool in 1964?
9 How much did Liverpool pay to sign the talented young Mancunian?
10 Who netted Liverpool's winner at United on the way to title glory in 1963/64?
11 Which United forward deputised in goal when Harry Gregg was injured?
12 Which native Mancunian scored twice against United at Anfield as Liverpool closed in on the Championship in April 1964?
13 How far behind Liverpool did second-placed United finish in 1963/64?
14 In April 1965, who scored twice for United as they beat Liverpool at Old Trafford on the way to replacing their rivals as champions?
15 Whose late winner gave Liverpool the points at Anfield on New Year's Day 1966?
16 When the two sets of Reds drew 2-2 at Old Trafford in December 1966, Ian St John netted twice for Liverpool. Who responded in kind for United?
17 Which Liverpool goalkeeper, affectionately dubbed 'The Flying Pig', frequently starred against United in the 1960s?
18 Which United centre-half made his senior debut at Anfield in October 1968?
19 Who was United's top scorer against Liverpool during the 1960s?
20 Which Anfielder hit the target most frequently against the Red Devils during the same decade?

ANSWERS

Pot Luck - 28 (see page 92)
1 1988/89. **2** Luton Town. **3** Northern Ireland. **4** 89 caps. **5** 31 years old. **6** £650,000.
7 Luton Town. **8** Stamford Bridge. **9** Ian Porterfield. **10** Malachy. **11** Burnley. **12** Third Division. **13** Norwich City. **14** £750,000. **15** Neil Webb. **16** Manchester United. **17** True. **18** 1993/94. **19** West Bromwich Albion. **20** Philip Neville.

Answers - see page 89

1   Who was United's first main shirt sponsor?
2   When did the Red Devils' agreement with that company start?
3   After what season was the arrangement changed?
4   Who replaced the original sponsors?
5   Which was the first replica strip which fans could buy?
6   What were the first colours worn by United's predecessor club?
7   What colour were the shirts worn later by that club, and which formed the basis of a new kit produced in 1992/93?
8   What colour shirts did the 1948 FA Cup winners wear?
9   When did United first wear red shirts and white shorts?
10 What colour was the shirt worn between 1922 and 1927?
11 A brief but radical change was made in 1934. Describe that new shirt.
12 Which away kit was jettisoned at half-time at Southampton in April 1996?
13 What colour shirts were the Red Devils wearing when they clinched the Premiership title in 1995/96?
14 When was the most recent season in which United shirts included laced collars?
15 When was a zip introduced?
16 When did Umbro begin producing United kit?
17 Who were Umbro's predecessors as suppliers to the club?
18 When were United first seen in all-black?
19 With which producers did United announce a new deal during 2000/2001?
20 What colour was on Bobby Charlton's back when he held aloft the European Cup in 1968?

ANSWERS

Pot Luck - 27 (see page 89)
1 Dennis Viollet. 2 Ten. 3 1968. 4 League title. 5 True. 6 Sporting Lisbon in March 1964.
7 0-5. 8 European Cup Winners' Cup. 9 Blackpool. 10 Stanley Matthews. 11 1956.
12 Manchester City. 13 Wyn the Leap. 14 Wrexham. 15 Bolton Wanderers. 16 Newcastle
United. 17 Blackpool. 18 Mark Dempsey. 19 John Doherty. 20 2002.

Answers - see page 90

1 During which season did Mal Donaghy join Manchester United?
2 From which club was the Irishman signed?
3 Does Mal hail from Northern Ireland or the Republic?
4 How many full international caps did he collect?
5 How old was Donaghy when he became a Red Devil?
6 How much did he cost the club he had idolised as a boy?
7 To which club did Alex Ferguson loan Donaghy during 1989/90?
8 Which ground became Mal's new HQ when he left Old Trafford in August 1992?
9 Who was his new manager?
10 What is Mal short for?
11 With which club did Mike Phelan begin his League career?
12 Which divisional title did he help to win in 1981/82?
13 With which club did he pocket a Second Division Championship gong in 1985/86?
14 How much did United pay for his services in July 1989?
15 Who did the Red Devils sign on the same day?
16 With which club did Phelan earn his sole England cap?
17 As a Red, Mike won a full set of major domestic medals plus one European. True or false?
18 At the end of which season was Phelan released on a free transfer?
19 Which club did Mike join after leaving Old Trafford?
20 Decipher the anagram: HIPLPI LEVILEN.

1   Shay is short for what first name?
2   In what position did Shay earn a European Cup winner's medal in 1968?
3   What was the unfamiliar role filled by the popular Brennan on his senior debut for United?
4   How did he mark the biggest occasion of his career to that point?
5   Who provided the opposition on that emotion-charged post-Munich evening?
6   In what competition was that memorable debut?
7   How many times did Shay play for the Republic of Ireland at full international level?
8   Where was Brennan born?
9   In what position did the rookie Shay earn an FA Youth Cup winner's medal in 1955?
10 Against which London club did Shay net in an FA Cup semi-final replay in 1958?
11 Was Shay selected for the subsequent final at Wembley?
12 Did Brennan ever play in an FA Cup Final?
13 What role did Shay fill for three-quarters of the 1959/60 season?
14 How many League Championship medals were in the Brennan collection?
15 Which young Scot was displaced by Shay for the second leg of the 1968 European Cup semi-final?
16 Which Real Madrid star was Brennan's experience thought necessary to counter?
17 Shay reached the fringe of England's 1962 World Cup squad. True or false?
18 In what year did Shay bow out of Old Trafford?
19 Which League of Ireland side did he manage to two Championships?
20 How old was Shay Brennan when he died in Tramore in June 2000?

Answers - see page 96

1　United played in five consecutive FA Cup semi-finals between 1962 and 1966. Bill Foulkes was one of two ever-present defenders; who was the other?

2　Bobby Charlton played in all of those consecutive semis; who was the other attacker who never missed a match?

3　The Reds lost four of those five semi-finals. True or false?

4　Where did United face Tottenham in 1962?

5　Who netted for the Reds as the Londoners triumphed 3-1?

6　Two Welsh wingers were on target for Spurs. One was Cliff Jones; who was the other?

7　A player with 44 goals for England scored Spurs' other goal. Name him.

8　The man who wore United's number-ten shirt in the 1962 semi was destined to captain an FA Cup Final side in 1964. Who was he?

9　The Reds fielded two Norberts against Spurs in 1962. True or false?

10　In the semi-final of 1963, United defeated a club who would beat them at Wembley 13 years later. Which club?

11　Who scored the only goal of that game?

12　What was the venue for that dour last-four encounter?

13　Which Scot, playing his third FA Cup tie for the Reds in April 1963, went on to be a colossal creative influence for the rest of the decade?

14　Who was the sole member of the victorious 1963 semi-final side to miss a Wembley place?

15　Where was the quagmire in which the Red Devils were submerged in 1964?

16　Who were United's conquerors on that muddy occasion?

17　Who netted United's only goal in a 3-1 defeat that year?

18　Who scored two for the victors, and then went on to score the 1964 Wembley winner?

19　Every time United lost a semi-final in the 1960s, their conquerors lifted the cup. True or false?

20　Which future England boss managed the side which beat the Reds in 1964?

Answers - see page 93

1   Which goalkeeper made a handful of Reds appearances in 1984/85 before becoming a stalwart for Middlesbrough?

2   Which marksman, who featured briefly for United, was said to be 'Black Magic in the box' during his Spurs prime?

3   Who was named in the programme to play for Clapton Orient against United in 1925, only to switch sides after a deal was struck shortly before kick-off?

4   From which Irish club did the Red Devils recruit Liam O'Brien in October 1986?

5   In what position did Liam specialise?

6   Is Liam a Northern or a Southern Irishman?

7   With which club did he flourish after leaving Old Trafford?

8   How much were United paid for his services?

9   With which club did he finish his League playing days?

10 At what ground was Liam dismissed in the opening minutes of a League encounter in January 1987?

11 Which Red was sent off against his former club at Old Trafford in August 1994?

12 Who were United's opponents that day?

13 Which United man was sent off at Bolton in September 1997, later to have the dismissal rescinded?

14 Which Trotter got his marching orders on the same occasion?

15 With which club did Ralph Milne kick off his senior career?

16 Which former United man sold Ralph to Alex Ferguson?

17 What was Milne's home ground prior to Old Trafford?

18 Which Salford-born goalkeeper played twice for the Reds as Jack Crompton's deputy, then departed to Torquay United?

19 Decipher this anagram: NIFBAE RHEBATZ.

20 With which club was Mike Phelan coaching in 2000/2001?

Answers - see page 94

1   Who were United playing when Wes Brown was summoned from the bench for his senior debut at Old Trafford in May 1988?

2   Who left the field to make way for the newcomer?

3   How old was Wes at the time of that Premiership entrance?

4   What was the result of the match?

5   Who were the opponents when he made his first senior start six days later?

6   Did Wes play enough games to qualify for a Championship medal in 1998/99?

7   How many Premiership starts had Brown made when he was called up for his full international debut in April 1999?

8   Who were the opposition?

9   Who replaced Wes after 73 minutes of that game?

10   Why did Wes miss the whole of 1999/2000?

11   Which player, who had experienced similar misfortune in 1997/98, offered advice which helped Wes through that ordeal?

12   Brown is a natural central defender but he has also excelled for the Reds in which other role?

13   Against which opponents did he score his first senior goal?

14   Wes supplied the cross for Ryan Giggs to open the scoring within two minutes of his European debut against which opposition?

15   Wes scored an own goal at Elland Road in April 1999. True or false?

16   United were three minutes from reaching the Champions League quarter-finals when Wes put through his own goal against which club in February 2001?

17   A week or so later Brown was spared similar trauma when his late 'own goal' was ruled out by an offside decision at which ground?

18   In which city was Wes Brown born?

19   Which club offered to sign Brown in the summer of 1998?

20   Which former United winger is credited with spotting Wes in junior football?

ANSWERS

FA Cup Semi-Finals - 2 *(see page 94)*

1 Tony Dunne, 2 David Herd. 3 True. 4 Hillsborough. 5 David Herd. 6 Terry Medwin. 7 Jimmy Greaves. 8 Nobby Lawton. 9 True, Messrs Stiles and Lawton. 10 Southampton. 11 Denis Law. 12 Villa Park. 13 Paddy Crerand. 14 Nobby Stiles. 15 Hillsborough. 16 West Ham United. 17 Denis Law. 18 Ronnie Boyce. 19 False. 20 Ron Greenwood.

Answers - see page 99

1 From which club did Matt Busby sign Paddy Crerand in February 1963?
2 What was the fee?
3 Paddy starred in that season's FA Cup Final against which opponents?
4 For whom did he create United's first goal in a 3-1 victory?
5 How many full Scottish caps did Crerand win?
6 During his spell as United's assistant manager, who was his boss?
7 Paddy had his own brief stint in the United hot seat during the 1970s. True or false?
8 In what famously tough area of Glasgow was Paddy raised?
9 Paddy's sole European goal for United was scored in what famous victory?
10 Only once, at Old Trafford in September 1964, did Crerand score twice in a game for United. Who were the opponents?
11 Paddy won two title medals with United. How many did he earn north of the border?
12 Of which club was Paddy the manager from July 1976 to January 1977?
13 Crerand was on the losing Celtic side in the 1961 Scottish Cup Final. Who took the trophy?
14 For which League club did his son, Danny, play three games during 1987/88?
15 Paddy was sent off playing for Scotland in Bratislava against which opponents?
16 Paddy was an ever-present during United's victorious 1967/68 European Cup-winning campaign. True or false?
17 Against which opponents did Crerand make his League entrance for United in February 1963?
18 In what season did Paddy make his final senior appearance for the Reds?
19 Which future United manager attempted to lure Crerand to Chelsea in 1961?
20 After leaving football, Paddy spent nine years as the landlord of which pub in Altrincham, near Manchester?

Answers - see page 100

1 How much did Manchester United pay to sign Ralph Milne?
2 Who did the affable Scot replace on the Red Devils' left wing?
3 Which was Ralph's first English club?
4 In which season did Milne win a Scottish title medal?
5 Ralph Milne scored 12 goals for his Scottish club in senior European competitions. True or false?
6 To which club did Alex Ferguson loan his countryman in January 1990?
7 From which club did United acquire Mick Martin in January 1973?
8 Who was the buying boss?
9 Mick is the son of which famous international?
10 Which Midlanders signed Mick in December 1975?
11 Who was the former Red Devil in charge at that club?
12 For which League club did Mick compile the highest number of League appearances?
13 Where did Mick Martin end his League playing days?
14 In which position did midfielder Mick sometimes play for his country?
15 Which former Old Trafford team-mate was his direct opponent at Wembley in 1976?
16 Which of his former clubs did Mick later serve as a coach?
17 Which Red Devil was sent off at home to Newcatsle in April 1998?
18 Decipher the anagram: ALPU CENI.
19 What was the last season in which United didn't miss a penalty in senior competition?
20 Who netted five out of five from the spot that term?

1 Who is the most recent United man to captain England?
2 Which United star won a century of England caps?
3 Which pair of United brothers have played for England?
4 Which Salford-born redhead notched a Wembley hat-trick against Poland?
5 How many times did Stuart Pearson play for England?
6 How many full England caps were won by Jimmy Greenhoff?
7 Brian Greenhoff won 28 England caps. True or false?
8 Against which country was Steve Coppell playing when an injury signalled the end of his career?
9 Was Paul Ince a West Ham or Manchester United player when first capped by England?
10 In what year did Lee Sharpe win his first full cap?
11 With which club did Gary Pallister win his first full England honours?
12 Did Steve Bruce receive a full cap?
13 Apart from Bobby Charlton, which United player helped to beat West Germany in the 1966 World Cup Final?
14 Which United winger played in the first game of the 1966 World Cup Final tournament, but then lost his place?
15 Which England centre-forward died in the Munich air crash?
16 Which future England star played only an hour of first team football for the Red Devils?
17 Which United defender made 33 consecutive appearances for England in the 1950s?
18 Which United midfielder ruptured an achilles tendon playing for England in 1989?
19 Ryan Giggs won schoolboy honours for England. True or false?
20 Which former Cambridge marksman left United and went on to play for England?

Answers – see page 98

1 What was Teddy Sheringham's first League club?
2 With what Republican of Ireland international did he form a prolific spearhead for that club?
3 Which manager took Teddy to the Midlands in 1991?
4 From which club did Alex Ferguson sign Sheringham in the summer of 1997?
5 Alongside which German star had Teddy thrived at that club?
6 Who did Sheringham face on his League debut for United?
7 He scored two goals that day. True or false?
8 Teddy excelled and scored twice at Highbury in November 1997. What was the result of the match?
9 Before his two famous cup final goals in 1998/99, how many times had Teddy hit the target for United that season?
10 In 1997/98, how many penalties did Sheringham miss before the job was taken away from him?
11 Teddy scored in United's opening League fixture of 1998/99 against which visitors to Old Trafford?
12 Sheringham made his full England debut in May 1993, in a World Cup qualifier in Katowice, against which country?
13 Which manager awarded Sheringham his first full England cap?
14 Which manager bought Teddy for the club he served before United?
15 At what ground did Teddy score his first goal for England against Sweden in June 1995?
16 Man-of-the-match Teddy scored twice in England's most memorable performance of Euro '96. Who lost 4-1 at Wembley that day?
17 Which former Manchester United player managed Teddy at his first League club?
18 What medal did Sheringham pocket after his first high-profile game for United?
19 Teddy scored in his only League Cup game for United in December 1998. Who were the opposition?
20 Teddy scored his first hat-trick for United in October 2000. Who were the victims?

Pot Luck - 30 *(see page 98)*

ANSWERS

1 £170,000. 2 Jesper Olsen. 3 Charlton Athletic. 4 1982/83. 5 False, he scored 15 goals.
6 West Ham United. 7 Bohemians. 8 Tommy Docherty. 9 Con Martin, who was capped by both the Republic of Ireland and Northern Ireland. 10 West Bromwich Albion. 11 Johnny Giles. 12 Newcastle United. 13 Preston. 14 Central defence. 15 Stuart Pearson.
16 Newcastle United. 17 Ole Gunnar Solskjaer. 18 Paul Ince. 19 1995/96. 20 Eric Cantona.

Answers - see page 103

Name the grounds of the following clubs, all of which Manchester United visited during 2000/2001:

1   Ipswich Town
2   West Ham United
3   Everton
4   Leicester City
5   Watford
6   Coventry City
7   Derby County
8   Sunderland
9   Sturm Graz
10 Charlton Athletic
11 Newcastle United
12 Fulham
13 Bradford City
14 Chelsea
15 Leeds United
16 Bayern Munich
17 Valencia
18 Middlesbrough
19 Southampton
20 Tottenham Hotspur

1   Name the stadium in which United humbled Benfica 5-1 in March 1966.
2   Who was the star of the show, netting twice in the first 12 minutes?
3   What headgear was that hero wearing on his return home?
4   Who made it 3-0 to the Red Devils after 15 minutes?
5   Benfica reduced the arrears with a United own goal. Who was the culprit?
6   He didn't net often for United, but he contributed the fourth in Lisbon. Name him.
7   Which England hero completed the rout with United's fifth?
8   The first leg at Old Trafford had ended in a 3-2 victory for United. Who made one of the Portuguese goals and scored the other?
9   From what unlikely source did United's third goal come?
10 What colour shirts were the Red Devils wearing that night at Old Trafford?
11 Who was United's goalkeeper in both those classic clashes?
12 United's semi-final opponents were Partizan Belgrade, from which country?
13 Which star Irishman was a passenger with an injured knee as the Reds went down 2-0 in the away first leg?
14 That defeat was United's first in any European game that season. True or false?
15 Who scored United's solitary reply in the 1-0 victory over Partizan at Old Trafford?
16 Which United man, together with a Partizan player, was sent off for fighting?
17 Who was the non-playing club captain who raced on to the field to escort the offender to safety?
18 Who was the deputy right-winger for the home game with Partizan?
19 In how many previous seasons had United reached a European semi-final?
20 Had they prevailed, United would have been Britain's first European champions, but who beat them to it in 1967?

ANSWERS

Pot Luck - 32 (see page 104)

1 Ian Storey-Moore. 2 Frank O'Farrell. 3 Paul Scholes. 4 Teddy Sheringham. 5 Carlo Nash. 6 Joe Spence. 7 Once, v Willem II in 1963. 8 Carrington. 9 The Cliff. 10 Derby County. 11 Brian Kidd. 12 Eric Cantona. 13 Fred The Red. 14 Ron Atkinson. 15 Ajax. 16 Bordeaux. 17 FA Cup winner's medal in 1985. 18 Johnny Sivebaek. 19 St Etienne. 20 Denis Law.

Answers - see page 101

1 The acquisition of Martin Buchan represented the finest signing of which United boss?

2 From which club was Martin recruited?

3 What was the transfer fee, which turned out to be such a bargain?

4 Among the many honours already garnered by Buchan was a Scottish title medal. True or false?

5 On what London ground did Martin make his Red Devils debut in March 1972?

6 When had Martin been voted Scottish Player of the Year?

7 How many of United's three FA Cup Finals during the 1970s did Buchan miss through injury?

8 Under how many United bosses did Martin serve?

9 Alongside which countryman did Buchan play at the heart of the Reds' rearguard in the late 1970s and early 1980s?

10 Did Martin become United skipper before or after their rise from the Second Division?

11 Who voted Martin Buchan First Division Player of the Year in 1977?

12 Which United manager decided the 34-year-old was surplus to requirements in 1983?

13 That August, Martin was freed to join which Lancashire club?

14 With which club was Buchan linked persistently by the press when it became clear he was leaving United?

15 Martin's younger brother followed him from the same Scottish club to Old Trafford. Name him.

16 How many times did Buchan play for Scotland?

17 In more than 450 senior outings for United, how many times did Martin score?

18 Of which club did Buchan become manager following his injury-enforced retirement from playing?

19 How long did he last in the job before resigning?

20 Martin's son is a professional footballer north of the border. What's his name?

Answers - see page 102

1 Which England winger did Brian Clough parade at the Baseball Ground as a prospective Derby player in 1972, when actually he was bound for United?

2 Who made that player one of his first signings for the Red Devils?

3 Who missed a penalty in the Manchester derby in April 2001?

4 Who scored from the spot in the same match?

5 Which keeper got a hand to that successful shot and almost kept it out?

6 Who was United's most prolific pre-war scorer?

7 How many times was David Herd sent off as a United player?

8 What is the location of the Reds' new state-of-the-art training ground?

9 What was the name of their previous training headquarters?

10 From which club did Steve McClaren join United as Alex Ferguson's number-two?

11 Who was Steve's predecessor in that role?

12 Who was chosen as United's greatest player of all time by readers of the club magazine?

13 United's mascot has his own regular page in the club programme. What's his name?

14 Which manager signed Jesper Olsen for the Reds in July 1984?

15 From what club was the talented little Dane recruited?

16 To which club was he transferred in November 1988?

17 What major club honour did Jesper earn as a Red Devil?

18 United signed another Dane in February 1986. Name him.

19 Who did that newcomer join in August 1987?

20 Decipher the anagram: SNIDE AWL.

Answers - see page 107

1   Who scored the goal at Old Trafford which tilted the title race Arsenal's way in March 1998?
2   Who was manager of the Arsenal side which went on to lift the League and FA Cup double that season?
3   Who netted the only goal of the game as the Reds knocked the Gunners out of the FA Cup in February 1951?
4   Who scored twice for United against Arsenal at Highbury in the nine-goal thriller a few days before the Munich crash?
5   What great Welsh goalkeeper was between the Gunners' posts that day?
6   Who left Highbury for Old Trafford in August 1981?
7   Who scored within a minute of making his Arsenal debut as a substitute at home to United in September 1998?
8   Who struck first for the Gunners in their 3-0 victory that afternoon?
9   Who scored to put United into the fifth round of the FA Cup in January 1962?
10   United practically clinched the 1964/65 title at home to Arsenal. Who scored twice in the Reds' 3-1 victory?
11   Arsenal beat United 4-0 at Highbury in 1970/71. Who scored a hat-trick that day?
12   Who missed a United penalty in the 1-1 home draw in February 1999?
13   Who left Highbury for Old Trafford midway through 1972/73, then made his United debut against his former employers?
14   Which of United's 1968 European Cup heroes was transferred to Arsenal in 1974?
15   Who scored a goal in each of the League clashes with Arsenal during 1975/76?
16   Who scored twice for Arsenal as they beat United in their first League Cup clash of 1977?
17   Who netted three times over the two legs of United's 1982/83 League Cup semi-final victory against Arsenal?
18   Which United keeper switched to Highbury in April 1974?
19   A Dutchman notched two goals at home to Arsenal in March 1984. Name him.
20   When United took the title in 1999/2000, how many more wins did they record than runners-up Arsenal?

Pot Luck - 33 (see page 107)

ANSWERS

1 Tottenham Hotspur. 2 Robert Pires of Arsenal. 3 1970. 4 Chelsea. 5 David Webb.
6 1911 7 Bradford City. 8 The Khaki Cup Final. 9 George Mutch. 10 Preston North End.
11 Canada. 12 Northern Ireland. 13 Alex Forsyth. 14 John Gidman. 15 Sunderland.
16 Glasgow Rangers. 17 Raith Rovers. 18 Millwall. 19 Bryan Robson. 20 The North Stand.

Answers - see page 108

1   What Brighton fanzine owes its name to an incident in this game?
2   What was the score when the incident occurred?
3   What footballing trauma had already befallen Brighton that season?
4   Which United and England winger missed the final through injury and soon would be forced into premature retirement?
5   What Welsh youngster replaced the missing star?
6   Which regular United midfielder was sidelined by suspension?
7   Which Brighton bulwark failed to overturn his suspension in the High Court, but was back for the replay?
8   Who opened the scoring for the Seagulls?
9   United's equaliser was netted by which Republic of Ireland international?
10   Which former Chelsea skipper contributed the goal of the game?
11   Brighton's late equaliser was scored by which future England utility player?
12   Who was the goalkeeping hero who kept the Reds in contention at the death?
13   Who netted twice for United in their 4-0 replay victory?
14   Who became the youngest goalscorer in FA Cup Final history?
15   What was the nationality of the man who completed United's triumph from the spot?
16   Who was the Scouser who led out the Seagulls?
17   Which former Anfielder had netted against his former club during Brighton's journey to Wembley?
18   To whom were the United fans singing 'Happy Birthday'?
19   Which Brighton stalwart was the brother of an England cricketer?
20   Which United midfielder, having played in the semi-final, was gutted to be dropped for Wembley?

Answers - see page 105

1 Who lost an FA Cup semi-final at Old Trafford in 2001?
2 Who scored the winning goal in that match?
3 In which year was the destination of the FA Cup last settled at Old Trafford?
4 In that year's replay, Leeds were the losers. Who were the winners?
5 Who scored the decisive goal?
6 When was the first time the FA Cup Final was replayed at Old Trafford?
7 Who were the victors on that occasion?
8 What was the tag given to the 1915 final between Sheffield United and Chelsea, also contested at Old Trafford?
9 Which former United and Scotland forward died in the spring of 2001 at the age of 88?
10 For which club did he score the winning goal in the 1938 FA Cup Final with a late penalty?
11 In what country was red-haired United full-back Jimmy Nicholl born?
12 For which nation did Jimmy win 73 full caps?
13 Which Scot did Nicholl replace as United's regular right-back in the mid 1970s?
14 Which newcomer ousted him from that slot in the early 1980s?
15 Which north-eastern club did Jimmy serve after leaving Old Trafford?
16 With which Scots did he enjoy two stints as a player?
17 Jimmy has put in two spells as manager of which Kirkcaldy club?
18 Nicholl spent a brief period guiding the fortunes of which London club?
19 Decipher the anagram: RANBY SORONB.
20 In what stand at Old Trafford is the United museum housed?

United v Arsenal - 2 *(see page 105)*

ANSWERS

1 Marc Overmars. 2 Arsene Wenger. 3 Stan Pearson. 4 Tommy Taylor. 5 Jack Kelsey. 6 Frank Stapleton. 7 Freddie Ljungberg. 8 Tony Adams. 9 Maurice Setters. 10 Denis Law. 11 John Radford. 12 Dwight Yorke. 13 George Graham. 14 Brian Kidd. 15 Stuart Pearson. 16 Malcolm Macdonald. 17 Steve Coppell. 18 Jimmy Rimmer. 19 Arnold Muhren. 20 Six.

Answers - see page 106

1   In what role did Lou Macari first make his reputation with club and country?
2   From which Scottish titans did United enlist little Lou in January 1973?
3   How much did the Red Devils pay for his signature?
4   Was the fee a record for a Scot?
5   Against which Londoners did Macari score on his United debut at Old Trafford?
6   Which club did Lou reportedly spurn to join United?
7   In which position did Lou Macari attain his greatest success?
8   How many times did he play for Scotland at full international level?
9   Lou was a non-smoking teetotaller. True or false?
10 Lou scored United's winner in the 1977 FA Cup Final. True or false?
11 How many Scottish title medals did Macari win with his first club?
12 How many times did Lou represent the Reds in FA Cup Finals?
13 Lou netted the goal which made certain of United's return to the top flight in 1974/75. On what ground was he at the time?
14 In which summer did Macari leave Old Trafford?
15 Of which club did he become player-manager?
16 Which former United goalkeeper became Lou's assistant in that job?
17 Lou's next management post was with which Londoners?
18 With which club has Macari put in two spells as manager?
19 The Macari management career has taken him to his homeland only once, to guide the fortunes of which club?
20 Lou Macari was attempting to lead which Yorkshire club out of relegation trouble in the spring of 2001?

ANSWERS

FA Cup Final 1983 *(see page 106)*

1 And Smith Must Score. **2** 2-2. **3** Relegation from Division One. **4** Steve Coppell. **5** Alan Davies. **6** Remi Moses. **7** Steve Foster. **8** Gordon Smith. **9** Frank Stapleton. **10** Ray Wilkins. **11** Gary Stevens. **12** Gary Bailey. **13** Bryan Robson. **14** Norman Whiteside. **15** Dutch (Arnold Muhren). **16** Jimmy Melia. **17** Jimmy Case. **18** Sir Matt Busby. **19** Steve Gatting, brother of Mike. **20** Ashley Grimes.

SECOND HALF

Answers - see page 113

1   From which club did United sign Paul Ince in September 1989?

2   How much did they pay for him?

3   Before leaving, what did Paul do which many of his old fans found unforgivable?

4   What number shirt did Paul wear in both installments of the 1990 FA Cup Final against Crystal Palace?

5   Ince helped United to lift a trophy all but one of his seasons at Old Trafford. At the end of which one was he empty-handed?

6   Paul succeeded Bryan Robson as skipper of the Red Devils. True or false?

7   In which game did Ince first captain his country?

8   Against who did Paul make his full international debut in September 1992?

9   How many full caps had he accumulated by the spring of 2001?

10   Against which London opponents did Paul net with a breathtaking overhead kick on the way to the 1992/93 Championship?

11   Ince missed the 1990/91 European Cup Winners' Cup Final through injury. True or false?

12   Paul was runner-up to which former Red Devil as the players' player of the year in 1993?

13   What was Ince's response to moronic abuse from his ex-fans when he visited the ground of his former club for the first time since his transfer?

14   Which famous boxer is Paul Ince's cousin?

15   To how many League and FA Cup doubles did Paul contribute?

16   Who bought Paul when he was allowed to leave Old Trafford in 1995?

17   The fee was . . .

18   Which manager brought Paul back to the Premiership with Liverpool in 1997/98?

19   Towards the end of which season did Paul relish striking a late equaliser for the Anfield Reds against United?

20   Which man who was Ince's skipper at Old Trafford was later to become his manager elsewhere?

ANSWERS

French Devils *(see page 113)*

1 Monaco. **2** £7.8 million. **3** Marseille. **4** 1992/93. **5** 1971. **6** His left. **7** Yes. **8** They won the World Cup. **9** False. **10** Eric Cantona. **11** Rugby. **12** Internazionale of Milan. **13** £3.5 million. **14** Liverpool. **15** Anfield. **16** The quarter-final. **17** Left-back. **18** Germany. **19** Rennes. **20** Left-footed.

Answers – see page 114

1   Who joined United from the Philadelphia Nationals in August 1950?
2   In what famous match had he captained a side that summer?
3   What was the score?
4   In what country did the encounter take place?
5   How many senior games did the above-mentioned skipper play for United?
6   What was his position?
7   To which club did United transfer Scott McGarvey in July 1984?
8   In what position did Scott play for the Reds?
9   Scott scored a hat-trick at home to Spurs in April 1982. True or false?
10 Decipher the anagram: RARHUT BLOTSINA.
11 Who scored on his United debut in a 4-2 away victory over Stoke in March 1968?
12 Which manager bought Arthur Graham for Manchester United?
13 From which club was the Scottish international winger signed?
14 With which club had Arthur been a teenage prodigy?
15 With which Yorkshire club did he complete his senior career?
16 Who was the Irish right winger whose only taste of senior football with United was a home encounter with Tottenham in February 1954?
17 Which Irishman who made one appearance in United's goal in 1934, became a massively successful scout for the Red Devils?
18 Which of the so-called Fergie's Fledglings was named after a Welsh village?
19 Which was the last club managed by former United defender Ian Greaves?
20 Ian's career as a manager also took in Wolverhampton Wanderers. True or false?

Answers – see page 111

1 From which club did United acquire Fabien Barthez in May 2000?
2 How much did they pay to sign the man they hope will prove a long-term replacement for Peter Schmeichel?
3 With which club did Fabien earn a European Cup winner's medal?
4 In what season was that?
5 In what year was Barthez born?
6 Does Fabien favour his left or his right foot?
7 He figured in the race for the French title in 1999/2000 but did he earn a winner's medal that term?
8 How did France fare in his first tournament as their regular keeper?
9 Fabien missed the 2000 European Championship Final against Italy through injury. True or false?
10 He is a close friend of which former Red Devil?
11 What sport did Fabien's father play at international level?
12 Mikael Silvestre was recruited from which club?
13 How much did he cost?
14 Which club did he reject to join the Red Devils?
15 At which ground did he make his Premiership debut a few days after his arrival in England in September 1999?
16 At which stage of the 1998/99 Champions League campaign had Mikael faced United?
17 In what role did Silvestre settle after spending chunks of his first season in central defence?
18 Early in 2001 Mikael made his full international debut against which opponents?
19 With which major French club did Mikael make an impact between 1996 and 1998?
20 Is Silvestre naturally right-footed or left-footed?

Answers – see page 112

1 Who did Tommy Docherty succeed as manager of Manchester United?
2 From what job did he resign to take the reins at Old Trafford in December 1972?
3 The Doc has claimed frequently that he has had more clubs than . . ?
4 Who succeeded Docherty in the United hot seat in 1977?
5 What was United's highest League position during the Docherty era?
6 Tommy is the only man since the war to lead United to relegation. True or false?
7 Which Arsenal and Scotland schemer, described by the Doc as 'another Netzer', became one of Tommy's first signings for the Reds?
8 Which stopper did Docherty snatch centre from lower-division obscurity, then presided over his rise to full international status?
9 By how many points did United escape the drop in the season of Docherty's arrival?
10 How many major semi-finals were reached by The Doc's Red Devils?
11 How many times were they victorious in finals?
12 Who did Tommy use as a Wembley substitute in two successive FA Cup Finals?
13 Who was the manager of the team beaten by Tommy's in the 1977 FA Cup Final?
14 With whom did Docherty replace Paddy Crerand as his assistant boss?
15 Which Greenhoff did Tommy buy, Brian or Jimmy?
16 Tommy was sacked by United in July 1977 over his love affair with the wife of the club physio. Name him.
17 With which club did Docherty spend the bulk of his splendid playing career?
18 Which of Tommy's many clubs did he serve the longest as manager?
19 To which club did he move on leaving Old Trafford?
20 Tommy Docherty's career as a Football League boss ended with his 1985 sacking by which club?

Answers – see page 117

1   Which one of the following have not finished as runners-up to United in the title race since 1993: Aston Villa, Arsenal, Liverpool, Newcastle, Blackburn?

2   Who was voted Player of the Century in the Rothmans Football Yearbook Millennium Awards?

3   The United side for which season received the Team of the Century accolade?

4   One of United's redesigned away shirts became what new colour for 2001/2002?

5   In both 1956/57 and 1958/59 United compiled their highest total of league goals. What was it?

6   Which actor who went on to play James Bond was offered a trial by Manchester United during the 1950s?

7   Over which League champions-to-be did United record a 6-5 away victory?

8   Who scored a hat-trick for the Red Devils in that match?

9   During which season did that amazing encounter take place?

10 Decipher the anagram: LAUP RAPERK.

11 Which club did United defeat four times in senior competition during 1993/94?

12 What was the first season the Reds beat every other side in their division, in either a League or cup encounter?

13 What was sent to Alex Ferguson to attract his attention to Dion Dublin?

14 From which club did United recruit the big Midlander?

15 What was the fee?

16 At which ground did Dion score on his first start for the club?

17 What happened to him in his next match a few days later?

18 To which club was Dion transferred in September 1994?

19 How much profit did the Reds make on that transaction?

20 At which ground was Dion based during 2000/2001?

Brian Kidd *(see page 117)*

ANSWERS

1 Nineteenth. 2 David Herd. 3 Australia. 4 George Best. 5 Once, the 8-1 win over QPR.
6 Two. 7 Northern Ireland. 8 Ecuador. 9 FA Cup third-place play-off. 10 Aston Villa.
11 None. 12 West Ham United. 13 Arsenal. 14 25 years old. 15 Tommy Docherty.
16 Manchester City. 17 Everton. 18 Preston North End. 19 Blackburn Rovers. 20 Leeds.

Answers – see page 118

1   Which Republic of Ireland international was captain of United in 2000/2001?
2   Which veteran Irish full-back announced his international retirement in 1999/2000, but played on for United?
3   Which goal-scoring inside-forward from Dublin died in the Munich air disaster?
4   Which Irish icon skippered United to FA Cup glory in 1948?
5   Which classy Eire central defender was allowed to join Aston Villa in the summer of 1989 after disagreements with the United manager?
6   Which Manchester-born European Cup winner won caps for the Republic during the second half of the 1960s?
7   Which young centre-half did United loan to Bournemouth during 1999/2000?
8   Dion Dublin was born in the Irish capital. True or false?
9   Which young United defender of the late 1980s shares his surname with a World Cup-winning country?
10 Which former Shamrock Rover shone with Newcastle and Tranmere after leaving Old Trafford?
11 Which Dubliner was United's regular left-back in 1958/59?
12 Which fellow native of that city was a United man before joining Bolton in 1973?
13 Which player, who went on to manage the Republic of Ireland, began his career with United?
14 Which Cork-born charmer was United skipper in the early 1960s?
15 Which combative Dubliner was plucked from Gaelic football by Dave Sexton in the late 1970s?
16 He played for Arsenal, United and the Republic, then later managed Bradford City. Name him.
17 Which curly-haired blond utility man arrived at Old Trafford from Bohemians for £20,000 in March 1977?
18 Which Irish international understudied both Alex Stepney and Gary Bailey?
19 Which slender Dubliner was United's penalty king in the mid 1970s?
20 Who was United's regular keeper when they lifted the title in 1964/65?

ANSWERS

Pot Luck - 36 (see page 118)

1 Oldham Athletic. 2 Sonny. 3 None. 4 AC Milan. 5 Upton Park. 6 Nicky Butt v Barcelona and Arsenal. 7 Andrei Kanchelskis. 8 Alan Foggon. 9 Sunderland. 10 Arsenal. 11 Partick Thistle. 12 Motherwell. 13 Hamilton Academical. 14 Lou Macari. 15 Tony Gill. 16 Bristol Rovers. 17 Manchester United. 18 Luton Town. 19 QPR. 20 Dave Sexton.

Answers – see page 115

1   On which of Brian's birthdays did he score in the 1968 European Cup Final?
2   Which veteran front-runner had Brian replaced in the United line-up during 1967/68?
3   Brian sprang to prominence on a 1967 summer tour of which country?
4   In his first season as a regular only one man scored more than Brian's 15 League goals for United. Who was that?
5   In his 29 League outings during 1968/69, how many times did Kiddo find the net?
6   How many full England caps did Brian win?
7   Against which country did he make his debut in April 1970?
8   He scored on his final full international appearance, after rising from the bench in Quito. Who were England's opponents?
9   Brian scored twice against Watford at Highbury in April 1970. What was the game?
10 Brian netted in both legs of the 1970/71 League Cup semi-final. Who were United's victorious Third Division opponents?
11 How many hat-tricks did Brian score for the Red Devils in senior competition?
12 Against which club did Kiddo grab the final two goals of his Old Trafford career in September 1973?
13 Which club did he join in August 1974?
14 How old was Brian when he made that surprise move?
15 Which manager allowed him to leave Old Trafford?
16 Which was Brian's third club as a player?
17 He joined a fourth top club in 1978/79. Name it.
18 Of which Lancashire club did he become manager for two months in 1986?
19 In 1998 he took over another Lancashire outfit. Which one?
20 Brian became chief coach of which United in 2001?

ANSWERS

Pot Luck - 35 *(see page 115)*

1 Liverpool. 2 George Best. 3 1998/99. 4 Gold. 5 103 goals. 6 Sean Connery. 7 Chelsea. 8 Dennis Viollet. 9 1954/55. 10 Paul Parker. 11 Sheffield Wednesday. 12 1998/99. 13 A video of his goals. 14 Cambridge United. 15 £1 million. 16 The Dell. 17 He broke a leg. 18 Coventry City. 19 £1 million. 20 Villa Park.

Answers – see page 116

1 With which club did Paul Edwards win a Third Division title medal in 1973/74?

2 By what nickname did fans and team-mates know post-war United goalkeeper John Feehan?

3 Apart from United, how many senior clubs did John Fitzpatrick serve?

4 Who were the opponents on the only occasion the abrasive Fitz was sent off in senior competition for United?

5 Ashley Grimes was dismissed in October 1982 On what ground were the Reds playing at the time?

6 Which Red Devil was sent off twice in four days during September 1998?

7 Who was the Reds' leading scorer in 1994/95?

8 Which Middlesbrough marksman was recruited by Tommy Docherty in July 1976?

9 To which club did that man move two months later after three appearances as substitute and no goals?

10 Alex Forsyth was on the groundstaff of which Londoners in 1967?

11 Which Scottish club did he join the following year?

12 Which was Forsyth's penultimate senior club?

13 And his final one?

14 Decipher the anagram: ULO CRIMAA.

15 Which versatile and promising young Yorkshireman was lost to United after a leg was shattered at Nottingham Forest in March 1989?

16 With which club did he later become one of the youngest coaches in the Football League?

17 Which was Don Givens' first League club?

18 Who bought him from United in April 1970?

19 With which London club did the Irishman finish as a championship runner-up in 1975/76?

20 Who was his manager during that thrilling campaign?

Red Republicans - 1 *(see page 116)*

ANSWERS

1 Roy Keane. 2 Denis Irwin. 3 Liam 'Billy' Whelan. 4 Johnny Carey. 5 Paul McGrath. 6 Seamus Brennan. 7 John O'Shea. 8 False. 9 Derek Brazil. 10 Liam O'Brien. 11 Joe Carolan. 12 Tony Dunne. 13 Johnny Giles. 14 Noel Cantwell. 15 Kevin Moran. 16 Frank Stapleton. 17 Ashley Grimes. 18 Paddy Roche. 19 Gerry Daly. 20 Pat Dunne.

Answers – see page 121

1   Was Roger Byrne a Mancunian or a Yorkshireman?

2   Matt Busby signed Roger from Manchester City. True or false?

3   Against which Merseyside club did Roger make his First Division debut as a young left-back in November 1951?

4   Who did the rookie Byrne replace in the number-three shirt?

5   In what position did Roger play the last six matches of that title-winning campaign?

6   How many goals did Roger contribute during that six-game springtime sequence?

7   How many Championship medals had Roger earned by the time of his death at Munich?

8   Which young deputy left-back, who also died in the crash, made the ill-fated trip because Byrne was carrying an injury?

9   Roger was the long-term successor of another great full-back as captain of United. Name him.

10 Who were England facing when Byrne made his full England entrance in April 1954?

11 Where was that game played?

12 Later in 1954 Roger took part in the World Cup Finals. Which country hosted that tournament?

13 How many consecutive England appearances did Roger make before losing his life?

14 Which teenage chum of Roger Byrne went on to become one of the finest fast bowlers in the history of English cricket?

15 Roger was two days short of which birthday when he was killed?

16 Roger once crashed his car into the garden of whose next-door neighbour?

17 How many times did Byrne represent the Football League?

18 How many penalties did Roger take for England?

19 How many of those international spot-kicks did he convert?

20 Who did Roger succeed as England's left-back?

ANSWERS

Pot Luck - 37 (see page 121)

1 Trafford Park industrial estate. 2 Main stand. 3 Bolton Wanderers. 4 United won 3-0.
5 1957. 6 Real Madrid. 7 1959. 8 1926. 9 Scotland. 10 Stand Up For The Champions.
11 1997. 12 Three. 13 Phil Hughes. 14 Ronny Johnsen. 15 Alan Gowling. 16 China.
17 1995/96. 18 False. 19 Arsenal. 20 164 times.

Answers – see page 122

1 In what year did George announce his first 'retirement'?

2 Who was the United manager at that time?

3 How many goals did George score in United's 5-1 thrashing of Benfica at the Stadium of Light in 1966?

4 In what year did George withdraw from an international because of threats on his life?

5 Which manager tempted George to return to United briefly during 1973/74?

6 Who were the opposition when George played his final League game for United, on New year's day 1974?

7 What was the result on that sad afternoon in London?

8 Against whom did George score his first full international goal in November 1964?

9 How many goals did George hit for his country?

10 He scored one hat-trick for Northern Ireland, in Belfast April 1971. Who were the opponents?

11 Who was the England keeper George netted past at Wembley in April 1970?

12 Against whom did George score his first FA Cup goal in February 1964?

13 Who were the opponents when George made his European debut at Old Trafford, also in February 1964?

14 Which Man. City player joined George in opening a clothes boutique in 1967?

15 George was sent off for the first time in his career in 1968 against which team?

16 George was suspended for bringing the game into disrepute after knocking the ball from which referee's hands in 1970?

17 Which Manchester City defender suffered a broken leg in a tackle with George in December 1970?

18 Best was dismissed at Stamford Bridge in August 1971 for arguing with which team-mate?

19 What was the name of the nightclub in Bootle Street, Manchester, in which George had a financial stake?

20 Of which former Miss World was George cleared of robbing in 1974?

Answers – see page 119

1   What were Hitler's bombers aiming at when they hit Old Trafford in 1941?
2   Which stand bore the brunt of the Germans' attack?
3   When the ground reopened for League football in August 1949, who were United opponents?
4   What was the result of that match?
5   In what springtime did United play their first League game under floodlights at Old Trafford?
6   Who were Old Trafford's first European visitors to be artificially illuminated?
7   In what year was the famous Stretford End terrace covered?
8   When was the first full international staged at Old Trafford?
9   Who were England's opponents that day?
10   Which song provoked problems with Trafford Borough Council during 2000/2001?
11   In what year did United open the towering new North Stand?
12   How many decks does that massive edifice contain?
13   Which young keeper reached no further than United's reserves but became a Northern Ireland international after leaving Old Trafford?
14   Decipher the anagram: NYNOR HEJNONS.
15   Which Red Devil played for Great Britain in the 1968 Olympics?
16   Who were the opponents when Gary and Phil Neville first played together for the full England side?
17   At the end of which club campaign did the Nevilles achieve that family landmark?
18   The Nevilles are the only brothers from the same club to win England caps together. True or false?
19   Which club has been Manchester United's most frequent League opponents?
20   By the end of 2000/2001, how many times had those two clubs met in League competition?

ANSWERS

Roger Byrne *(see page 119)*

1 Mancunian. **2** False. **3** Liverpool. **4** Billy Redman. **5** Outside-left. **6** Seven. **7** Three.
8 Geoff Bent. **9** Johnny Carey. **10** Scotland. **11** Hampden Park. **12** Switzerland.
13 33. **14** Brian Statham. **15** His 29th. **16** Matt Busby's. **17** Six. **18** Two. **19** Neither.
20 Bill Eckersley.

Answers – see page 120

1   United reached Wembley only three months after the Munich crash. Which survivor played in goal?

2   Which other survivor was the new skipper?

3   Two more men had recovered from their Munich injuries in time to play. One was Bobby Charlton; who was the other?

4   With Matt Busby still not fit, who was in charge of the Reds?

5   Who scored both Bolton goals in a 2-0 victory.

6   What was controversial about Bolton's second?

7   Who hit a Bolton upright with a ferocious shot shortly before the clinching goal?

8   Who played at centre-half for United and gave a magnificent performance?

9   Which relation of the late Duncan Edwards was playing for Bolton?

10 Which England keeper was between the posts for Wanderers?

11 Who did the United defeat in their replayed semi-final?

12 What was Bolton's nickname?

13 What was the score at the break?

14 Who was the victorious manager?

15 Who was the emergency signing employed as United's midfield general?

16 Who played for Villa in the 1957 FA Cup Final, then for United against a year later?

17 Which fellow Lancastrians did Bolton overcome in their semi-final?

18 Which Welshman on United's left flank went on to do well in that summer's World Cup Finals?

19 Who received tumultuous applause as he took his place on the Wembley bench?

20 Who presented the trophy to Nat Lofthouse?

George Best - 2 (see page 120)

ANSWERS

1 1972. **2** Frank O'Farrell. **3** Two. **4** 1971. **5** Tommy Docherty. **6** QPR. **7** 3-0 to QPR. **8** Switzerland. **9** Nine. **10** Cyprus. **11** Gordon Banks. **12** Barnsley. **13** Sporting Lisbon. **14** Mike Summerbee. **15** Estudiantes. **16** Jack Taylor's. **17** Glyn Pardoe. **18** Willie Morgan. **19** Slack Alice. **20** Marjorie Wallace.

Answers – see page 125

1 Which Greenhoff brother is the elder, Brian or Jimmy?
2 From which town do the brothers hail?
3 At which club did Jimmy begin his professional career?
4 Brian's first League club was . . .
5 How many full England caps are in Brian's collection?
6 How many does Jimmy have to his name?
7 Both men featured in two FA Cup Finals for United, but only in one of them did they play together. Which one?
8 In what role did Brian break into the United side in 1973/74?
9 Who was Brian's most regular partner when he settled in central defence?
10 Who was manager at Jimmy's second League club, Birmingham City?
11 From which club did Tommy Docherty recruit Jimmy Greenhoff in November 1976?
12 What was the fee?
13 How old was Jimmy at the time of his move?
14 Which of Jimmy's former clubs bought Brian in the summer of 1979?
15 What did they pay for their second Greenhoff?
16 Against which opposition did Jimmy rattle in an Old Trafford hat-trick some three months after his arrival?
17 Which club signed the 34-year-old front-man in December 1980?
18 Which was Jimmy's penultimate League club?
19 For which club did Brian play under Jimmy's management during 1982/83?
20 Did Jimmy ever pocket a winner's medal in European competition?

ANSWERS

Nicky Butt (see page 125)
1 Paul Ince. 2 1975. 3 Oldham Athletic. 4 Paul Ince. 5 The Dell. 6 Yes. 7 Semi-final.
8 Eric Cantona. 9 Leicester City. 10 The Stadium of Light. 11 Borussia Dortmund.
12 Newcastle United. 13 Leeds United. 14 Twice. 15 Mexico. 16 Steve McManaman.
17 Chile. 18 Vasco da Gama. 19 West Ham United. 20 Handball on the goal line.

Answers — see page 126

1   Against which club did United play the first League game to be arranged for a Saturday night?

2   In what season did that unusual encounter take place?

3   What was the result of the match?

4   Where did the Saturday night meeting take place?

5   When was the last time the Red Devils played on Christmas Day?

6   Who did they face on that yuletide occasion?

7   Where was the game played?

8   And the outcome?

9   Which new goalkeeper was making only his second appearance for the Red Devils on that Christmas Day?

10   Who scored in that match, then did so again against the same opponents on Boxing Day?

11   Decipher the anagram: ELE RASPEH.

12   Who is the most-capped keeper to play represent Manchester United?

13   Did Don Gibson make enough appearances to merit a title medal in 1951/52?

14   In what position did Don operate?

15   When Gibson lost his place, who took on his former shirt?

16   Against which club were United drawn in both the FA Cup and the League Cup in the same season?

17   In what season did that occur?

18   Who won both ties?

19   Which club did the Red Devils face in both domestic cup competitions in 1984/85?

20   The same thing happened the following season. Who were the familiar opponents that time around?

Answers – see page 123

1   Nicky Butt won a regular place in the United side after the departure of which midfield dynamo in the summer of 1995?

2   In what year was Nicky born?

3   Who were the Reds' opponents when he made his senior debut in 1992?

4   That afternoon Nicky rose from the bench to replace which colleague?

5   On which ground did Nicky score his first senior goal for United?

6   Did Butt start in the 1996 FA Cup Final against Liverpool?

7   At what stage did Nicky make his only FA Cup appearance in 1994?

8   Which returning hero laid on Nicky's early goal against Liverpool at Old Trafford in October 1995?

9   Who were the opponents at Old Trafford in November 1996 when Nicky scored his only senior brace to date for United?

10   Butt scored a late equaliser after United had fallen two behind at which Stadium in December 1999?

11   Against which European Cup semi-final opponents did Nicky shoot against an upright in April 1997?

12   Nicky netted with a flying header against which opposition in the 1996 Charity Shield encounter?

13   A brilliant Butt goal sealed a 3-2 victory over which fierce rivals at Old Trafford in November 1998?

14   How many goals did Nicky score in the two-legged 1992 FA Youth Cup final?

15   Who were England's opponents when Nicky became a full international at Wembley in March 1997?

16   Who was Nicky sent on to replace during the second half of that game?

17   Who were the opposition when Butt made his first England start in February 1998?

18   Who did Nicky score against during the Club World Championships in Rio?

19   Who were the Reds playing when Nicky was dismissed for the first time in senior competition, in January 1996?

20   Why was Nicky Butt sent off against Barcelona in September 1998?

The Greenhoffs *(see page 123)*

ANSWERS

1 Jimmy. **2** Barnsley. **3** Leeds United. **4** Manchester United. **5** 18 caps. **6** None. **7** The 1977 final. **8** Midfielder. **9** Martin Buchan. **10** Stan Cullis. **11** Stoke City. **12** £120,000. **13** 30 years old. **14** Leeds United. **15** £350,000. **16** Newcastle United. **17** Crewe Alexandra. **18** Port Vale. **19** Rochdale. **20** Yes, in the Fairs Cup with Leeds United.

Answers — see page 124

1 Willie Morgan was the second international right-winger Matt Busby signed from which club?
2 Who was the United manager's previous capture?
3 What did the Red Devils pay for Willie?
4 Against which Londoners did the skillful Scot make his League debut in August 1968?
5 Willie's opening League goal for United was the first of a hat-trick in March 1969. Who were the opponents?
6 What was the result of that one-sided Old Trafford encounter?
7 Under how many Manchester United managers did Willie Morgan serve?
8 Willie supplied United's only goal of the two-legged World Club Championship clash with Estudiantes in 1968. Was it home or away?
9 What was the sole club honour Willie won during his time as a Red Devil?
10 Which manager switched Morgan from a conventional winger to midfield?
11 Who did Willie succeed as United captain?
12 Who once described Morgan as 'the best right winger in the world'?
13 To whom did Willie lose custody of United's number-seven shirt during the spring of 1975?
14 With whom did Morgan win a court confrontation in 1978?
15 Willie fell out with the famously abrasive chairman of his first club. Name that chairman.
16 How many times did Willie represent his country at full international level?
17 To which club was Morgan transferred in the summer of 1975?
18 With which club did he pocket a second Division Two title gong in 1978?
19 With which club did Willie conclude his League career in 1982?
20 In which season did Willie score the only goal of United's home clash with Liverpool, then go on to net as the Red Devils triumphed 4-1 at Anfield?

Pot Luck - 38 *(see page 124)*
ANSWERS
1 Wolverhampton Wanderers. 2 1958/59. 3 Wolves won 4-0. 4 Molineux. 5 1957. 6 Luton Town. 7 Old Trafford. 8 United won 3-0. 9 Harry Gregg. 10 Tommy Taylor. 11 Lee Sharpe. 12 Peter Schmeichel (129 Danish caps). 13 Yes. 14 Right-half. 15 John Carey. 16 Leeds United. 17 1991/92 18 Manchester United. 19 Everton. 20 West Ham United.

Answers – see page 129

1 What was the number on the open-top bus in which United brought their Treble trophies home to Manchester in May 1999?

2 Who was the first player to be sent off at Wembley when playing for England?

3 Who were the opposition that day?

4 Decipher the anagram: MIRE SMESO.

5 In May 2001, only one current League club had beaten United more often in League meetings than United had beaten them. Name that club.

6 Who scored exactly a century of League and FA Cup goals for the Reds between 1893 and 1900?

7 Who equalled that feat between 1907 and 1914?

8 Which FA Cup-winning Red Devil left Old Trafford for Parkhead in January 1994?

9 Which former United favourite bought him for Celtic?

10 What was the fee?

11 That same player suffered appaling fitness problems. With which West Country club was he serving when a back injury ended his League career?

12 Which left winger of Italian extraction jumped from part-timers Histon United to the Old Trafford senior squad during 1988/89?

13 When was the winger freed from his United contract?

14 Which former United winger is the father of a successful film and TV actor?

15 Who is that acting star?

16 For what long-running TV series is he arguably best known?

17 What film did he make about a professional footballer?

18 Name the United-supporting host of the TV show Have I Got News For You?

19 Which TV chef is a rabid Red?

20 To which club did Matt Busby sell full-back Tommy McNulty in February 1954?

Answers – see page 130

1   Which Poles dumped United out of the UEFA Cup in the first round in 1980/81?

2   United were beaten at the same stage of the same competition in 1982/83 Who were their conquerors?

3   In the first round of the Cup Winners' Cup in 1983/84 the away-goals rule worked in United's favour against which opponents?

4   Who netted an equaliser for the Reds with a penalty in the last minute of the first leg on his 27th birthday?

5   Who did United vanquish beside the Black Sea in the second round of the Cup Winners' Cup?

6   Who was the bull-like young Welshman who made his European debut in the home leg of that contest against Bulgarian opposition?

7   Which Irishman scored both goals in a 2-0 second-leg victory at Old Trafford?

8   Who was the manager who led United proudly to the Nou Camp for their Cup Winners' Cup quarter-final against Barcelona in March 1984?

9   Who scored an own goal as the Spanish giants recorded a 2-0 home advantage?

10 At that time, who was the jewel in the Barcelona crown?

11 Who scored twice as United triumphed 3-0 in the Old Trafford second leg, one of their greatest European performances?

12 Who grabbed United's aggregate winner on that never-to-be-forgotten night?

13 Who was the Dutch master at the heart of United's heady triumph?

14 Which young Welsh substitute notched United's goal in the 1983/84 Cup Winners' Cup semi-final first-leg draw against Juventus?

15 Which French maestro schemed Juventus' 2-1 second-leg triumph?

16 Who equalised for United after Boniek had put Juve in front?

17 Who plundered the Italians' last-minute winner?

18 Whose extra-time penalty saw United through against PSV Eindhoven in the second round of the 1984/85 UEFA Cup?

19 Which gallant Scots held United at Old Trafford before bowing to the Reds by 3-2 at Tannadice in the third round?

20 Which club beat United on penalties in the 1984/85 UEFA Cup quarter-final?

Answers – see page 127

1 How many members of the 1948 FA Cup-winning side earned title medals in 1951/52?

2 Who skippered United to the Championship?

3 Who scored 14 goals for the Red Devils in the first seven games?

4 Who pocketed a medal for playing the first 18 games at left-back?

5 Which winger played nearly half the Championship games, then joined Carlisle for £5,000 the following September?

6 Which former Bradford Park Avenue star prospered in both inside-forward positions?

7 By what margin did United carry off the title?

8 Who were the runners-up?

9 When United played Fulham on Christmas Day and Boxing Day, two Reds scored in both matches. One was Jack Rowley; who was the other?

10 Which future United captain featured at both left-back and outside-left?

11 United's Championship came after they had finished runners-up in the five previous seasons. True or false?

12 Which future England manager contributed to the Reds' home victory over Spurs with an own goal?

13 Which Salford-born inside-right played eight consecutive games but could not claim a regular berth?

14 Who was United's leading First Division goal-scorer?

15 The father of which TV star made a dozen appearances during the season?

16 Who was the Reds' first-choice goalkeeper in 1951/52?

17 Which England amateur international inside-forward enjoyed consecutive League outings in the autumn?

18 Against which opponents did the Reds score eight goals in August?

19 United fell how many short of a century of League goals?

20 How many times were the Reds beaten during the League campaign?

Answers – see page 128

What are the predominant colour (s) of the first-choice shirts favoured by the following opponents of Manchester United (not necessarily what they wore when the faced the Red Devils during 2000/2001)?

1 Panathinaikos
2 Charlton Athletic
3 Watford
4 Anderlecht
5 Aston Villa
6 Ipswich Town
7 Bradford City
8 Valencia
9 Coventry City
10 Leicester City
11 Newcastle United
12 PSV Eindhoven
13 Derby County
14 Sunderland
15 Southampton
16 Bayern Munich
17 West Ham United
18 Dynamo Kiev
19 Middlesbrough
20 Everton

ANSWERS

Reds in Europe - 1980s *(see page 128)*
1 Widzew Lodz. 2 Valencia. 3 Dukla Prague. 4 Ray Wilkins. 5 Spartak Varna. 6 Mark Hughes. 7 Frank Stapleton. 8 Ron Atkinson. 9 Graeme Hogg. 10 Diego Maradona. 11 Bryan Robson. 12 Frank Stapleton. 13 Arnold Muhren. 14 Alan Davies. 15 Michel Platini. 16 Norman Whiteside. 17 Paolo Rossi. 18 Gordon Strachan's. 19 Dundee United. 20 Videoton.

1   Who provided the opposition when Eric made his first League start for the Reds?

2   Against which opponents did he score his first United goal?

3   Which Liverpool defender once attempted to upset Eric by turning down his collar?

4   Against which club did Eric score a Charity Shield hat-trick in 1992?

5   Which shirt number became Eric's personal property at Old Trafford?

6   What is the name of Eric's footballing younger brother?

7   For what English team did Cantona Jnr make three League appearances?

8   How many senior goals did Eric contribute to the Reds' cause during his first full season with the club?

9   Did Eric ever score 20 League goals in one season for United?

10 Which man who guided Eric at international level and recommended him to Alex Ferguson went on to become a Premiership manager?

11 At which ground did Cantona launch his infamous kung-fu-style kick at an abusive fan?

12 Who were United playing that evening?

13 Cantona had been sent off for clashing with which opponent in that game?

14 What was the result of the match?

15 Eric was sent off for stamping on which Swindon Town midfielder at the County Ground in March 1994?

16 Immediately prior to signing Cantona, Alex Ferguson had been foiled in a bid to acquire which Sheffield Wednesday spearhead?

17 To what tune did Manchester United fans adapt the chant of Ooh Aah Cantona?

18 Eric is the only man to score two penalties in an FA Cup Final. True or false?

19 Against which opponents did a black-clad Eric mark his opening League game of 1993/94 with a sumptuous first-time chip-shot?

20 In September 1994, Eric hit the bar with a 45-yard lob at which stadium?

Pot Luck - 41 *(see page 133)*

ANSWERS

1 Derby County. 2 Malcolm Christie. 3 Danny Higginbotham. 4 Georgi Kinkladze. 5 They were safe from relegation. 6 Jim Smith. 7 One. 8 He was suspended. 9 Sir Alex Ferguson. 10 Luke Chadwick. 11 Four. 12 A giant shirt. 13 Paul Scholes. 14 Ronnie Wallwork. 15 True. 16 Ray Wilkins. 17 Steve Coppell. 18 Gianluca Vialli. 19 Graham Taylor. 20 Brian Kidd.

1   Which Welshman starred in United's treble-winning side of 1998/99?
2   Which fire-breathing United marksman became manager of Wales?
3   Which United assistant manager led Wales to the quarter-finals of the World Cup in 1958?
4   Which winger's 48-cap Welsh international career was spread over 25 years?
5   With which other top club did that fabulous performer spend two spells?
6   During which season did Ryan Giggs win his first full international cap?
7   Who provided the opposition that day?
8   Which United and Wales utility man began his full international career in 1985/86?
9   Which Busby Babe figured in the 1958 World Cup Finals?
10 Which Welsh forward did United sign from Chelsea in November 1963?
11 Which Welsh under-23 international winger survived the Munich air crash but never won a full cap?
12 Mark Jones, who died at Munich, was a Welsh international. True or false?
13 Which workaholic Welshman joined United from Wrexham in 1978?
14 How many Welshmen have been in charge of United since the war?
15 Which United youngster made his debut for Wales a few days after helping to lift the FA Cup in 1983?
16 Which Welsh legend joined United from Portsmouth in exchange for George Graham?
17 Which Welsh centre-forward was known as 'Wyn The Leap'?
18 What rookie centre-half won Welsh under-23 honours in 1974?
19 Which Welsh international wing-half was on the fringe of United's 1948 FA Cup-winning side?
20 Against which country did Mark Hughes make his full international entrance in May 1984?

Answers – see page 131

1 Which party-poopers won at Old Trafford on the day United received the Premiership trophy for 2000/2001?

2 Which childhood United fan scored the only goal of the game?

3 Which former Red Devil played in the visitors' defence?

4 Which one-time Manchester City idol featured prominently in the opposition's midfield?

5 What did victory mean to the visitors?

6 Who was the triumphant manager?

7 How many previous home defeats had the Reds suffered in the League campaign?

8 Why did skipper Roy Keane miss that game?

9 After the match, who received the Premiership trophy along with Keane?

10 The second player to hold aloft the trophy dropped the lid. Who was the Red Devil with careless hands?

11 Sir Alex Ferguson did a lap of honour with how many grandchildren?

12 What did the players pass into the crowd as part of the celebrations?

13 Which Red had missed the week's training and that day's match because he was awaiting the birth of his second child?

14 Which young United defender won his first title medal in 2000/2001?

15 In 2001 United were crowned as champs on April 14, the earliest date the Premiership race had ended. True or false?

16 Which former United and England man took a job with Watford early in May 2001?

17 Which ex-Red Devil turned down a similar approach from the same club?

18 Who was the new Vicarage Road manager offering employment?

19 Who did he replace?

20 Decipher the anagram: RANIB DIKD.

Answers – see page 132

1 Name the United skipper who was missing from the final due to suspension.
2 Which gifted redhead was unable to face Bayern Munich, also because of suspension?
3 Who didn't play in the final but topped the pyramid of joyful players during the post-match celebrations?
4 In which stadium did United face the recently-crowned German champions?
5 On what plane did the United party fly from England?
6 Both teams had qualified for the competition as domestic runners-up. True or false?
7 When was the last time Bayern Munich had won the European Cup?
8 Who was the Germans' manager?
9 Which key Bayern player was nicknamed 'Stinkfinger'?
10 Who lined up in the centre of United's midfield after excelling there in the FA Cup Final?
11 Who conceded what proved to be a costly free-kick in the sixth minute?
12 Who curled the ball past Schmeichel and into United's net?
13 Which 38-year-old German star was substituted ten minutes from the end?
14 Who delivered the corners which led to both of United's goals?
15 Who rose from the bench to replace Jesper Blomqvist after 67 minutes?
16 Whose departure with nine minutes left heralded the arrival of Ole Gunnar Solskjaer?
17 Who charged the length of the pitch in a late bid to avert a United defeat?
18 Whose miscued shot set up the Reds' dramatic equaliser?
19 Whose goal made extra-time appear inevitable?
20 Who put the ball in the Germans' net for the sensational winner?

Answers – see page 137

1   As United chased their first title for more than quarter of a century, who gave City the lead in the crucial Maine Road derby in March 1993?
2   Whose exquisite cross set up Eric Cantona's late equaliser?
3   Who was the City player-manager that season?
4   Who was United's non-playing substitute keeper for the Old Trafford meeting with City in December 1992?
5   The son of which former Maine Road hero faced United at Maine Road in April 1996?
6   The offspring of a European Cup-winning manager was also in the City line-up that day. Name him.
7   Which teenage City keeper made his League debut at Old Trafford in May 1991?
8   Season 1990/91 was the last time City have finished above United in the League table. True or false?
9   Who put City 3-1 in front with 11 minutes remaining at Maine Road in October 1990?
10 Whose scored two late goals to secure an unexpected draw for United?
11 Which Manchester manager shocked his club by walking out nine days later?
12 Who was sacked as City boss just two months after the so-called 'Maine Road Massacre', in which United had been thrashed 5-1?
13 Who scored twice for City on that grisly afternoon in September 1989?
14 Who gave United the lead in the 1-1 encounter at Old Trafford in February 1990?
15 Which future City boss scored an own goal against the Reds at Old Trafford in March 1987?
16 His friend and England colleague also registered for United. Name him.
17 Which Manchester manager was dismissed ten days after the 1-1 draw at Maine Road in October 1986?
18 Which United FA Cup-winner started that game for City?
19 Which former City star was on United's left wing that day?
20 Which future Republic of Ireland manager supplied the City equaliser with a powerful header?

ANSWERS

Wilf McGuinness (see page 137)
1 Clarrie Hilditch. 2 Duncan Edwards. 3 Wolves. 4 Peter Broadbent. 5 1956/57.
6 1958/59. 7 Twice. 8 Northern Ireland. 9 22 years old. 10 Sir Alf Ramsey (with England).
11 1966/67. 12 June 1969. 13 June 1970. 14 December 1970. 15 Seven. 16 Leeds
United. 17 Greece. 18 York City. 19 Bury. 20 Paul McGuinness.

QUIZ 26

Pot Luck - 42

SECOND HALF

Answers – see page 138

1 How many home League defeats did United suffer in the first nine seasons of the Premier League/Premiership?
2 Who is the youngest of only two Red Devils to have claimed a title medal in each of United's Championship campaigns under Sir Alex Ferguson?
3 And who is the veteran with an identical record?
4 Two Liverpool men hold the record of winning eight title medals. One is Alan Hansen; who is the other?
5 Decipher the anagram: YARG VELNILE.
6 Who did the Professional Footballers Association honour as their player of the year in 2001?
7 With which club did Nobby Lawton wind up his playing career?
8 Who, in May 1982, became United's youngest post-war goalscorer in senior competition?
9 How old was that marksman?
10 Who were United's opponents that day?
11 Who was the first United substitute to score on his debut?
12 Who provided the opposition that day in August 1996?
13 What was the venue?
14 What was the result of that match?
15 Who scored a hat-trick for the Red Devils in his first FA Cup outing for the club?
16 Who were his victims?
17 On what ground did he achieve his memorable feat?
18 In what season did it occur?
19 United went on to capture the trophy in that campaign. True or false?
20 Which otherwise prolific marksman had to wait for his 25th meeting with the Red Devils before registering his first goal against them?

ANSWERS

The Neville Brothers *(see page 138)*
1 Phil. 2 Chris Casper. 3 Eric Cantona. 4 Phil. 5 David Beckham. 6 Bury. 7 Neville Neville.
8 1992 9 1995. 10 Glandular fever. 11 Gary. 12 Wrexham. 13 19 years old. 14 Phil.
15 Torpedo Moscow. 16 1995. 17 Gianfranco Zola. 18 Phil. 19 Vasco de Gama.
20 Middlesbrough.

Answers – see page 135

1   Wilf McGuinness was the second former United player to manage the club. Who was the first?

2   Which Busby Babe stood between Wilf and a regular first-team place in the mid 1950s?

3   Against which top opponents, wearers of old gold and black, did the 17-year-old McGuinness make his senior United debut in October 1955?

4   Which player, a future England player, was Wilf marking that day?

5   In which of United's Championship seasons did Wilf enjoy 13 Division 1 outings?

6   In which campaign did Wilf miss only three matches as the Red Devils finished as runners-up?

7   How many times was McGuinness capped by England at senior level?

8   Who were the opponents when he entered the international arena?

9   How old was Wilf when his senior playing days were ended by a broken leg?

10 Wilf coached under two soccer knights during the 1960s. One was Sir Matt Busby, who was the other?

11 During what season did Wilf attempt a playing comeback, getting as far as the United substitute's bench?

12 When did McGuinness become United's chief coach in charge of first-team affairs?

13 When was he given the title of manager?

14 When was Wilf sacked as the Red Devils' boss?

15 During his short reign at the Old Trafford helm, into how many senior semi-final games did Wilf lead his side?

16 That total included three in a twice-replayed FA Cup encounter with which bitter rivals in 1969/70?

17 In which country did Wilf coach successfully after leaving Old Trafford?

18 Which club suffered consecutive relegations under Wilf's management?

19 Which club did McGuinness serve as coach, physio and caretaker boss from 1980 to 1991?

20 Which of Wilf's sons became director of United's School of Excellence?

Answers – see page 136

1 Which Neville has a twin sister, Tracey, who is an international netballer?
2 With whom did Gary form a hugely promising central defensive partnership at youth level?
3 Who did Phil pick out with a pinpoint cross which led to a hugely important goal at St James' Park in March 1996?
4 Which Neville played throughout the whole of the 1996 FA Cup Final?
5 The other rose from the bench near the end. Who did he replace?
6 The Nevilles' father is the commercial manager of which club?
7 What's his name?
8 In which year did Gary captain United to victory in the FA Youth Cup?
9 When did Phil emulate that achievement?
10 To what debilitating illness did Phil fall prey during 1996/97?
11 Which Neville was selected for the PFA Premiership team in four successive seasons from 1995/96 to 1998/99?
12 Phil made his senior debut in the FA Cup. Who were United's opponents that day?
13 How old was Phil when he won his first full England cap?
14 Which Neville can double effectively as a midfielder?
15 Who were the opponents when Gary made his senior entrance for the Red Devils in September 1992?
16 In what summer did Gary win his first full England cap after making only 17 Premiership starts?
17 Which Chelsea star did Phil man-mark out of the game when United ejected Chelsea from the FA Cup at Stamford Bridge in March 1999?
18 Which Neville was a last-minute omission from England's party for the 1998 World Cup Finals?
19 Against which Brazilians did Gary drop two uncharacteristic clangers during the Club World Championship in 2000?
20 Gary's first League goal was a crucial one against which opponents during the 1996/97 title race?

ANSWERS

Pot Luck - 42 *(see page 136)*
1 11 home defeats. **2** Ryan Giggs. **3** Denis Irwin. **4** Phil Neal. **5** Gary Neville. **6** Teddy Sheringham. **7** Lincoln City. **8** Norman Whiteside. **9** 17 years old. **10** Stoke City. **11** Ole Gunnar Solskjaer. **12** Blackburn Rovers. **13** Old Trafford. **14** 2-2. **15** Tommy Reid. **16** Stoke City. **17** Victoria Ground. **18** 1930/31 **19** False. **20** Ian Rush.

Answers – see page 141

1 Which Bermuda-born marksman, who never made the grade with United, went down from the Premiership with Manchester City in 2000/2001?

2 Which other ex-Red Devil was on City's books throughout that term but played senior football only for Sheffield Wednesday?

3 Which Ukrainian, a former Old Trafford favourite, was pitched into the relegation dogfight with City during a spell on loan from Ibrox?

4 How many points did United take in their two Premiership clashes with City during 2000/2001?

5 Decipher the anagram: VESTE RUBEC.

6 When did United suffer the longest run of consecutive League defeats at the start of a campaign by any club in the top division?

7 How many games did that nightmare sequence last?

8 United's longest run of successive League reverses is even more depressing. Exactly how lengthy was that?

9 What is the longest run of home League defeats recorded by the Reds?

10 When did that take place?

11 Not surprisingly, the lengthiest sequence of away League reverses is more extensive still. How many matches did it involve?

12 When was that gloomy period in Old Trafford history?

13 What is United's longest unbeaten run in League competition?

14 When did that glorious sequence occur?

15 What about the longest cluster of games in all senior competitions, excluding the Charity Shield and the UEFA Super Cup, without being beaten?

16 Who inflicted United's final defeat, in December 1998, before that run began?

17 What was the score that day at Old Trafford?

18 Who shattered that successful sequence comprehensively in October 1999?

19 What was the score that day?

20 Who was keeping goal for the Reds on that unhappy occasion?

FA Cup Semi-Finals - 3 *(see page 141)*

ANSWERS

1 City Ground, Nottingham. 2 No, in a replay. 3 Billy Bremner. 4 Liverpool. 5 Johnny Giles. 6 Pat Dunne. 7 Burnden Park. 8 Everton. 9 Colin Harvey. 10 Ray Wilson. 11 Alex Young. 12 Willie Anderson. 13 Partizan Belgrade. 14 Bobby and Jackie Charlton. 15 Wilf McGuinness. 16 One. 17 Billy Bremner again! 18 Bolton Wanderers. 19 Carlo Sartori. 20 Paul Edwards.

Answers – see page 142

1 In what city did Stan Pearson first see the light of day?

2 How old was Stan when he enlisted with United in December 1935?

3 Stan set up four goals on debut in a 7-1 victory at Saltergate. Who were United's opponents?

4 In giving United the lead for the first time in the 1948 FA Cup Final, which of the Reds' four goals did Pearson contribute?

5 Who were United's opponents in that enthralling Wembley encounter?

6 How old was Stan when he received an overdue international call-up?

7 Who did he face in his first game for England?

8 That day Stan was at inside-left, alongside which plumber from Preston on the left wing?

9 In his eight games for England, how many goals did Stan score?

10 He netted twice in the 9-2 demolition of Northern Ireland in Manchester in November 1949. On what ground was that World Cup qualifier played?

11 Stan bagged an FA Cup semi-final hat-trick against which opponents in 1948?

12 How many times did Stan line up for England alongside his United partner Jack Rowley?

13 Every time the pair played together for their country the outcome was the same. Were those matches won, drawn or lost?

14 Stan won two First Division title medals with United. True or false?

15 Pearson hammered his first senior hat-trick at home to which rival Reds in September 1946?

16 Stan struck three times against Blackburn in the last League match of 1947/48 to clinch United's position as runners-up to which champions?

17 Stan left Old Trafford for Gigg Lane in February 1954. Which club did he join?

18 Of which club did Pearson subsequently become player-manager?

19 After which season did Stan end his playing days?

20 How old was Stan Pearson when he died in 1997?

Answers – see page 139

1 Where did the Red Devils lose to Leeds in a 1965 FA Cup semi-final?
2 Were United beaten at the first time of asking by their main title rivals that season?
3 Who contributed Leeds' winner?
4 Leeds lost the title to United on goal average, then lost in extra time at Wembley to which opponents?
5 Which player who had helped United to lift the FA Cup in 1963 was instrumental in their defeat by Leeds two years later?
6 Who kept goal for the Reds in both 1965 last-four encounters?
7 What was the scene of United's semi-final defeat in 1966?
8 Who were their FA Cup conquerors in that year of England's World Cup glory?
9 Who scored the only goal of a fearfully tight contest?
10 Which member of the team which scuppered United was to play a part in England's finest hour?
11 Which 'Golden Vision' contributed to the Reds' 1966 semi-final downfall?
12 Which precocious young winger wore United's number-seven shirt on that occasion?
13 To whom had Matt Busby's men lost a European Cup semi-final three days earlier in April 1966?
14 Which brothers were on opposite sides when United encountered Leeds again in 1970?
15 Who selected the Mancunians' side for the 1970 semi-final?
16 How many goals were scored in 300 minutes of attrition between the Uniteds of Manchester and Leeds?
17 Whose goal settled that epic contest?
18 Which club hosted the decisive showdown in 1970?
19 For whom was Denis Law introduced as a substitute in that match?
20 Who played at right-back for United in each of the three games with Leeds?

Pot Luck - 43 (see page 139)

ANSWERS

1 Shaun Goater. 2 Terry Cooke. 3 Andrei Kanchelskis. 4 Four points. 5 Steve Bruce.
6 1930/31. 7 12 games. 8 14 games, including the last two of 1929/30. 9 Six games.
10 May to October 1930. 11 17 matches. 12 Between April 1930 and February 1931
13 26 games. 14 February to October 1956. 15 45 matches. 16 Middlesbrough.
17 United 2 Middlesbrough 3. 18 Chelsea. 19 5-0 to Chelsea. 20 Massimo Taibi.

Answers – see page 140

1 How many times have United remained unbeaten at home over a whole League campaign?

2 When was the last time?

3 When was the last time the Reds achieved that feat but were not rewarded with the Championship?

4 Who was the Old Trafford manager that term?

5 Decipher the anagram: NIRBA LIMCARC.

6 How many times had United lifted the League title after their triumph in 2000/2001?

7 How many clubs have recorded more such triumphs?

8 Which one holds the record?

9 What is the highest total of Championships achieved by an English club?

10 How many goalkeepers did the Red Devils use in senior matches during 2000/2001?

11 How many of them were English?

12 How many different nationalities were involved?

13 Who was appointed as United's communications director during 2000/2001?

14 Who won the Denzil Haroun award as United's most outstanding reserve of 2000/2001?

15 Who was voted the club's young player of the year?

16 After which famous United figure is the last-mentioned award named?

17 United faced Celtic in a testimonial match for which Scottish international in May 2001?

18 How many United players have been elected as Footballer of the Year by the game's writers?

19 How many Red Devils have received the PFA accolade?

20 Who was the first United man to become players' player of the year?

1   Gary Lineker equalled Bobby Charlton's England goal-scoring record. True or false.
2   How many goals did Bobby score for his country in full internationals?
3   Against which country did Bobby made his final appearance for England?
4   During which competition did that game take place?
5   In what country was the tournament being held?
6   Apart from Bobby, who else has played more than 600 League games for the Red Devils?
7   Bobby is United's record League scorer. How many times did he hit the target?
8   In what season did Charlton score 29 League goals for the Reds?
9   In what year did England's favourite footballing son become Sir Bobby?
10 Against which country did Bobby score England's first goal of the 1966 World Cup Finals?
11 How many times did Bobby net in the 1966 World Cup semi-final against Portugal?
12 How many of England's four in the World Cup Final came from the boot or head of Bobby Charlton?
13 In what year did the teenage Charlton turn professional with Manchester United?
14 How many times did Bobby finish on the losing side in an FA Cup Final?
15 When was Bobby voted both English and European Footballer of the Year?
16 How many times did Bobby score in the 1968 European Cup Final?
17 Apart from in the final, did Bobby score during that European campaign?
18 At the end of which season did Bobby retire as a Red Devil?
19 How old was he when he ended his playing days at his beloved Old Trafford?
20 After Sir Alf Ramsey was sacked, Bobby was England's caretaker manager for a brief period. True or false?

Answers – see page 146

1   In what Irish city was Sammy born?

2   Against which opponents did Sammy score as a 17-year-old debutant in November 1971?

3   Sammy started his Old Trafford career as a striker, but in what position did he settle and thrive?

4   The young McIlroy's development was temporarily halted by serious injuries suffered in a car accident in what year?

5   Which United manager gave Sammy his senior break?

6   Sammy was United's top scorer in League games when they were relegated in 1973/74. What was his tally?

7   With what marksman did McIlroy form a potent dual spearhead during the Reds' season in the Second Division?

8   When Sammy switched roles during 1976/77, who replaced him in the front line?

9   Sammy retained a first-team slot, but who lost out in the subsequent reshuffle?

10 In which of Sammy's three FA Cup Finals did he head against the woodwork when the score was 0-0?

11 In another of those three Wembley occasions, he supplied a brilliant late equaliser. When was that?

12 How old was 'Super Sam' when he left United in February 1982?

13 Who was the Red Devils boss who discarded him?

14 Which club did he join?

15 What was the fee?

16 How many times was Sammy capped by Northern Ireland?

17 Though he will always be remembered as a Red, McIlroy had two spells with Manchester City. True or false?

18 With which club did McIlroy close his illustrious playing career?

19 As a manager, which club did Sammy lead from non-League status to the Second Division?

20 Of which team did Sammy assume control during 2000?

Answers – see page 143

Name the League clubs with which these former United men first started work as first-team managers:

1 Steve Bruce
2 Harry Gregg
3 Bryan Robson
4 George Graham
5 Steve Coppell
6 David Herd
7 Maurice Setters
8 Jack Rowley
9 Lou Macari
10 Noel Cantwell
11 Peter Davenport
12 Nobby Stiles
13 Jim Ryan
14 Viv Anderson
15 Ian Greaves
16 Gordon Strachan
17 Pat Crerand.
18 Dennis Viollet
19 Jimmy Greenhoff
20 Johnny Giles

ANSWERS

Bobby Charlton - 2 (see page 143)
1 False. 2 49. 3 West Germany. 4 The 1970 World Cup Finals. 5 Mexico. 6 Nobody.
7 199. 8 1958/59. 9 1994. 10 Mexico. 11 Twice. 12 None. 13 1954. 14 Twice. 15 1966.
16 Two. 17 No. 18 1972/73. 19 35. 20 False.

Answers – see page 144

1. Tommy Taylor was born in which Yorkshire town?
2. Name the headquarters of his first club.
3. Tommy averaged better than a goal every two games for his first employers. True or false?
4. Towards the end of which season did he sign for Manchester United?
5. What was the fee when he moved to Old Trafford?
6. When the transaction was complete, who benefited unexpectedly from the deal?
7. Against which Lancashire club did Taylor make his Red Devils debut?
8. How many times did he score in United's 5-2 victory that afternoon at Old Trafford?
9. Tommy netted 22 League goals in his first full season, despite missing the last six games through injury. But was he the Reds' top scorer?
10. Two men contributed 20 First Division strikes in 1954/55. One was Tommy, but who was his partner in goals?
11. Against which nation did Tommy make his full England debut in May 1953?
12. In which city did the game take place?
13. Against which Scandinavians did Tommy grab his first England hat-trick?
14. Between November 1956 and May 1957, Tommy played in four internationals, scoring how many goals?
15. How many times did the ebullient Yorkshireman play for his country?
16. To which Bolton dreadnought did he appear to be the natural successor?
17. How many times did Tommy find the net for England?
18. Against which country did Tommy take the field for his last England appearance in November 1957?
19. That day at Wembley, how many times did Taylor hit the target in a 4-0 victory?
20. How old was Tommy when he died at Munich?

Answers – see page 149

Who said the following:

1 I played for the prison team. There were no away games.

2 When an Italian tells me it's pasta on the plate, I check under the sauce to make sure.

3 Football is a very simple game – 22 players run after a ball and in the end the Germans win.

4 I'm often seen as an atypical player, because I began a degree, have left-wing politics and read books.

5 The whole of my career flashed before me in the blink of an eye.

6 Nobby Stiles doesn't so much tackle people as bump into them.

7 I could have bought a row of houses in Manchester with what the Colombians gave me.

8 I gave them the Cup and they gave me the sack.

9 I didn't get angry enough. They told me I needed more aggression.

10 I have one rule on the field. I never, ever, talk to the opposition.

11 Name on the trophy!

12 What do they want me to do? Go out and smash up some bar?

13 He was so small it was like picking up a baby. But that didn't stop him scoring eight goals in one game, all with his head.

14 I'll give Bill Shankly the credit for making sure he went for genuine talent.

15 Charlee Meeten, numero uno. If we have heem, we never need Gento!

16 I went for the ball, that was all I could see, it was definitely playable.

17 It shouldn't happen to a dog.

18 Peter Schmeichel returned from his operation today, but it hasn't worked. He still won't admit it when he makes a mistake!

19 One goal and suddenly he's a superstar!

20 I can't believe it. Football. Bloody hell!

Reds in Europe 1976 to 1978 *(see page 149)*

ANSWERS

1 Tommy Docherty. 2 All blue. 3 Ruud Krol. 4 Stuart Pearson. 5 Lou Macari. 6 Sammy McIlroy. 7 Gordon Hill. 8 Dino Zoff. 9 Roberto Boninsegna. 10 Don Revie. 11 Steve Paterson. 12 Arthur Albiston. 13 Dave Sexton. 14 Gordon Hill. 15 Home Park, Plymouth. 16 Because of hooliganism by United fans in France. 17 Stuart Pearson. 18 Steve Coppell. 19 0-4. 20 Porto won 6-5.

Answers – see page 150

1   Danny Wallace had how many brothers who played League football?
2   With what club was Danny playing when he made his full international debut?
3   How many full caps did Danny collect?
4   Decipher the anagram: DEDYT GRENHISMAH.
5   How many times did Bobby Charlton appear for the Football League?
6   Who was the only United man who reached that same total?
7   Who holds the United record for England under-23 appearances?
8   How many did he make?
9   Which Republic of Ireland under-21 international defender's sole United appearance was as a substitute for Kevin Moran during 1980/81?
10 Which future chairman of the Reds played for the United Kingdom in the 1908 Olympics?
11 In what city were those Games staged?
12 Two United men played for the Rest of Europe against Scandinavia in 1964. One was Bobby Charlton; who was the other?
13 Who was United's keeper when they lost the FA Youth Cup Final in 1986?
14 Which member of that team would go on to score the winning goal in an FA Cup Final?
15 Who were United's conquerors in the 1986 FA Youth Cup Final?
16 United were beaten in their previous FA Youth Cup Final in 1982. Who won the trophy that year?
17 What was the aggregate score in the final?
18 Before that, United had won all six of the FA Youth Cup Finals in which they had appeared. True or false?
19 Whose first autobiography, entitled 'Living For Kicks', was published in 1963?
20 Which marksman scored 67 times in 101 League and FA Cup outings for United between 1929 and 1933?

ANSWERS

John Connelly (see page 150)
1 Burnley. 2 £56,000. 3 1959/60. 4 Number seven. 5 True. 6 20. 7 HJK Helsinki. 8 Leeds United. 9 20. 10 Uruguay. 11 Terry Paine. 12 Two. 13 Blackburn Rovers. 14 £40,000.
15 Bury. 16 Joiner. 17 28 years old. 18 St Helens. 19 1962 for Burnley v Spurs.
20 Connelly's Plaice.

1 Who was United manager when they played their first European tie of the 1970s?
2 What colours did United wear for their UEFA Cup encounter with Ajax in Amsterdam in September 1976?
3 Which world-class footballer scored the only goal of that game?
4 Which key United marksman was missing from the return leg because of injury?
5 Which Scot shot the Red Devils into the lead at Old Trafford?
6 Who was the Irishman who scored the goal which knocked out Ajax?
7 United then defeated Juventus at Old Trafford. Who struck the only goal?
8 Who was the Juventus keeper, who would one day manage Italy?
9 Which Italian marksman scored twice as Juventus won the second leg 3-0?
10 The game, played in November 1976, was watched by the reigning England manager. Name him.
11 Which future boss of Inverness Caledonian Thistle was used as a substitute away to Juventus?
12 Which teenage left-back excelled for United in both legs against the Italians?
13 Who had taken over as United manager when they faced St Etienne in the Cup Winners' Cup of 1977/78?
14 Who scored United's goal in the 1-1 draw in France after having two earlier efforts disallowed for offside?
15 Where did the Red Devils play the return leg?
16 Why was it not played at Old Trafford?
17 Who netted the Red Devils' opener in the 2-0 home victory over St Etienne?
18 Who added the goal which saw United through to the second round?
19 United were thrashed by FC Porto in Portugal. What was the score?
20 United scored five at home but lost on aggregate. What was the overall result?

Answers – see page 148

1 From which club did Matt Busby sign John Connelly in April 1964?
2 What was the fee?
3 In what season did John earn the first Championship medal of his career?
4 What number shirt did Connelly wear as he helped United to the title in his first season at Old Trafford?
5 John was one of three ever-presents during that memorable campaign. True or false?
6 How many senior goals did John contribute in 1964/65?
7 Against which opponents did John notch a European Cup hat-trick in September 1965?
8 On the title run-in in 1964/65, John scored the only goal in a crucial away encounter with which of United's chief rivals for the crown?
9 How many full England caps adorn the Connelly trophy cabinet?
10 John struck the woodwork twice in England's goalless opening to the 1966 World Cup Finals. Who provided the Wembley opposition?
11 To whom did John lose his place for the next game?
12 How many full seasons did Connelly spend at Old Trafford?
13 To which club was he transferred?
14 How much money did United bank from his sale?
15 Which was John's fourth and last Lancashire club?
16 When John won his first England cap in 1959 he was a part-timer. What was his trade outside football?
17 How old was Connelly when he bowed out of Old Trafford?
18 John hailed from a rugby league heartland. In what town was he born?
19 In which FA Cup Final did John Connelly appear?
20 What was the name of the fish-and-chip shop John opened in Brierfield?

Answers – see page 153

1 Which former United central defender spent four seasons with Chicago Sting in the late 1970s?

2 Which earlier United pivot, the Chicago coach, had taken him to Chicago?

3 The prospects of which Manchester-born Red Devil were shattered by a broken leg after he had made two substitute appearances in 1975/76?

4 Which marksman netted in the first minute of his debut for United in 1908?

5 Which Mancunian half-back made his United entrance in the FA Cup quarter-final replay clash with West Bromwich Albion in 1958?

6 What was the outcome of that match?

7 For which injured newcomer to the Reds' squad was that half-back deputising?

8 To which club was he transferred the following year?

9 How many FA Cup medals did David McCreery earn as a Red Devil?

10 They were both collected as a loser. True or false?

11 To which club was David transferred in August 1979?

12 Which manager allowed him to leave Old Trafford?

13 Who was the buying manager?

14 With which club did McCreery excel throughout most of the 1980s?

15 Which Scottish outfit did he join in 1989?

16 For which club did David make his final League appearance?

17 Which club gave McCreery a start in management?

18 What was David's nickname during his Old Trafford years?

19 How many times was David McCreery capped by the Republic of Ireland?

20 Decipher the anagram: AXLE NESTYPE.

Matt Busby - 2 *(see page 153)*

ANSWERS
1 1909. 2 The FA Cup in 1934. 3 Frank Swift. 4 David Herd's father, Alex. 5 Jean. 6 1936. 7 Player-coach at Liverpool. 8 United chairman James Gibson. 9 Running the British Olympic football team. 10 Tottenham Hotspur. 11 Not to enter the European Cup. 12 Ten weeks. 13 The CBE. 14 Manager of Scotland. 15 Denis Law. 16 1967. 17 False – he came seventh. 18 1971 19 1982. 20 1980 – 1994.

Answers – see page 154

1 Charlie Mitten played on which wing for Matt Busby's first great post-war United side?

2 In what Burmese city was Charlie born?

3 Mitten was the only one of United's swashbuckling 1940s 'Famous Five' forward line who was not a full international. True or false?

4 Charlie was a renowned penalty expert, but did he ever fail to convert for United?

5 How many times did he net from the spot against Aston Villa at Old Trafford in March 1950?

6 Charlie earned only one major honour as a Red Devil. What was it?

7 For which country was Mitten selected as 12th man in an unofficial wartime international?

8 To which Colombian club did Charlie move in 1950 in contravention of FIFA rules?

9 How many seasons did he spend in South America?

10 What was the title of Charlie's biography, published in 1996 and reflecting his Colombian adventure?

11 To which club was he transferred after serving a ban for his 'defection'?

12 Charlie made his United debut in August 1946 against the Mariners. What is that club's more formal name?

13 Of which club did Mitten become player-manager in 1956?

14 Who played on the opposite wing to Charlie during his prime years with United?

15 During his halcyon days on United's left flank, who was Charlie's most frequent inside-forward partner?

16 Of which north-eastern giants did Charlie become boss in 1958?

17 What happened to Mitten's side in 1961?

18 Which Scottish club offered the teenage Charlie a trial before he joined United?

19 The eldest of Charlie's two sons played for six League clubs. Name him.

20 At the end of which campaign did Charlie retire as a player?

ANSWERS

Pot Luck - 48 (see page 154)

1 Chelsea. 2 Sheffield Wednesday. 3 Everton. 4 1976. 5 Wolves. 6 Halifax Town.
7 Seamus Brennan. 8 £60,000. 9 Frank Kopel. 10 Blackburn Rovers. 11 Harry Gregg.
12 Charlton Athletic. 13 Tommy Heron. 14 Mark Higgins. 15 John Higgins. 16 Stoke City.
17 Graeme Hogg. 18 Portsmouth. 19 Hearts. 20 Brentford.

Answers – see page 151

1   In what year was Matt Busby born?
2   What club honour did Matt win as a player with Manchester City?
3   Which of Matt's playing team-mates at Maine Road died in the Munich air crash?
4   The father of which Manchester United star played alongside Busby at City?
5   What was the name of Sir Matt's wife?
6   When did Matt leave Manchester City to join Liverpool?
7   What job did Matt turn down to become United manager?
8   Who gave Busby the Old Trafford job?
9   What extra assignment did the United manager take on in the summer of 1948?
10 Which London club offered Matt their hot seat in April 1949?
11 What advice from the Football League did Matt ignore in 1956?
12 How long did Busby remain in a German hospital after nearly losing his life at Munich?
13 What honour came Busby's way in June 1958?
14 From 1958 to 1959, Matt was involved in what extra-curricular footballing activity?
15 Which illustrious pay rebel did Busby transfer-list briefly in 1966?
16 In what year was Matt Busby accorded the Freedom of Manchester?
17 In 1969 a Gallup poll found Sir Matt to be the eighth most popular man in Britain – true or false?
18 When did Sir Matt join the United board?
19 What was his last year as a director?
20 When was his reign as club president?

Answers – see page 152

1 For which club did Jim McCalliog make his League debut?
2 For whom did he score after only four minutes of the FA Cup Final in 1966?
3 That year, he collected a loser's medal. Who won the match?
4 When did he make up for his disappointment by helping to lift the trophy, against United?
5 For which club did Jim make the most League appearances?
6 Which club did McCalliog manage in the early 1990s?
7 Decipher the anagram: MASSUE NARNBEN.
8 How much did Tommy Docherty pay for Jim McCalliog in a desperate bid to avoid relegation in March 1974?
9 Which former United full-back enjoyed a successful decade with Dundee United, starting in 1972?
10 To which club had he been transferred by United for £25,000 in March 1969?
11 Whose book, published in 1961, was entitled 'Wild About Football'?
12 Matt Busby sold promising centre-half Frank Haydock to which club in 1963?
13 Which Scottish utility man had played League football in Scotland and Northern Ireland before he joined United from Portadown in March 1958?
14 Which former Everton centre-half and skipper revived his injury-ravaged career with United during 1985/86?
15 His father, also a stopper, had played against the Red Devils for Bolton in the 1958 FA Cup Final. Name him.
16 With which League club did the son end his League playing days?
17 Which Scottish centre-half missed just one tie as the Reds reached the FA Cup Final in 1985, only for injury to rule him out of Wembley contention?
18 After leaving Old Trafford in 1988, that Scottish under-21 international made a century of League appearances for which south-coast club?
19 He returned north of the border to play for which Edinburgh club in the early 1990s?
20 This tall stopper finished his League career with which Londoners?

Charlie Mitten (see page 152)

ANSWERS

1 The left. 2 Rangoon. 3 True. 4 Yes, four times, according to the cuttings and contrary to widespread belief. 5 Three. 6 FA Cup winner's medal in 1948. 7 Scotland. 8 Santa Fe of Bogota. 9 One. 10 Bogota Bandit. 11 Fulham. 12 Grimsby Town. 13 Mansfield Town. 14 Jimmy Delaney. 15 Stan Pearson. 16 Newcastle United. 17 They were relegated from Division One. 18 Glasgow Rangers. 19 John Mitten. 20 1957/58.

1 Which marksman, recently recalled by England, contributed a hat-trick to the 5-0 demolition of Southampton at Old Trafford?

2 Which young centre-half impressed hugely in the League Cup win at Watford?

3 Which United keeper was sent off that night at Vicarage Road?

4 Which Scottish teenager made his senior United debut against the Hornets?

5 Who put United ahead at Highfield Road to cap an exquisite flowing move?

6 Whose Old Trafford goal ensured the Reds' progress to the second stage of the Champions League?

7 Which Dynamo Kiev striker missed a golden chance to eliminate United in the dying moments of that match?

8 Which fellow Frenchman beat Fabien Barthez to put Middlesbrough in front at Old Trafford?

9 Some 90 seconds into the resumption of hostilities with Manchester City, who struck the game's decisive blow?

10 Whose late double, including a fabulous chip which followed a 32-pass move, saw off plucky Panathanaikos at Old Trafford?

11 Who put United ahead at Derby with his 15th goal of the season?

12 Whose curling, Beckhamesque 25-yarder doubled the Reds' lead over the Rams?

13 Who was sent off as United exited the League Cup at the Stadium of Light?

14 Who played his first senior game for the Red Devils that night?

15 Against which opponents did United claim the first away win of their European campaign?

16 Name the stadium in which this triumph was accomplished.

17 Whose shot from the centre circle rebounded off the bar to set up a goal for Ole Gunnar Solskjaer at Charlton?

18 Who scored the only goal as Liverpool inflicted United's first home Premiership defeat of the campaign?

19 How many previous League defeats had the Reds suffered since Alex Ferguson became boss?

20 Who was sent off in the dying moments of Liverpool's visit?

Answers – see page 158

1 Who did Ron Atkinson succeed as manager of Manchester United in June 1981?

2 From which club did the Reds recruit Big Ron?

3 Is Atkinson a native of Birmingham, Manchester or Merseyside?

4 What was the lowest United finished in the League table during Ron's five complete seasons in control?

5 And what was the highest?

6 Which campaign did Ron's Red Devils begin with ten straight League victories?

7 Who was the chairman when Ron Atkinson was sacked in November 1986?

8 Who replaced Ron at Old Trafford?

9 Soon after arriving, Ron signed Bryan Robson and which other midfielder from his former club?

10 In Atkinson's first season as United boss, the Reds bowed out of the FA Cup in the third round to which Second Division opposition?

11 Which Third Division side eliminated them at the same stage in 1983/84?

12 The Reds' last match before Ron's departure was a 4-1 League Cup thrashing at which ground?

13 Who scored United's goal on that sorry night?

14 Including Charity Shield clashes, in how many games did Ron guide United's fortunes at Wembley?

15 How many times did Atkinson lead the Red Devils to the last four of a major European competition?

16 As a dynamic wing-half, of which club was Ron the driving force on their journey from the Southern League to Division Two?

17 As a manager, which club did Atkinson guide to the Fourth Division crown in 1977?

18 With which club did Ron challenge United for the League title in 1992/93?

19 Which Spanish club did Atkinson boss for 96 days during 1988/89?

20 How many clubs did Ron Atkinson lead to Wembley glory over United after he left Old Trafford?

Answers – see page 155

1 Which 1920s United full-back served the club as a trainer from 1934 until his retirement in 1961?

2 What his his first senior club as a player?

3 Decipher the anagram: MONNAR TIDESHEW.

4 With which club did Northern Ireland international Tommy Jackson begin his League career?

5 Which was Jackson's first English club?

6 In which season did Tommy pocket a title medal?

7 With which club did he spend the first half of the 1970s?

8 After leaving United in 1978, he re-crossed the Irish Sea to join which club?

9 How many full caps did Tommy win for Northern Ireland?

10 Which former United full-back won a Fourth Division title medal with Stockport in 1966/67?

11 His sole senior outing as a Red Devil had been in a 3-0 home defeat by which opponents in October 1957?

12 Which former United striker helped his club reach the Division One play-offs in 2000/2001?

13 With which club did the Northern Irish international achieve this distinction?

14 Which countryman of Sir Alex Ferguson was that marksman's new club boss after his move from Old Trafford?

15 With which club did on-loan United goalkeeper Nick Culkin feature in an unsuccessful relegation battle in 2000/2001?

16 Which ex-United midfielder helped his Lancastrian employers reach the Division Three play-offs in 2000/2001?

17 Which Scottish under-21 international striker finished United's treble-winning campaign on loan at Aberdeen?

18 To which club was he loaned during 1999/2000?

19 Wes Brown spent a month of 1997/98 on loan at Preston. True or false?

20 Which club featured four former Red Devils in their promotion-winning squad of 2000/2001?

ANSWERS

Season 2000/2001 - 2 *(see page 155)*
1 Teddy Sheringham. 2 John O'Shea. 3 Raimond van der Gouw. 4 Michael Stewart. 5 Andrew Cole. 6 Teddy Sheringham. 7 Demetradze. 8 Christian Karembeu. 9 David Beckham. 10 Paul Scholes. 11 Teddy Sheringham. 12 Nicky Butt's. 13 Dwight Yorke. 14 Danny Webber. 15 Sturm Graz. 16 The Arnold Schwarzenegger Stadium. 17 Ryan Giggs'. 18 Danny Murphy. 19 99 defeats. 20 Luke Chadwick.

1 From which club did Alex Ferguson sign Dwight Yorke in August 1999?
2 What was the fee?
3 Was that fee a record between two British clubs?
4 On what ground did Dwight make his Premiership debut for United?
5 Dwight netted twice in his first match at Old Trafford as a Red Devil. Who were the opponents?
6 Yorke's first hat-trick for Manchester United was scored on what ground?
7 In 1999/2000 Dwight struck 20 League goals. Who was the previous United man to reach that mark in one season?
8 Against which opponents did he register his landmark strike?
9 For which side does Dwight play his international football?
10 Dwight netted twice in United's FA Cup quarter-final replay victory over which club in the spring of 1999?
11 With what part of his anatomy did Yorke score twice at home to Inter Milan in March 1999?
12 Which manager, who went on to lead England, discovered Dwight while touring the West Indies in 1989?
13 Who made the tongue-in-cheek comment about Dwight: 'If I had a gun I'd shoot him'?
14 What United shirt number has Dwight made his own?
15 Yorke was upset about missing which Wembley confrontation with Manchester United?
16 Who was the manager who didn't pick Dwight for that big match?
17 Yorke had won one major club honour before joining United. What was it?
18 Which keeper picked the ball out of the net three times as Dwight bagged his second hat-trick for the Reds in March 2000?
19 How many goals did Dwight score in his 11 Champions League appearances during 1998/99?
20 At what ground did Dwight score twice, for the first time of that European campaign?

ANSWERS

Big Ron *(see page 156)*

1 Dave Sexton. 2 West Bromwich Albion. 3 Merseyside. 4 Fourth. 5 Third. 6 1985/86.
7 Martin Edwards. 8 Alex Ferguson. 9 Remi Moses. 10 Watford. 11 Bournemouth.
12 The Dell. 13 Peter Davenport. 14 Six times. 15 Once, in the 1984 Cup Winners' Cup.
16 Oxford United. 17 Cambridge United. 18 Aston Villa. 19 Atletico Madrid. 20 Two, Sheffield Wednesday and Aston Villa in League Cup Finals.

Answers – see page 161

1   Which United marksman overtook Denis Law's European Cup club goals record during season 2000/2001?

2   How many times did Denis hit the target in that competition?

3   Why did Denis miss the 1968 European Cup Final?

4   In what year was Law voted European Footballer of the Year?

5   Who were the opponents when Denis Law backheeled his final League goal?

6   Which United manager gave Denis a free transfer in the summer of 1973?

7   After which season did Law hang up his boots?

8   How many times was Denis capped by his country?

9   Who were Scotland's opponents in the Lawman's final international?

10 In which tournament did that game take place?

11 How many goals did Denis score for Scotland?

12 Law's total was a record. Who equalled it in later years, having played in almost twice as many games?

13 In 2000, Denis Law was voted the greatest Scottish player of all time. True or false?

14 How many hat-tricks did Denis score at full international level?

15 Who were the opponents when Law made his League debut on Christmas Eve 1956?

16 Under how many managers did Denis play as a Red Devil?

17 Which Stoke City keeper, a fellow Scottish international, did Denis beat four times at Old Trafford in December 1963?

18 In what side did Denis line up alongside Alfredo di Stafano, Puskas and Eusebio in 1963?

19 Did Denis Law ever enter club management?

20 For which national League team did Denis play during 1961/62?

Answers – see page 162

Name the seasons in which these Red Devils make their senior debuts for
Manchester United:

1 Peter Schmeichel
2 Dennis Viollet
3 Paul Scholes
4 Arthur Albiston
5 Jim Holton
6 Roger Byrne
7 Ryan Giggs
8 Reg Hunter
9 John Curtis
10 Bobby Noble
11 Mark Hughes
12 Stan Pearson
13 Darren Ferguson
14 Colin Webster
15 Brian Greenhoff
16 Allenby Chilton
17 Remi Moses
18 Phil Neville
19 Tony Gill
20 George Best

ANSWERS

Title Trail 1996/97 *(see page 162)*
1 Eric Cantona. 2 Jordi Cruyff. 3 David Unsworth. 4 Newcastle United. 5 The Dell.
6 The White Feather (Fabrizio Ravanelli). 7 Michael Clegg. 8 Julian Dicks'. 9 Wimbledon.
10 Coventry City. 11 Andy Melville own goal. 12 Derby County. 13 Leicester City.
14 Middlesbrough. 15 Solskjaer. 16 Seven points. 17 Newcastle United. 18 Peter
Schmeichel. 19 True. 20 Karel Poborsky.

160

Answers – see page 159

1 Which former Burnley idol scored the only goal as United beat Liverpool at Old Trafford in September 1969?

2 A big, blond Scottish stopper scored one of United's goals as they thrashed Liverpool 4-1 at Anfield in December 1969. Name him.

3 Who made the last of nearly 500 senior outings for Liverpool as a late substitute in that match?

4 Who was the composed young full-back who made one of his few Liverpool appearances, against United at Anfield in September 1970?

5 Which United centre-half scored an own goal as Liverpool won 2-0 at Old Trafford in April 1971?

6 Who struck an equaliser for United, to claim a 2-2 draw in September 1971?

7 Who was the manager at United's helm for that tumultuous encounter?

8 What new star was galvanising Liverpool that season?

9 What was the humiliating result of Liverpool's visit to Old Trafford in April 1972?

10 Who scored the opening goal as bottom-placed United upset League leaders Liverpool 2-0 at Old Trafford in November 1972?

11 Which Scot created that first goal, then scored the second?

12 The lesser-known brother of a United stalwart went on as a substitute against Liverpool at Old Trafford in September 1973. Name him.

13 United performed abominably in a 2-0 defeat at Anfield in December 1973 under what manager?

14 Arnold Sidebottom was one of United's two rookie centre-halves that day. Who was the other?

15 Why did United not face Liverpool during 1974/75?

16 Who was Liverpool's manager when hostilities were resumed in 1975/76?

17 Who netted United's consolation goal in the 3-1 defeat in November 1975?

18 Who was United manager when they lost 3-0 on Boxing Day 1978?

19 Which United keeper hit the Liverpool bar with a clearance during a 2-0 reverse at Anfield on Boxing Day 1979?

20 How many points adrift of Liverpool did runners-up United finish in 1979/80?

ANSWERS

Denis Law - 2 (see page 159)

1 Andrew Cole. 2 14 3 A knee injury. 4 1964. 5 Manchester United. 6 Tommy Docherty. 7 1973/74. 8 55. 9 Zaire. 10 The 1974 World Cup Finals in West Germany. 11 30. 12 Kenny Dalglish. 13 True. 14 Three. 15 Notts County. 16 Four. 17 Lawrie Leslie. 18 Rest of the World. 19 No. 20 The Italian League.

Answers – see page 160

1 Who scored United's first goal of the Premiership campaign, against Wimbledon at Selhurst Park?

2 Who made his League debut for the Reds in that away encounter with Wimbledon?

3 To whom were United indebted for the late own goal which saved a point against Everton at Old Trafford?

4 Who thrashed United 5-0 in October?

5 Six days later they conceded six goals at which ground?

6 What was the nickname of the big Italian who equalised against United at the Riverside?

7 Which United youngster made his debut away to Middlesbrough in November?

8 Whose penalty cost the Reds two points at Upton Park?

9 Who knocked United out of the FA Cup only six days after being beaten in the Premiership at Old Trafford?

10 Which club conceded two own goals in the first five minutes at Old Trafford?

11 United lost 2-1 at Roker Park in March. Who scored their only goal?

12 Who caused the Reds to stutter on the title trail, winning 3-2 at Old Trafford in early April?

13 Who took a 2-0 lead against United in May, only for the game to finish 2-2?

14 Which opponents netted three times in the first half at Old Trafford on Easter Monday?

15 In the final game against, West Ham, a Paul Scholes effort crossed the line before Ole Gunnar Solskjaer made sure. Who was credited with the goal?

16 By what margin did the Reds claim the title?

17 Who were runners-up?

18 Two players made the most (36) Premiership appearances for United. One was Eric Cantona, who was the other?

19 Six opponents scored own goals against United during the season. True or false?

20 Which Czech international pocketed a title medal in his first term as a Red Devil?

Answers – see page 165

1   Who scored an own goal when United lost 5-0 at Stamford Bridge in 1999?

2   Who netted twice for Chelsea on that painful afternoon for United fans?

3   Which United man was dismissed following a clash with Chelsea's Dennis Wise?

4   Who netted twice as the Reds triumphed in the return encounter in April 2000?

5   Who scored United's only goal when the Reds met the Blues at Old Trafford in December 1998?

6   What was the score in the return fixture when Chelsea travelled north 13 days later?

7   Another United own goal against Chelsea was conceded by which Red Devil at Old Trafford in September 1997?

8   Who put Chelsea in front midway through the second half of that contest?

9   Who popped up with a late equaliser for United?

10 In February 1998 a goal at Stamford Bridge from which unlikely source appeared (wrongly) to give United an unassailable lead in the title race?

11 Who grabbed the Reds' late consolation goal when Chelsea won 2-1 at Old Trafford in November 1996?

12 Later that season United took a point away from Stamford Bridge, thanks to a second-half equaliser. Who grabbed it?

13 The Red Devils' 4-1 victory at Stamford Bridge in October 1995 featured two early goals from which marksman?

14 Who contributed Chelsea's sole reply that day?

15 Who capped United's triumph with a stunning solo goal near the end?

16 Decipher the anagram: NATS ARPNOSE.

17 Whose late winner gift-wrapped United's Boxing Day victory at Stamford Bridge in 1994?

18 During their first League and FA Cup double-winning campaign, how many points did the Reds take from Chelsea?

19 Who scored for Chelsea in both Premiership games with the Londoners that season?

20 How did United fare in that term's final meeting with Chelsea?

Answers – see page 166

1 What landmark did United achieve when they beat Chelsea 4-0 at Wembley?
2 Who scored two penalties to put the Reds on the glory trail?
3 Which United player was upended to concede the first spot-kick?
4 Who bet the penalty-taker £100 that he would miss?
5 Who grounded Andrei Kanchelskis to give away the second penalty?
6 Who was the wrong-footed Chelsea keeper?
7 Who was the referee who made the fateful decisions?
8 Who hit the bar for Chelsea when the score was 0-0?
9 Which future Chelsea favourite notched the Red Devils' third?
10 Who poked the ball into an empty net for United's fourth?
11 Who was the Chelsea player-manager, who had claimed that morning that God was on his side?
12 Who lifted the FA Cup for Manchester United?
13 Which of the Reds' three named substitutes was not used?
14 Who took the field as Chelsea's first substitute?
15 What was the Londoners' consolation prize?
16 What was the title of United's Cup Final song?
17 Footballers of how many nationalities took the field for the Reds?
18 Who played at right-back for United?
19 Who was the kit-man in the centre of the celebration pictures?
20 Which United legend was disappointed not to be given a place on the bench?

ANSWERS

Pot Luck - 52 *(see page 166)*
1 Dwight Yorke's. 2 Harry Kewell. 3 David Beckham. 4 Lucas Radebe. 5 Lee Bowyer.
6 Jimmy Floyd Hasselbaink. 7 Nigel Martyn. 8 Paul Robinson. 9 Roy Keane. 10 Nicky
Butt. 11 Jimmy Floyd Hasselbaink. 12 Andrew Cole. 13 Dwight Yorke. 14 David Wetherall.
15 Wes Brown. 16 Denis Irwin. 17 Leeds manager Howard Wilkinson. 18 Eric Cantona.
19 Eric Cantona. 20 Nicky Butt.

Answers – see page 163

1   By the end of season 2000/2001, how many men had played more senior games for United than Tony Dunne?

2   With whom did Tony form a successful long-term full-back partnership for club and country?

3   In what capital city was Tony Dunne born?

4   From which club was Tony signed by Matt Busby in April 1960?

5   What was the bargain-basement fee which secured the services of the pacy little defender?

6   During which campaign did Dunne win a regular place in United's first team?

7   What was Tony's first major club honour as a Red Devil?

8   On the day that he secured that prize, who was his full-back partner?

9   Tony is the brother of Pat Dunne, a goalkeeper in front of whom he played many a time for the Reds. True or false?

10 How many matches did Tony miss as United lifted the title in 1964/65?

11 How many full caps did Dunne win for his country?

12 Against which nation did he make his debut for the Republic in April 1962?

13 Which Portuguese international right-winger was Tony's direct opponent in the 1968 European Cup Final?

14 How many times did Dunne help the Red Devils lift the League title?

15 How old was Tony when he was allowed to leave Old Trafford in July 1973?

16 Who was the manager who let him go when he was arguably still the best full-back at the club?

17 Which club was delighted to employ the released Irish international?

18 In what season did Tony help the Trotters to the Second Division Championship?

19 Which former United full-back was Dunne's boss as those Trotters rose to the top flight?

20 In which country did Tony Dunne coach successfully after retiring as a player?

Answers – see page 164

1 Whose two headers in the second half thwarted Leeds at Old Trafford in 1999?

2 Which Elland Road-based Aussie had rapped the Reds' post before the home side seized the initiative?

3 Who was the shock omission by Sir Alex Ferguson for the return encounter in February 2000?

4 Who was the defender outpaced by Andrew Cole before the England marksman struck that game's only goal?

5 Which Leeds midfielder missed from close range with the empty goal gaping near the end of that torrid encounter?

6 With United embarked on the treble trail in 1998/99, which Leeds striker put his side in front at Old Trafford?

7 Which injured goalkeeper had to be replaced at half-time in that encounter?

8 Who was the substitute custodian?

9 Who netted in the first minute of the second half?

10 Who claimed all three points for the Reds with a brilliant shot on the turn with 12 minutes remaining?

11 When United visited Elland Road in April 1999, they fell behind to a goal from which Leeds man in the first half?

12 Who equalised for the Reds ten minutes after the interval?

13 Who missed a golden opportunity to seal victory with the last kick of the match?

14 Who contributed the only goal when the two Uniteds met at Elland Road in September 1997?

15 Which future England defender made his debut at home to Leeds in May 1998?

16 On that same day, which former Leeds player netted against his former club?

17 Who lost his job shortly after United's four-goal demolition of Leeds at Elland Road in September 1996?

18 A former Leeds player finished the scoring in the last minute. Name him.

19 A penalty settled the Manchester-Leeds clash at Old Trafford that December. Who scored it?

20 Decipher the anagram: YINCK TUBT.

Answers — see page 169

1   Which Poles did United face in their Champions League qualifier?
2   Who headed United in front against Barcelona at Old Trafford?
3   A wondrous free-kick from the partner of which pop star put United 3-2 in front?
4   Who was sent off for conceding the penalty by which the Catalans equalised?
5   Whose late blunder cost United victory against Bayern Munich in the Olympic Stadium?
6   Who had earlier given the Reds a 2-1 lead?
7   Which midfielder made his European debut as a substitute for Dwight Yorke in the 6-2 away victory over Brondby?
8   Who scored with his first touch after going on as a substitute in that Copenhagen encounter?
9   What was United's half-time lead in the home encounter with the Danes?
10   United went behind in the first minute at the Nou Camp. Who was the scorer?
11   Who bagged a pair for the Red Devils that night?
12   Who reciprocated with a double for Barcelona?
13   Who scored for United in their 1-1 home draw with Bayern Munich?
14   Who delivered both crosses for Dwight Yorke to head the Reds into a two-goal quarter-final lead at home to Inter Milan?
15   Which Argentinian, an old acquaintance of David Beckham's, had a 'goal' disallowed controversially that night?
16   Who equalised for United after Ventola had put Inter in front in Italy?
17   Who cracked the last-minute goal which put the Reds on level terms in their Old Trafford semi-final against Juventus?
18   Which 'Captain Courageous' delivered the Reds' first goal in response to two early strikes by Juventus at the Stadio Delle Alpi?
19   Who stooped to nod United's equaliser?
20   Who ensured the Red Devils' place in the final with a goal in the 84th minute?

1 United were the first holders of the Charity Shield after they beat QPR in 1908. True or false?

2 Whose hat-trick secured the trophy in a replay?

3 Who netted six times as United defeated Swindon Town 8-4 in 1911?

4 How did QPR and Swindon qualify to battle for the Charity Shield?

5 With which club have the Red Devils shared the Shield on three occasions?

6 Which keeper netted sensationally against United in the 1967 game?

7 Which 16-year-old United keeper was summoned from the crowd as an impromptu substitute to face Manchester City in 1956?

8 Who notched a hat-trick in the Reds' 1957 victory over Aston Villa?

9 Which champions thrashed United 4-0 in the 1963 event?

10 Which inspirational captain contributed both goals as United beat Liverpool in 1983?

11 The Reds beat Arsenal on penalties after a 1-1 draw in 1993. Who scored United's goal with an adroit volley?

12 In that match, which England keeper saw his spot-kick saved?

13 In 1994, a Cantona penalty put United ahead against Blackburn. Which England midfielder made the final score 2-0?

14 Which £15 million centre-forward did the Reds face in the 1996 Charity Shield encounter?

15 What was the result of that game?

16 In 1997, who gave Chelsea the lead against United?

17 Which Norwegian supplied the equaliser by heading his first goal for the Reds?

18 What was the outcome of the match?

19 Which Dutchman was given a torrid welcome to English football by Nicolas Anelka in the 1998 Charity Shield clash?

20 In 1999 against Arsenal, David Beckham's shot hit the bar and crossed the line before Dwight Yorke nodded home to make sure. Who was given the goal?

ANSWERS

David Beckham - 2 *(see page 170)*

1 Rivaldo. 2 No. 3 Gary Neville. 4 Italy. 5 Colombia. 6 Argentina. 7 Diego Simeone.
8 1997/98. 9 Nine in 1997/98. 10 Away to Leeds United. 11 Leicester City. 12 Ian Walker of Tottenham Hotspur. 13 Central midfield. 14 Peter Taylor. 15 Italy. 16 Nottingham Forest. 17 Chelsea. 18 Newcastle United. 19 Leicester City. 20 Anfield, against Finland.

168

Answers — see page 167

1 Who scored the first goal of United's 1999/2000 title campaign, against Everton at Goodison Park?

2 Whose header cannoned off Jaap Stam for the Toffees' late equaliser?

3 Who hit Everton with a four-goal blitz in fewer than 30 minutes at Old Trafford in December 1999?

4 Who scored the first goal of that match, which United won 5-1?

5 Which goalkeeper was substituted because of injury shortly after that goal?

6 Which Everton defender's misdirected header put United two up at Goodison Park in October 1998?

7 Who scored only the second goal of his United career when the Red Devils chewed up the Toffees at Old Trafford in March 1999?

8 Which towering Evertonian grabbed a brilliant brace at Old Trafford in 1996?

9 Who notched his first League goal as the Reds fought back to take a point?

10 Who netted twice as United won at Goodison on the way to their second League and FA Cup double?

11 Which Toffee who had grabbed an FA Cup Final winner against the Reds scored against them again on that occasion?

12 Who scored the only goal of the game at Goodison in February 1995 to dent United's title hopes?

13 Whose stunning volley earned three points for the Reds away to Everton in 1993?

14 What moving event took place before United's home meeting with Everton in January 1994?

15 Who contributed the only goal of the match on that sombre afternoon?

16 Which former United man opened the scoring as Everton triumphed 3-0 at Old Trafford in the second match of United's 1992/93 title campaign?

17 Whose two goals gave United victory in his first home clash with the Toffees, then the reigning champions, in December 1987?

18 Who scored twice in a 5-0 win over United at Goodison in October 1984?

19 Which Everton manager presided over that humbling of the Red Devils?

20 Decipher the anagram: NADNUC SRADWED.

Answers – see page 168

1 David was runner-up to which great player in the polls for European and World Footballer of the Year in 1999/2000?

2 Has David ever been voted Footballer of the Year by his peers or the writers?

3 Who was best man when Beckham married Victoria Adams?

4 David helped England qualify for France '98 with a goalless draw in which country?

5 During that tournament David scored his first international goal with a spectacular free-kick against which opponents?

6 Famously, he was sent off in the next game, against which nation?

7 Who was the opposition midfielder with whom the Beckham boot made contact, thus causing his dismissal?

8 David topped United's Premiership appearance tally, missing only one game, in which season?

9 Before 2000/2001, what is the most Premiership goals David had scored in one campaign?

10 For which big game in February 2000 was Beckham controversially omitted?

11 Who were the opponents in March 2000 when David first appeared with a cropped head?

12 David scored United's penultimate Premiership goal of the Treble-winning campaign. Which keeper did he beat?

13 In what position was David deployed for the 1999 European Cup Final?

14 Who was in charge of the England team when David first captained his country?

15 Who provided the opposition that night in November 2000?

16 The first time David scored twice in a Premiership match was at Old Trafford in April 1996. Who did United thump 5-0 that day?

17 David notched two goals in an FA Cup tie in January 1998 against which side?

18 The first time David netted a penalty in senior competition for United was against which team in December 2000?

19 Who were Old Trafford's visitors when Beckham answered his critics by scoring in his first League game after his 1998 World Cup trauma?

20 At what venue did David net his first goal as England skipper?

ANSWERS

Charity Shields (see page 168)
1 True. 2 Jimmy Turnbull's. 3 Harold Halse. 4 As Southern league champions. 5 Liverpool. 6 Pat Jennings of Spurs. 7 David Gaskell. 8 Tommy Taylor. 9 Everton. 10 Bryan Robson. 11 Mark Hughes. 12 David Seaman. 13 Paul Ince. 14 Alan Shearer. 15 United beat Newcastle 4-0. 16 Mark Hughes. 17 Ronny Johnsen. 18 United won on penalties. 19 Jaap Stam. 20 Dwight Yorke.

Answers – see page 173

1 Who was the two-goal hero of United's 1976 semi-final triumph?

2 Who were the opponents on that happy Hillsborough afternoon?

3 Apart from the scorer, which United player would go on to play for those opponents?

4 Who was the reigning Old Trafford boss, who would also make the same journey?

5 Who played alongside Martin Buchan in the centre of the Reds' defence?

6 Which former Manchester City idol went on as a substitute for the losing 1976 semi-finalists?

7 Which influential United midfielder would miss the semi through injury, but recover in time to face the Saints at Wembley?

8 Who stood in for that dynamic absentee?

9 When United beat Leeds in the 1977 semi-final, which Red opened the scoring against his former employers?

10 Who doubled the lead against the men from Elland Road?

11 Which England striker reduced the deficit with a penalty?

12 Which fearsome future Old Trafford spearhead was on the opposite side on that afternoon at Hillsborough in April 1977?

13 The Leeds marksman's pal, who was also Old Trafford-bound, was at centre-half for the Yorkshiremen. Name him.

14 In 1979, United drew 2-2 with Liverpool on a ground where the Mancunians had once played home matches. Name it.

15 Kenny Dalglish put the Merseysiders ahead; who equalised?

16 Which Liverpool midfielder struck a post with a penalty?

17 After Brian Greenhoff had nudged United in front, whose goal set up a replay?

18 Where was the second semi-final meeting of these two northern giants?

19 Whose cross created the only goal of the replay?

20 Who wrong-footed Ray Clemence with an adroit header to assure United's place in the 1979 FA Cup Final?

Answers – see page 174

1 Who scored twice as United raced to a three-goal lead in the first 20 minutes at West Ham in December 1999?

2 Who else contributed two goals for United that day?

3 Which Italian kept the game alive with two goals of his own?

4 There were eight goals in the return between the two clubs. Who scored three of them?

5 In that game, who saw his penalty saved, then knocked in the rebound?

6 Who opened and closed the scoring for the Hammers in the 11th minute?

7 After that match, how many goals had keeper Craig Forrest conceded in his last two games at Old Trafford?

8 Which Red Devil and England star received an hysterical greeting from the West Ham fans at Upton Park in August 1998?

9 Whose brace was sandwiched by goals from Yorke and Solskjaer as United beat West Ham at Old Trafford on the road to the Treble?

10 Who gave West Ham the lead before United claimed a 2-1 home win in 1997?

11 Whose goal set the Hammers on the way to a point after the Reds had taken a two-goal lead at Upton Park in December 1996?

12 Whose own goal did not prove decisive when the Hammers visited Old Trafford in August 1995?

13 Whose sublime strike kept United on track at Upton Park in January 1996?

14 In what appropriate colour were United playing as their Championship hopes died at Upton Park on the last day of the 1994/95 League season?

15 Who put the Hammers ahead in that game?

16 Who headed United's equaliser?

17 An inspired display by which keeper denied United the winner they needed?

18 Who scored West Ham's first goal against the Reds in the 2-2 draw at Upton Park in the 1993/94 League and FA Cup double campaign?

19 What were West Ham celebrating as United claimed their first title for 26 years in 1992/93?

20 Decipher the anagram: TAMT BYSUB.

Answers – see page 171

1 What unique distinction would United have claimed had they beaten Aston Villa?
2 Who was the United keeper whose cheekbone was fractured after six minutes?
3 Who was the Villa man with whom he collided?
4 Who deputised between the posts for United?
5 Which player, who often kept goal in training, expected to be landed with the job?
6 In which position did the crocked keeper eventually return as a passenger?
7 Following the injury, who spent the rest of the match at centre-half?
8 Who put the Midlanders into a two-goal lead?
9 What was the score at half-time?
10 Whose late header for United set up grandstand finish?
11 Which United man had a 'goal 'disallowed in the dying minutes?
12 In what colours did the Red Devils take to the Wembley turf?
13 Who was the captain who hoisted the trophy aloft for Villa?
14 Who was United's skipper?
15 Which United forward was absent with a groin injury?
16 Who replaced the missing star?
17 Which club did Matt Busby's side defeat in the semi-final?
18 What was unusual about the make-up of the two semis?
19 Which Villa man had once been the subject of a British record transfer fee?
20 Who was the Villa manager?

FA Cup Semi-Finals - 4 *(see page 171)*

ANSWERS

1 Gordon Hill. 2 Derby County. 3 Gerry Daly. 4 Tommy Docherty. 5 Brian Greenhoff.
6 Francis Lee. 7 Lou Macari. 8 David McCreery. 9 Jimmy Greenhoff. 10 Steve Coppell.
11 Allan Clarke. 12 Joe Jordan. 13 Gordon McQueen. 14 Maine Road. 15 Joe Jordan.
16 Terry McDermott. 17 Alan Hansen. 18 Goodison Park. 19 Mickey Thomas.
20 Jimmy Greenhoff.

Answers – see page 172

1 Against which country did Wes Brown make his full international debut in, April 1999?

2 With whom did Teddy Sheringham form the SAS combination for England?

3 Who were the opponents when Phil Neville made the ill-fated tackle which led to England's elimination from Euro 2000?

4 In what season did Nicky Butt make his full England entrance?

5 Who was the first black footballer to play for England?

6 How many players have scored more goals for England than Bobby Charlton?

7 Albert Quixall won five caps as a Sheffield Wednesday star, but did he receive any as a Red Devil?

8 What was Bill Foulkes doing the day before he won his only England cap?

9 Only one post-war United manager is a full England international. Name him.

10 Which 21-year-old who died at Munich had already earned 18 full England caps?

11 Was Andrew Cole a full international when he joined United from Newcastle?

12 Did England full-back Paul Parker play again for his country after his arrival at Old Trafford?

13 How many England caps are in Bryan Robson's collection?

14 During which campaign did Mike Phelan win his sole full England honour?

15 Who were England's opponents on Phelan's big day?

16 Which former Real Madrid and England winger spent two months on loan with United in the spring of 1983?

17 Which left-winger perished at Munich with only one full cap to his name?

18 Which veteran schemer, capped once by England, was an emergency signing from Blackpool in the wake of the Munich tragedy?

19 Ray Wilkins won England caps while serving three clubs. Chelsea, United and which other?

20 Were any of Garry Birtles' three caps won as a Red Devil?

Answers – see page 177

1 Who made his sole senior appearance for Manchester United at Villa Park in a Worthington Cup tie in October 1999?

2 Which future Northern Ireland international also made his entrance as a Red Devil that night?

3 Which former United marksman was leading Villa's attack?

4 What was the result of the game?

5 Who put United in front against leaders Aston Villa at Villa Park in December 1998?

6 Which Villan scored in both League meetings with the Red Devils during their Treble-winning campaign?

7 Who netted United's winner at home to Villa on Mayday 1999?

8 Which Scottish redhead sat on United's bench but was not called on for his first senior outing at Villa Park in May 2000?

9 Whose lone goal gave United a home victory over Villa in December 1997?

10 Both League meetings between United and Villa during 1996/97 yielded the same result. What was it?

11 Who scored the Reds' winner in a 2-1 triumph at Villa Park in October 1994?

12 Who netted twice as United completed a 3-1 home Premiership victory over Aston Villa on the way to the 1993/94 League and FA Cup double?

13 Who managed Villa to the League runners-up spot behind United in 1992/93?

14 In the March of that memorable campaign, what was the result when United and Villa met at Old Trafford?

15 Earlier in the season, the Reds had lost 1-0 at Villa Park. Who scored that goal?

16 Three days earlier Villa had beaten United by the same score in a League Cup tie at Villa Park. Who supplied that goal?

17 Whose own goal enabled Aston Villa to claim a point from their visit to Old Trafford in December 1990?

18 Who grabbed both United's goals in a 2-0 home victory over Villa in April 1990?

19 Who netted twice for the Red Devils when they beat Villa 2-1 at Old Trafford during their only post-war season in the second flight?

20 Decipher the anagram: BYOBB LARCHNOT.

Answers – see page 178

1 With what club did Denis Irwin kick off his League career?

2 From which club was the quiet Irishman signed by Alex Ferguson in June 1990?

3 How much did he cost?

4 Who was the selling manager?

5 How many Republic of Ireland caps had Denis accumulated when he retired from international football in 1999?

6 The arrival at Old Trafford of which newcomer in 1991 saw the versatile Irwin switch from right-back to left-back?

7 Who did Denis replace as United's regular penalty-taker in the autumn of 1997?

8 A sending-off against which opponents cost Denis the chance of an FA Cup Final appearance in 1999?

9 An Irwin strike against which opposition secured the Reds' first point of their 1992/93 title-winning campaign?

10 How many times has Denis picked up League and FA Cup winners' medals in the same season?

11 Whose foul on Denis led to the Cantona penalty which put the Reds ahead in the 1994 FA Cup Final?

12 Against which club did Denis score his first penalty in senior football (excluding shoot-outs)?

13 What personal landmark did Irwin pass during the 2000/2001 season?

14 Did Denis make his full international debut before or after his move to United?

15 How many times has Denis finished on the losing side in League Cup Finals?

16 When was the first of those occasions?

17 Denis was in the United side the day they won their first major honour under Alex Ferguson. True or false?

18 At what sport did Denis excel before taking up soccer?

19 Under how many managers did Irwin play for the Republic at full international level?

20 In what competition did Denis pick up the first winner's medal of his senior career?

Answers – see page 175

1 Of which comedian has Gordon Hill perfected a brilliant impersonation?
2 By what nickname was Hill known?
3 With which club did Gordon make his Football League entrance?
4 Which coach of Chicago Sting, a former United stalwart, took Gordon for a fruitful loan stint in the States in 1975?
5 Which manager signed Hill for three different League clubs?
6 How much did United pay for Gordon's signature in November 1975?
7 Who once boxed Gordon's ears during a match?
8 On which flank did the speedy trickster thrive, right or left?
9 Gordon started in both FA Cup Finals of 1976 and 1977, but did he last the full 90 minutes of either?
10 Hill ensured United's place at Wembley in 1976 with two goals against which opponents?
11 Though operating on the flank, Gordon topped the Reds' scoring tallies in senior competition in both his full seasons at Old Trafford. True or false?
12 Which manager dispensed with Gordon's services in April 1978?
13 To which club was he sold?
14 What was the fee?
15 Which contrasting player did the United boss draft in as a replacement?
16 Which was Gordon's final Football League club?
17 How many times was Hill capped by England at the top level?
18 How old was Gordon when his international career ended?
19 Gordon scored two European goals for United, one of them against St Etienne. What other opponents picked a Hill shot out of their net?
20 Gordon served what leading non-League club as caretaker-manager during 1986/87?

Answers – see page 176

1 On Christmas Eve 1995, United lost 3-1 at Elland Road. Who put Leeds in front with a sixth-minute penalty?

2 Who equalised for the Red Devils?

3 The crucial springtime '96 return fixture, as the Reds closed in on their second double, was settled by a goal from which midfielder?

4 After that tight game, Alex Ferguson controversially voiced the hope that Leeds would work just as hard against which opponents?

5 Who was memorably upset by Fergie's remarks?

6 Who gave United a second-minute lead in their FA Cup encounter with Leeds at Old Trafford in February 1995?

7 Who doubled that advantage in the fifth minute?

8 Which Leeds substitute ignited brief hope before the Reds won 3-1?

9 Which flankman put United in front in their crucial clash with Leeds at Elland Road, on the trail of their first League and FA Cup double in April 1994?

10 Another winger sealed the victory late in the game. Name him.

11 In 1991/92, when Leeds pipped the Reds for the title, the two games between the Uniteds ended in the same score. What was it?

12 Who supplied United's equaliser in the Old Trafford encounter in August 1991?

13 Who put United ahead at Elland Road just after the break in the following February?

14 The two clubs met in that season's League Cup. What was the final score?

15 The pair encountered each other in that term's FA Cup, too. Who scored the only goal of their meeting at Elland Road?

16 Lee Sharpe scored three times as the Reds won the two-legged League Cup semi-final against Leeds in 1990/91 True or false?

17 What was the most recent season in which Manchester United and Leeds did not meet in League competition?

18 Have the Red Devils ever met Leeds in senior European competition?

19 Who was the last Red Devil to score against Leeds before their most recent relegation to the second flight?

20 Decipher the anagram: MIMYJ FRENEGFOH.

Answers – see page 181

1   With which fellow Scottish international did David Herd form a prolific dual spearhead for United in the 1960s?

2   In how many seasons was David the leading League scorer for the Red Devils?

3   How many times did David score in the 1963 FA Cup Final?

4   Herd is an Aberdonian. True or false?

5   For which club did David make his League debut?

6   That day David played at outside-right. Who played alongside him at inside-right?

7   To which London giants was Herd transferred in 1954?

8   What major domestic honours did he lift with that club?

9   How many times did Herd play for Scotland?

10   How much did Matt Busby pay to sign David Herd in the summer of 1961?

11   David broke a leg in the act of scoring against which opponents on the way to the title in 1966/67?

12   What was unusual about David's four-goal display against Sunderland in November 1966?

13   In November 1963 at Old Trafford, David took over in goal after which keeper broke his collarbone?

14   Who scored the only goal of that game?

15   David scored on his United debut in five out of six of the three major domestic and three European competitions. Which was the odd one out?

16   Alongside which childhood chum did David play his early games for United?

17   David was freed to join which Potteries club in July 1968?

18   With which League of Ireland outfit did Herd end his playing days?

19   David had one stab at management. Who were his employers?

20   In what trade did David Herd spend more than three decades after leaving football?

ANSWERS

Pot Luck - 57 *(see page 181)*

1 Wesley Brown. 2 Andy Goram. 3 Ryan Giggs. 4 Four times. 5 Because Southanmpton were leaving The Dell at season's end. 6 Dwight Yorke. 7 Matthew Le Tissier. 8 Massimo Taibi. 9 3-3. 10 Ole Gunnar Solskjaer. 11 Jordi Cruyff's. 12 Roy Keane. 13 David Beckham. 14 Henning Berg. 15 Kevin Davies. 16 Eyal Berkovic. 17 Phil Neville. 18 6-3 to Southampton. 19 Eric Cantona. 20 Mark Hughes.

1 Noel Cantwell skippered United to FA Cup glory in which season?
2 What number shirt did the captain where at Wembley that day?
3 Though primarily a defender, Noel could also operate effectively in what other position?
4 From what London club was Cantwell recruited in November 1960?
5 How much did Matt Busby pay for him?
6 In what Irish city was Noel born?
7 Noel was still club captain in 1966/67, but how many title medals did he earn?
8 Aside from his club responsibilities, which office did the eloquent Irishman hold during his playing days?
9 Of which newly-promoted top-flight club did he become boss in 1967?
10 Cantwell managed one other Football League club. Name it.
11 How many full caps did he earn with the Republic of Ireland?
12 Which honour did Noel win with his first League club in 1957/58?
13 In what county did tough-nut Maurice Setters first see the light of day?
14 Name his first League club.
15 From which Midlands club did Matt Busby recruit Maurice in January 1960?
16 In which position was Setters an FA Cup winner with the Red Devils?
17 Who replaced Maurice as United hit title-winning form in the mid 1960s?
18 To which club did Matt Busby sell Setters in November 1964?
19 Maurice managed one Football League club. Which one?
20 To which successful international boss was Maurice Setters the assistant in the 1990s?

Answers – see page 179

1. Who headed Southampton in front against United at The Dell in May 2001?
2. Four minutes later, which veteran keeper picked the ball out of his net for the second time in the first quarter of an hour?
3. Which United skipper-for-the-day pulled back a goal in the second half?
4. After losing that day, the Reds had been beaten in how many times out of their last six visits to the Dell?
5. Why would United never get the chance to improve on their dismal Dell record?
6. Who netted twice against Southampton at Old Trafford in September 1999?
7. Who responded with two goals for the Saints?
8. Which goalkeeper dropped an excruciating clanger in that game?
9. What was the result of the game?
10. In the return at The Dell in April, who grabbed United's third goal as they wrapped up the title?
11. Whose immaculate volley sealed United's 3-0 victory at The Dell in October 1998?
12. A goal from which substitute set the Red Devils on the way to triumph over the Saints at Old Trafford in February 1999?
13. Who was called from the bench to supply the winner against Southampton at Old Trafford in August 1997?
14. Which other substitute made his senior debut for United that evening?
15. The Reds lost to a third-minute strike from which Saint at The Dell in January 1998?
16. Two Saints each scored a brace against United at The Dell in October 1996. One was Egil Ostenstad; who was the other?
17. Who scored an own goal that day?
18. What was the final score?
19. Who contributed the 79th-minute winner which gave United a measure of revenge at Old Trafford the following February?
20. Decipher the anagram: KAMR SUGHEH.

Answers – see page 180

1 Who was the manager of United's opponents, Sheffield Wednesday?
2 Who netted the only goal of the game for the Owls?
3 Where was the match-winner born?
4 Whose knee was cut to the bone in a collision?
5 What was the accident victim's reaction when asked to leave the field?
6 What was the half-time score?
7 For whom was Mike Phelan a 55th-minute replacement?
8 Who remained on the United bench throughout the 90 minutes?
9 Which England star with more than half a century of caps was Wednesday's unused substitute?
10 Who did United conquer in their two-legged semi-final?
11 Who were the Owls' semi-final opponents?
12 Which former United keeper kept a clean sheet for Sheffield?
13 Which of Wednesday's finalists would later become a high-profile transfer target for Alex Ferguson?
14 Who was the Swedish international in the Yorkshiremen's number-two shirt?
15 United captain Bryan Robson never lifted the League Cup? True or false?
16 Who sponsored the League Cup in 1990/91?
17 Who was the future Hillsborough manager who turned out for Wednesday in midfield?
18 Which North American was substituted by the Owls?
19 How many Yorkshire clubs had United vanquished on their way to the final?
20 Denis Irwin was playing in his third major final for United. True or false?

ANSWERS

FA Cup Heroes - Noel Cantwell & Maurice Setters *(see page 180)*

1 1963. 2 Number three. 3 Centre-forward. 4 West Ham United. 5 £29,500. 6 Cork.
7 None. 8 Chairman of the Professional Footballers Association. 9 Coventry City.
10 Peterborough United. 11 36 caps. 12 Second Division title medal. 13 Devon.
14 Exter City. 15 West Bromwich Albion. 16 Left-half. 17 Nobby Stiles. 18 Stoke City.
19 Doncaster Rovers. 20 The Republic of Ireland's Jack Charlton.

Answers – see page 185

1 When United beat Spurs in May 1999, it was the first time Alex Ferguson's team had clinched the title at Old Trafford. True or false?

2 Who was the United skipper that day?

3 Which winger netted twice for United in a 4-3 defeat by Spurs at Old Trafford in November 1958, the clubs' last meeting before the Munich tragedy?

4 Who scored the game's only goal, a penalty, in their first encounter after the crash?

5 Who supplied the crosses for both Sol Campbell headers which secured a point for Spurs against United in London in December 1998?

6 Who had shot the Reds into an early two-goal lead?

7 The captain of Tottenham's fabulous League and FA Cup-winning side of 1960/61 was the brother of which United star?

8 Which Scottish striker joined United from Spurs for £700,000 in June 1984?

9 Who opened United's scoring at White Hart Lane in the first League game of 1997/98?

10 Who doubled their tally in that game a minute later?

11 Which left-back who was an FA Cup Final loser with United in 1976 went on to become Tottenham's assistant manager?

12 Which Belfast-born winger played for both Spurs and United in the 1970s?

13 Whose header and volley condemned Spurs to a 2-0 League defeat at Old Trafford in January 1998?

14 Which diminutive marksman joined United from Coventry in January 1986?

15 When did United last face Spurs in the Charity Shield?

16 Two goals from which recently signed Norwegian sunk Spurs at Old Trafford in September 1996?

17 By what margin did United eject Spurs from the FA Cup in 1997?

18 Seven days later United rubbed it in with a 2-1 victory at White Hart Lane. Who netted Spurs' consolation goal?

19 Though Spurs won the League and FA Cup double in 1960/61, United beat them 2-0 at Old Trafford. Nobby Stiles scored one goal, who got the other?

20 Who was the manager of Spurs during that season?

ANSWERS

Sheer Class on the left - Arthur Albiston & Stewart Houston (see page 185)

1 Six men. **2** Chelsea. **3** Brentford. **4** Tommy Docherty. **5** Manchester United. **6** Scotland. **7** Once. **8** Fourteen. **9** Second Division title medal in 1974/75. **10** Stewart had broken a leg. **11** He offered Houston his winner's medal. **12** Three. **13** Sheffield United. **14** West Bromwich Albion. **15** Ron Atkinson. **16** Colchester. **17** Arsenal. **18** QPR. **19** Dundee. **20** Chester City.

Answers — see page 186

1 Whose four-goal salvo destroyed Newcastle at Old Trafford in August 1999?
2 Who was sent off that day?
3 Did the Reds complete the League double over the Magpies that term?
4 What was the most recent occasion that United met Newcastle in senior knockout competition?
5 Who was the Magpies' manager at that time?
6 Who gave Newcastle the lead against the Reds with a sublime free-kick at St James' Park in March 1999?
7 From which country does that gifted individual hail?
8 Who hit back with two goals against his former employers?
9 Who replaced Peter Schmeichel for the second half of that game?
10 Manchester United needed only one goal to win on Tyneside four days before Christmas in 1997. Who supplied it?
11 The Reds couldn't force a home victory over Newcastle during the following spring, despite a goal from which midfielder?
12 Who was Newcastle's boss when they finished as title runners-up to United in 1996/97?
13 Who had been guiding the Magpies when they had occupied an identical position at the end of the previous campaign?
14 Whose controversial opener set the Magpies on the way to a comprehensive defeat of United at St James' Park in October 1996?
15 Who scored a magnificent second for Newcastle?
16 What was the score at the final whistle?
17 United thrashed the Magpies by a similar margin when the two clubs met again at Old Trafford in the spring. True or false?
18 Who netted the Reds' second goal when they beat Newcastle 2-0 at Old Trafford during the Christmas break in 1995?
19 Whose shot shivered Peter Schmeichel's bar in the crucial return at St James' Park the following March?
20 Decipher the anagram: NORGENUAL JOSKLERAS.

Reds in Europe 1956/57 *(see page 186)*

ANSWERS

1 Matt Busby. 2 Chelsea. 3 Anderlecht. 4 2-0 to United. 5 Dennis Viollet. 6 Duncan Edwards. 7 10-0. 8 Maine Road. 9 Dennis Viollet. 10 David Pegg. 11 Ray Wood. 12 0-0. 13 Liam Whelan's. 14 Tommy Taylor. 15 Johnny Berry. 16 Francisco Gento. 17 Alfredo di Stefano. 18 Tommy Taylor. 19 Tommy Taylor. 20 Bobby Charlton.

1 How many men have played more senior games for Manchester United than Arthur Albiston?

2 With which club did Houston start his League career?

3 From which club did the Red Devils sign Stewart?

4 Who was the United boss who took Houston to Old Trafford?

5 With which club did Arthur begin his senior career?

6 Which country have both left-backs represented at international level?

7 How many times was Stewart thus honoured?

8 How many full international appearances did Arthur make?

9 What was Stewart's sole club honour as a Red Devil?

10 Why did Arthur replace Stewart to make his FA Cup debut in the 1977 final?

11 What magnanimous gesture did Albiston make after the game?

12 How many times did Arthur finish on the winning side in an FA Cup Final?

13 For which club did Stewart sign on leaving the Reds in July 1980?

14 Where did Arthur go after being freed by Alex Ferguson in 1988?

15 Who was Arthur's first manager at his new club?

16 With what United did Houston finish his playing days?

17 Of which club did Stewart become caretaker boss in 1995 and again in 1996?

18 In 1997 he became a fully-fledged manager at which club?

19 Arthur played senior football north of the border for which club during 1989/90?

20 Arthur's senior career ended with a spell at which English club?

Answers – see page 184

1 Who was United's manager during their first European campaign?
2 Which English champions had spurned the invitation to enter the previous term's European Cup?
3 At the home of which Belgian champions did United play their first ever European game?
4 What was the result of that historic encounter?
5 Who scored the Red Devils' first goal in European competition?
6 Which colossus was missing from the English club's ranks in that opening game?
7 United won the home leg heavily, but by what margin?
8 Which ground hosted that first European Cup match on English soil?
9 Who hit the target four times for United in their home meeting with the Belgians?
10 Who was the only United forward not to score on that occasion?
11 Who was the keeper who conceded United's first goal in Europe, at home to Borussia Dortmund?
12 What was the result of the second meeting with the German champions?
13 United lost 5-3 in Spain to Athletic Bilbao, but whose brilliant late goal gave hope to the Reds?
14 Who levelled the scores for United back in Manchester?
15 Who grabbed the Red Devils' dramatic late winner?
16 Who was the Spanish speed merchant who terrorised the United defence in the first leg of the semi-final against Real Madrid?
17 Who was the great Argentinian who played as Real's deep-lying centre-forward?
18 Who scored United's only goal in a 3-1 defeat at the Bernebeu?
19 Back at Old Trafford, who opened United's account in the 2-2 draw?
20 Who scored United's late consolation goal in a fabulous match?

ANSWERS

Pot Luck - 58 (see page 184)
1 Andrew Cole's. 2 Nikolaos Dabizas. 3 No, they lost 3-0 at St James' Park. 4 The 1999 FA Cup Final. 5 Ruud Gullit. 6 Nolberto Solano. 7 Peru. 8 Andrew Cole. 9 Raimond van der Gouw. 10 Andrew Cole. 11 David Beckham. 12 Kenny Dalglish. 13 Kevin Keegan. 14 Darren Peacock's. 15 David Ginola. 16 5-0 to Newcastle. 17 False, it was a 0-0 draw. 18 Roy Keane. 19 Philippe Albert's. 20 Ole Gunnar Solskjaer.

Answers – see page 189

1 Who opened United's scoring at Highfield Road in August 1999?
2 What was the result that day?
3 Who netted twice in the return fixture at Old Trafford in February 2000?
4 What was the tally that day when the final whistle sounded?
5 Who notched the only goal of the game at Coventry in February 1999?
6 Who scored United's final goal in the last minute of a 3-0 home victory over Coventry in August 1997?
7 Which former Red Devil equalised from the spot against United with three minutes remaining of their December 1997 clash at Highfield Road?
8 Who plundered a brilliant winner for the Sky Blues a minute later?
9 United were two up in five minutes against Coventry at Old Trafford in March 1997 without a Red Devil scoring. True or false?
10 Who scored two as United slammed Coventry 4-0 at Highfield Road in November 1995?
11 Whose second-half brace at Coventry on Mayday 1995 kept the Reds in the hunt for a hat-trick of title triumphs?
12 Whose goal on the hour at Highfield Road settled United's confrontation with Coventry in November 1994?
13 United thrashed Coventry in their last League game of 1992 Who got the first of the Reds' five goals at Old Trafford on the day Joe Ponting was born?
14 Which on-loan keeper, never used by the Reds at senior level, occupied their bench that day?
15 Who struck United's winner at Coventry during the run-in to their first Championship in more than a quarter of a century?
16 Whose late equaliser earned a point for United at Highfield Road in December 1990?
17 In what season did the Red Devils last confront Coventry in the FA Cup?
18 What was the result of that game?
19 Who scored the winner?
20 Decipher the anagram: AYRG SALPTRILE.

ANSWERS

Jim Holton *(see page 189)*
1 Big Jim Holton's after you! 2 Tommy Docherty. 3 Shrewsbury Town. 4 £80,000. 5 False. 6 1973 7 Martin Buchan. 8 15 caps. 9 Celtic. 10 West Bromwich Albion. 11 Lou Macari. 12 West Ham United. 13 None. 14 Yes. 15 Hillsborough. 16 Sheffield Wednesday 6, United 4. 17 Sunderland. 18 Coventry City. 19 Sheffield Wednesday. 20 42 years old.

Answers – see page 190

1 On the opening day, United came from two down to draw with which visitors to Old Trafford?

2 The second game of the campaign, in London, marked the debut of which newcomer?

3 United's first League win of the season was 4-1 at home to Charlton. Who scored for the Addicks?

4 The Reds salvaged a point with a late goal at Derby. Who supplied it?

5 Who scored his only League goal for United in the 4-1 victory at Goodison Park?

6 Which Lancashire club fought back from a three-goal deficit to leave United hanging on for a win at Old Trafford?

7 Who netted twice for Sheffield Wednesday as they defeated the Reds 3-1 at Hillsborough?

8 Against which table-topping side did United claim an away point in December?

9 Whose two headers earned Spurs a home draw with the Reds?

10 Who managed the club who inflicted United's final defeat of the campaign?

11 Which central defender lit up Boxing Day with two goals against Nottingham Forest?

12 Against which opponents did Jaap Stam register his first goal for the club?

13 Whose 89th-minute winner made it a pleasant Valley Sunday for United?

14 United scored eight at Forest in February, but who netted for the hosts?

15 Which Villan set the Reds on their way to victory at Old Trafford with a May Day own goal?

16 Whose late goal for Leeds at home to Arsenal in May eased United's title task?

17 Which manager was condemned to relegation after his side drew 0-0 with the Reds?

18 By how many points did United clinch the title?

19 The Reds conceded 25 more goals than runners-up Arsenal. True or false?

20 How many goals did Teddy Sheringham score during the League campaign?

Answers – see page 187

1 Six foot two, eyes of blue . . . complete the chant.
2 Which manager recruited Jim to the Old Trafford cause?
3 From which club was Holton signed by United?
4 What was the fee?
5 The Reds were relegated in the season Jim was signed. True or false?
6 In what year did the big stopper make his full international debut?
7 Alongside which United colleague did Jim play in the centre of Scotland's defence during the 1974 World Cup Finals?
8 How many full caps did Holton win?
9 With which Scottish giants did Jim fail to make the grade as a teenager?
10 With which Midlands club, known as The Baggies, did the young Holton fail to make a senior breakthrough?
11 Jim Holton made his United debut on the same day as which fellow Scot?
12 Who were the Red Devils' opponents on that murky afternoon in January 1973?
13 How many times did Jim run out at Wembley for an FA Cup Final?
14 Did Jim play enough games in 1974/75 to earn a Second Division title medal?
15 On what ground did Holton suffer a broken leg while playing for United in December 1974?
16 What was the score in that match?
17 To which club was Jim transferred in the autumn of 1976?
18 He moved on again in spring 1977. Who were his new employers?
19 In 1981 Jim joined a Yorkshire club but injuries prevented him from making a debut. Name that club.
20 How old was Jim Holton when he died prematurely in October 1993?

Answers – see page 188

Name the club for which each of these Red Devils played the most League games:

1 Paul Parker
2 Albert Quixall
3 John Doherty
4 Mike Phelan
5 Frank Stapleton
6 Jim Holton
7 Ian Greaves
8 Joe Jordan
9 Gordon McQueen
10 Les Sealey
11 Garth Crooks
12 Liam O'Brien
13 Ray Wood
14 Terry Gibson
15 Ernie Taylor
16 Joe Carolan
17 Gordon Strachan
18 Maurice Setters
19 John Gidman
20 Ray Wilkins

Answers – see page 193

1 Who described Frank as 'the best centre-forward in Europe' after signing him for United in August 1981?
2 Alongside which fellow striker had Frank made his name at Arsenal?
3 When Stapleton left Highbury for Old Trafford, what transfer tribunal fee was decided?
4 How many championship medals did Frank collect with Arsenal?
5 In what Wembley final did Gunner Stapleton find the net against the Red Devils?
6 How did the scoreline in that final read after his goal?
7 What was Frank's highest League goal tally in his six years at Old Trafford?
8 During what season did the Irishman achieve that total?
9 Frank had a trial with United as a teenager. True or false?
10 What did Frank become when he scored for United against Brighton in the 1983 FA Cup Final?
11 In November 1983 Frank scored his sole senior hat-trick for the Red Devils against which opposition?
12 In what semi-final did Stapleton score for United against his former employers?
13 In which European final did Frank appear?
14 How many times did Stapleton appear for the Republic of Ireland?
15 To which position was Frank switched successfully for United in the latter stages of two cup finals?
16 Which club signed Frank when he was freed by the Red Devils in July 1987?
17 Who recommended Stapleton to his new employers?
18 Apart from Arsenal and United, for which club did Frank make most League appearances?
19 Which club did Frank manage between 1991 and 1994?
20 Which former United marksman was his assistant in the post?

Answers – see page 194

1 In what year did Manchester United first employ a manager (even though his official title was secretary)?

2 Who was that first occupant of the boss's seat?

3 In what season under their new leader did United earn a place in the First Division?

4 They won promotion as champions of Division Two. True or false?

5 When did United lift their first League title?

6 Who were runners-up as United claimed the Championship?

7 In which season did United reach their first FA Cup Final?

8 Who were their opponents on that landmark occasion?

9 What was the venue of United's first FA Cup Final?

10 Who scored the only goal to land the club's first senior knockout trophy?

11 Which future United manager refereed their FA Cup quarter-final tie with Burnley in 1909?

12 Soon after the turn of the century, United signed several players from a club penalised by the FA for financial irregularities. Which club?

13 During which summer did United's players hover on the brink of a strike over union membership before the authorities caved in?

14 When did Manchester United move to Old Trafford?

15 Who were United's first opponents in their new stadium?

16 In which campaign did United clinch their second League title?

17 For which club did the successful United boss leave the club?

18 When did that same secretary/manager depart?

19 Who was the first man to receive the official title of manager?

20 From which club was the new boss recruited?

Answers – see page 191

1 Whose two goals, including a brilliant bicycle kick, defeated Leicester at Old Trafford in November 1999?

2 Which young United full-back made an assured full League debut against the Foxes that day?

3 Which former United youngster was patrolling midfield for Leicester in that encounter?

4 Whose new haircut had the cameramen working overtime at Filbert Street one Saturday afternoon in March 2000?

5 How did the wearer of that haircut celebrate that day?

6 What was the outcome of that meeting between Foxes and Red Devils?

7 Who put Leicester in front against United at Old Trafford on the first day of the 1998/99 Premiership campaign?

8 Which former Hammer and Toffee made it 2-0 to the Foxes?

9 Which England star reduced the deficit to 2-1?

10 A last-minute free-kick from which man-of-the-moment salvaged a point for United?

11 Who was the Leicester boss at that time?

12 What was the result when the two teams met again at Filbert Street later in United's Treble-winning season?

13 Who was the Greek international who netted for Leicester that day?

14 Whose first goal as a Red Devil was United's last of the afternoon?

15 Who helped himself to a hat-trick that day?

16 Another marksman contributed two goals. Name him.

17 Who scored the only goal of the game when United faced Leicester at Old Trafford on the last day if January 1998?

18 Who scored twice in United's 4-0 away triumph over the Foxes in April 1995?

19 How many times have the Reds faced Leicester in senior cup finals?

20 Decipher the anagram: LEYBLAN NOCLITH.

Answers – see page 192

1 Whose fabulous volley gave United victory over Arsenal in their 1983 FA Cup semi-final?

2 Who created the goal with an intelligent lofted pass from the left flank?

3 Who had put the Gunners ahead with a scrambled first-half effort?

4 Who supplied the United equaliser?

5 Which club hosted the contest in which the Reds reached Wembley in May 1983?

6 United's victory over Arsenal qualified them for their second Wembley final of the season. True or false?

7 Who was United's manager during the 1983 FA Cup run?

8 Which left-sided midfielder excelled in the semi-final but didn't win a Wembley place?

9 Another United man had shone in the semi but was ruled out of the final through suspension. Name him.

10 Who was the Arsenal manager in 1983?

11 Which Gunners goalkeeper was beaten by United's two magnificent shots?

12 Where did United and Liverpool draw 2-2 in the 1985 semi-final?

13 Bryan Robson put United in front before which Irishman curled a late equaliser for the Merseysiders?

14 Frank Stapleton's deflected effort restored during extra time, but which Liverpool man's last-minute larceny set up a replay?

15 Who was the relieved Liverpool manager who said: 'We were outplayed and got away with it.'

16 Where did the two sets of Reds meet for their 1985 FA Cuo semi-final replay?

17 Whose headed own-goal gave Liverpool a first-half lead?

18 Whose magnificent long-range effort levelled the scores just after the interval?

19 Whose cute through-ball set up the United winner?

20 Who thrashed home the goal which took Ron Atkinson's men to Wembley in 1985?

Early Days - 2 (see page 192)

1 1903. 2 Ernest Mangnall. 3 1906. 4 False, Bristol City were champions. 5 1907/08. 6 Aston Villa. 7 1908/09. 8 Bristol City. 9 Crystal Palace. 10 Sandy Turnbull. 11 Herbert Bamlett. 12 Manchester City. 13 1909. 14 1910. 15 Liverpool. 16 1910/11. 17 Manchester City. 18 1912. 19 John Robson. 20 Brighton.

Answers – see page 197

1 Who were United's opponents when they returned to European competition in 1963 for the first time since Munich?

2 Who netted for the Reds in that 1-1 draw in Holland?

3 A hat-trick from which Scot led the way in the 6-1 demolition of the Dutch side at Old Trafford?

4 In what competition were the Red Devils involved in 1963/64?

5 Another hat-trick lit up the home leg of the quarter-final against Sporting Lisbon. Who bagged it?

6 The return in Portugal produced the most humiliating reverse in the Reds' European history to that point. What was the score?

7 United's first Inter-Cities Fairs Cup campaign in 1964/65 kicked off against which Stockholm club?

8 What was the Red Devils' margin of aggregate victory over the Swedish side?

9 Who contributed five goals to United's 10-1 aggregate annihilation of Borussia Dortmund in the next round?

10 Which English opponents did the Reds meet in the third round?

11 Which former Burnley winger contributed two goals to the 3-2 aggregate triumph?

12 Against Strasbourg in the quarter-final, United won 6-0 away but could only draw 0-0 at home. True or false?

13 Which goalkeeper preserved clean sheets in both matches against the French club?

14 The semi-final against which Hungarian club needed three matches to complete?

15 United won the first leg 3-2 Who scored twice?

16 After an aggregate 3-3 draw, the decider was played at the home of which club?

17 What was the outcome of that tight contest?

18 Back in the European Cup in 1965/66, who were the Reds' first opponents?

19 Who contributed four goals to the 9-2 aggregate victory over those opponents?

20 A hat-trick from which Scottish international sharpshooter steamrollered ASK Vorwaerts at Old Trafford in the next round?

Answers – see page 198

1   Which former United and Northern Ireland winger helped Blackburn gain promotion to the Premiership in 2001?

2   One of the most popular of all Red Devils, a Welshman, also was in that successful Rovers squad. Name him.

3   Which former Blackburn defender returned to Ewood Park from Old Trafford during 2000/2001?

4   Who was the fourth former Red who played regularly as Rovers surged into the top flight?

5   The man who led Blackburn back to the Premiership was Sir Alex Ferguson's one-time assistant, Brian Kidd. True or false?

6   What was the score when United met Blackburn at Ewood in the penultimate League match of their Treble-winning campaign?

7   What was the consequence of that result for Rovers?

8   Who scored twice for United as they beat Blackburn at home in November 1998?

9   Whose goal made it 3-2 and set up a grandstand finish to that clash?

10 Which England international was sent off during the game?

11 Who was the soon-to-be-sacked Blackburn manager at the time?

12 Who scored twice as United beat Rovers 4-0 at Old Trafford in November 1997?

13 Which future Liverpool defender scored an own goal that day?

14 Which Dutchman scored his second League goal for the Reds in the 2-2 home draw with Blackburn in August 1996?

15 Which emerging star curled United's winner a 2-1 victory in August 1995?

16 A crucial home win over Rovers in February 1996 kept the Reds in touch with table-topping Newcastle. Who supplied the only goal of that contest?

17 United did the League double over Blackburn in the season that Rovers lifted the title. True or false?

18 Who scored twice in the thrilling 4-2 win at Ewood in the October?

19 What was Blackburn's result on the day they wrestled the Championship from United's grasp in 1994/95?

20 Decipher the anagram: DEEDI LAMNOC.

United v Liverpool - 5 *(see page 198)*

1 1-1. **2** Gordon McQueen's. **3** Ron Atkinson. **4** Arthur Albiston. **5** Frank Stapleton's.
6 United won 4-3. **7** Joe Fagan. **8** Frank Stapleton. **9** Paul McGrath. **10** Jan Molby.
11 Johnny Sivebaek. **12** Norman Whiteside's. **13** Peter Davenport's. **14** Ian Rush.
15 Gordon Strachan. **16** Mark Hughes. **17** Russell Beardsmore. **18** John Barnes.
19 Ronnie Whelan (own goal). **20** Peter Beardsley.

ANSWERS

196

Answers – see page 195

1   From which club did United sign Steve Coppell in February 1975?
2   Who was the selling manager?
3   How much did Steve cost the Red Devils?
4   Steve made his debut in March 1975 against Cardiff as a substitute for which popular right-winger?
5   When Coppell rose from the bench that day the game was goalless. What was the score half an hour later at the final whistle?
6   United won all their remaining matches as they lifted that season's Second Division crown. True or false?
7   Between January 1977 and November 1981, Steve set what record?
8   Steve netted in both legs of the League Cup semi-final against which opponents in 1982/83?
9   Which was Steve's most bountiful scoring season, in which he struck a dozen times for United in senior competition?
10 Under how many United bosses did Coppell serve?
11 Against which nation did Steve make his full England debut in a World Cup qualifier?
12 Which Mancunian, and future United player, was afforded his international entrance on the opposite flank that night?
13 Who was the England boss who gave the two young wingers their chance?
14 How many caps did Steve accumulate before injury cut short his career?
15 How many goals did he contribute to his country's cause?
16 Who were England's opponents in November 1981 when Coppell suffered the foul challenge that was to lead eventually to his premature retirement?
17 How old was Steve when he played his last game for the Red Devils in the spring of 1983?
18 How old was Steve when he became the League's youngest manager at that time?
19 Which club has he served in three separate spells?
20 At which club did he last as manager for only 33 days during 1996?

Answers – see page 196

1 In 1980/81, what was the result of United's and Liverpool's third successive Boxing Day meeting?

2 Whose powerful header won the game for United at Anfield in April 1981?

3 Which Liverpudlian took over as United boss in the summer of 1981?

4 Who was the unlikely scorer of United's winner at Anfield in October 1981?

5 Whose penalty was saved by Bruce Grobbelaar in United's 1-0 defeat at Old Trafford in April 1982?

6 What was the outcome of a testimonial game in Belfast in August 1983?

7 Which Liverpool manager presided over three defeats by United within a few months of taking the job?

8 Who scored United's winner at Old Trafford in September 1983?

9 Whose goal held Liverpool to an Old Trafford draw in October 1985, thus stretching table-topping United's unbeaten sequence to 13 games?

10 Which Dane's double dumped United out of the League Cup in 1985/86?

11 Which Dane made his United debut at Anfield in February 1986?

12 Whose goal lit up Alex Ferguson's yuletide by beating Liverpool on Boxing Day?

13 Whose winner at Old Trafford in April 1987 effectively ended Liverpool's title hopes?

14 Which prolific marksman left Liverpool in the summer of 1987 after failing to score against United in 15 outings?

15 Who pretended to puff on a cigar in front of the Kop after netting the final goal of a 3-3 draw at Anfield in April 1988?

16 In 1988/89 both clubs had re-signed illustrious Welsh old boys. Ian Rush returned to Anfield; who reappeared at Old Trafford?

17 Which slight Lancastrian starred in United's 3-1 demolition of Liverpool on New Year's Day 1989, making two goals and scoring another?

18 Which Watford winger was monitored by United but became a superstar with Liverpool?

19 Who lobbed the ball over Bruce Grobbelaar in a 2-1 home defeat in March 1990?

20 Which former Red scored a hat-trick in United's 4-0 reverse at Anfield in September 1990?

ANSWERS

Pot Luck - 62 *(see page 196)*

1 Keith Gillespie. **2** Mark Hughes. **3** Henning Berg. **4** John Curtis. **5** False. **6** 0-0.
7 Relegation. **8** Paul Scholes. **9** Nathan Blake's. **10** Tim Sherwood. **11** Roy Hodgson.
12 Ole Gunnar Solskjaer. **13** Stephane Henchoz. **14** Jordi Cruyff. **15** David Beckham.
16 Lee Sharpe. **17** True. **18** Andrei Kanchelskis. **19** They lost 2-1 to Liverpool.
20 Eddie Colman.

Answers – see page 201

1   United lost by the only goal of the game at home to Everton in December 1983. Who scored that goal?

2   United shared the points in a six-goal thriller at Goodison Park in April 1982. Who struck twice for the visitors?

3   Who scored in both games as United did the double over Everton in 1980/81?

4   A rare strike from which defender secured a home point against Everton in September 1978?

5   United's uplifting 6-2 Boxing Day triumph at Goodison in 1977 included a pair of strikes from which wee Scot?

6   Who scored both United's goals in a 2-1 away win over Everton in April 1977?

7   Who was Everton's new manager at that point?

8   Who was picking the Red Devils' team at that time?

9   Season 1974/75 was the only season since the war in which United didn't meet Everton in League competition. True or false?

10 Which new signing netted twice as United raised false hopes of avoiding the drop by beating Everton 3-0 at Old Trafford in the spring of 1974?

11 What was the score when they met again at Goodison eight days later?

12 An England full-back scored the only goal as Everton beat United at Goodison in February 1970. Name him.

13 Which future Manchester City boss was on target as champions-to-be Everton inflicted a 3-0 home defeat on the Red Devils in autumn 1969?

14 Who netted twice for United as they beat Everton 5-1 in August 1963?

15 What was the result when the two sides met in that year's Charity Shield?

16 What was the score months later when United met the reigning champions?

17 Which newly-signed marksman found the net in both United's League encounters with Everton during 1961/62?

18 In which season did United lose 4-0 to Everton one week, then beat them by the same score the next?

19 Who scored twice for the Red Devils in the second of those contests?

20 Decipher the anagram: EPTRE DRABEYLES.

Ryan Giggs - 2 *(see page 201)*

ANSWERS

1 1993/94. **2** 17 goals. **3** None. **4** 1993. **5** Blackburn Rovers. **6** IFK Gothenburg. **7** Middlesbrough. **8** He tore off his shirt and waved it round his head. **9** None. **10** The right flank. **11** Jan Stejskal. **12** Juventus. **13** Barcelona. **14** David Beckham. **15** Brondby. **16** Jesper Blomqvist. **17** Antonio Conte. **18** Second. **19** Rhodri Giggs. **20** Joseph.

Answers – see page 202

1 In what position did John Aston Snr make the bulk of his 282 League and FA Cup appearances for United?

2 In what berth did he make his First Division debut for the Red Devils in 1946/47?

3 Who was John Snr's footballing partner and skipper when United won the FA Cup in 1948?

4 How many title medals went the way of John Snr?

5 In what role did the versatile senior Aston spend the second half of the 1950/51 campaign?

6 Against which country did John Snr make his full England debut in September 1948?

7 Which United colleague played ahead of him at left-half that day?

8 John Snr played for England against the USA in the 1950 World Cup Finals. Who won?

9 That day in Belo Horizonte, which future England boss played alongside the older Aston?

10 What illness ended John Snr's career prematurely in his early thirties?

11 Later John Aston Snr was chief scout for United under how many managers?

12 In which season did John Jnr earn an FA Youth Cup winner's medal?

13 When did Aston the younger win his only League title medal?

14 What number was on John Jnr's back when he starred in the 1968 European Cup Final?

15 Aston Jnr broke a leg in a collision with which Manchester City and England man in August 1968?

16 In which year did young John win his sole England under-23 cap against Wales?

17 In 1972 John moved to Kenilworth Road. What was his new club?

18 How much did it cost his new employers to sign him?

19 What did he help those employers to achieve in 1974?

20 With what Lancashire club did John Aston Jnr finish his League career?

ANSWERS

Pot Luck - 64 *(see page 202)*

1 Paul Scholes. 2 Teddy Sheringham. 3 Niclas Alexandersson. 4 3-1 to Wednesday. 5 Teddy Sheringham. 6 Jon Newsome. 7 Bruce Grobbelaar. 8 Paolo di Canio. 9 David Herd at Old Trafford in December 1963. 10 United won 3-1. 11 Tommy Taylor in 1953. 12 It was on Christmas Day. 13 Karel Poborsky. 14 Eric Cantona. 15 David Hirst. 16 David May. 17 1993/94. 18 5-1 to United. 19 Trevor Francis. 20 Liam Whelan.

Answers – see page 199

1 Which has been Ryan's most prolific goal-scoring season to date?
2 What was his tally in senior competition for United that term?
3 How many senior hat-tricks has Ryan contributed to the United cause?
4 When was Giggs voted Young Player of the Year by his fellow professionals?
5 On the night that United were presented with the 1992/93 Premier League trophy, Ryan celebrated with a stunning free-kick against which opponents?
6 Ryan notched a brace in the opening game of the Reds' 1994/95 Champions League campaign. Who were the opposition?
7 Who did Ryan score against as United regained their title on the final day of the 1995/96 campaign?
8 How did Giggs celebrate his wondrous goal against Arsenal in the 1999 FA Cup semi-final replay?
9 How many times has Ryan netted in an FA Cup Final?
10 In what position did Giggs play most of the 1999 European Cup Final?
11 Who was the QPR keeper beaten by Ryan at the end of an unforgettably enchanting dribble at Loftus Road in February 1994?
12 Which Italian giants did Ryan shock with a near-post screamer in the dying stages of a Champions League encounter at Old Trafford in October 1997?
13 In September 1998, Giggs netted with a far-post header against which Spaniards?
14 Who supplied the cross for that majestic finish?
15 Ryan grabbed two goals in the first 21 minutes at the home of which Danes on the Treble trail?
16 In 1998, which Swede was bought as a left-flank alternative to Giggs?
17 Ryan scored a late equaliser against Juventus in the first leg of the 1999 Champions League semi-final. Who had put the Italians in front?
18 Since Giggs became a United regular, what is the lowest the Reds have finished in the Premiership?
19 What is the name of Ryan's younger brother, who was once on the books of Torquay United?
20 What is Ryan Giggs' middle name?

Answers – see page 200

1   Who grabbed United's opener in the 4-0 demolition of Sheffield Wednesday at Old Trafford in August 1999?

2   Who was the only man to hit the target in the return encounter at Hillsborough in February 2000?

3   Which Swedish international benefited when Peter Schmeichel dropped an uncharacteristic clanger at Hillsborough in November 1998?

4   What was the result of the match?

5   Who scored the 250th senior goal of his career in the 3-0 home victory over the Owls in April 1999?

6   Which ex-Leeds player put through his own goal as United hit Wednesday for six at Old Trafford in November 1997?

7   Who was the unused substitute goalkeeper on the Wednesday bench that day?

8   Which flamboyant Italian scored Sheffield Wednesday's clincher when they beat United 2-0 at Hillsborough in March 1998?

9   Who was the last Red Devil to score a senior hat-trick against Wednesday?

10   What was the outcome of that match?

11   Who contributed United's only other post-war hat-trick against the Owls?

12   What made that one easy to remember?

13   Who chipped in with United's second goal when they defeated Sheffield Wednesday 2-0 at Old Trafford on the way to the title in March 1997?

14   A brace from which marksman earned United a home point against Sheffield Wednesday in December 1995?

15   Which sometime transfer target of Alex Ferguson scored the only goal of United's visit to Hillsborough in October 1994?

16   A goal by which United stopper kept the Reds' title hopes alive when they entertained Wednesday in May 1995?

17   In what season did United meet Wednesday in the League Cup semi-final?

18   What was the aggregate score?

19   Who was the Sheffield Wednesday boss at that time?

20   Decipher the anagram: MILA LAWNEH.

ANSWERS

The Astons (see page 200)

1 Full-back. **2** Inside-right. **3** Johnny Carey. **4** One. **5** Centre-forward. **6** Denmark. **7** Henry Cockburn. **8** The USA. **9** Alf Ramsey. **10** Tuberculosis. **11** Three. **12** 1963/64. **13** 1966/67. **14** Number eleven. **15** Francis Lee. **16** 1969. **17** Luton Town. **18** £30,000. **19** Promotion to the First Division. **20** Blackburn Rovers.

Answers – see page 205

1   David Pegg hailed from which county?

2   How many times did David play for England?

3   Which flank did Pegg patrol, right or left?

4   How old was David when he was killed at Munich?

5   Which inside-forward made his United debut in the same match as Pegg, at home to Middlesbrough in December 1952?

6   Though older than most of his colleagues, Johnny Berry was still dubbed a Babe. What age was he when Matt Busby signed him in August 1951?

7   From which club did United acquire Berry?

8   Johnny might have won far more than his four England caps but for the magic of which 'Wizard of Dribble'?

9   Berry grabbed a late and brilliant winner in a 1957 European Cup quarter-final against which Spanish opponents?

10   Johnny survived the Munich air disaster, but was he able to play again?

11   How many times did Johnny help United to lift the Championship?

12   How many times was left-flank flyer Albert Scanlon capped by England at the top level?

13   At the time of the Munich disaster, Albert had unseated David Pegg from the United side on merit. True or false?

14   After being plucked from the wreckage of Munich, did Scanlon recover in time to face Bolton in the FA Cup Final three months later?

15   In 1958/59 Albert was an ever-present on the Reds' left wing as they finished in what League position?

16   To which club was Albert transferred, rather surprisingly, in November 1960?

17   Which other former Old Trafford winger was the manager who bought him?

18   Who wore United's number-seven shirt against Red Star Belgrade in the last game before the Munich tragedy: Johnny Berry or Kenny Morgans?

19   When Kenny bowed out of Old Trafford in March 1961 he joined his hometown club. Name it.

20   What international honours did Kenny win during his time as a Red Devil?

ANSWERS

Pot Luck - 65 *(see page 206)*

1 Bobby Charlton. 2 1957/58. 3 7-2 to United. 4 1-1 at Old Trafford. 5 Andrew Cole.
6 Gary Pallister. 7 Nine goals. 8 None: Bolton were still at Burnden Park. 9 Paul Scholes.
10 Paul Scholes. 11 Division Three. 12 Mark Hughes. 13 1979/80. 14 Steve Coppell.
15 Gordon McQueen. 16 Ian Greaves. 17 Frank Worthington. 18 Tony Dunne. 19 Alan
Gowling. 20 Willie Morgan.

Answers – see page 206

1 Apart from United, for which League club did Steve make the most appearances?
2 Was Steve the first Englishman to captain a side to the League and FA Cup double in the 20th century?
3 How many times did he receive both trophies in the same season?
4 Which England manager failed to pick Steve Bruce, then later admitted that he should have done?
5 With which famous associate does Steve Bruce share 31 December as a birthday?
6 From which club did United acquire Steve in December 1987?
7 Which trophy did Bruce help that club to lift in 1985?
8 What title medal did Steve pocket in 1985/86?
9 What did Steve break on his United debut against Portsmouth?
10 Who was his central defensive partner that day?
11 Against which nation did Steve skipper England 'B' in Valletta in 1987?
12 Which was the first major trophy won by United under the captaincy of Steve Bruce?
13 Steve thought he had scored in the 1991 Cup Winners' Cup Final against Barcelona, but who forced his goalbound header over the line?
14 How many senior goals did Steve score for United that term?
15 How many of them were penalties?
16 Against which opponents did Steve Bruce head two late goals to claim an unforgettable late victory as the 1992/93 title race neared a climax?
17 Which international boss investigated the possibility of picking Steve, but was frustrated by a Bruce appearance for England youth?
18 Who was selected ahead of 35-year-old Steve for United's 1996 FA Cup Final clash with Liverpool?
19 Which club did Bruce join that summer?
20 With which club did he end his playing days?

Answers – see page 203

1 Who is the only man since the war to score a hat-trick for United in senior competition against Bolton Wanderers?
2 In what season did Old Trafford witness that feat?
3 What was the result of the match?
4 What was the result of the 20th century's last meeting between United and Bolton?
5 In that game, who grabbed United's late equaliser?
6 When the two teams met in a goalless draw at the Reebok Stadium during the previous autumn, which United defender was dismissed?
7 How many League goals did United shoot past Bolton during the Reds' 'double double' campaign of 1995/96?
8 How many of those were scored at the Reebok Stadium?
9 Who scored twice for United in that term's meeting at Bolton?
10 Who scored twice in the Old Trafford encounter in September 1995?
11 In what division were Bolton playing when they met United in the FA Cup during 1990/91?
12 Who scored the only goal of that Old Trafford encounter?
13 In what campaign did the Red Devils and the Trotters enjoy their final encounters in the old First Division?
14 Who was the England international who scored for United in both League games that term?
15 That feat was equalled by a Scottish international. Name him.
16 What former United man started that season as Bolton boss, but was sacked in January?
17 In 1978/79, who scored four goals for the newly-promoted Trotters as they did the League double over United?
18 Who wore Bolton's number-three shirt in both of those games?
19 Which ex-Red netted against United in the Burnden Park match in 1978?
20 A former United skipper excelled in both that term's matches for Bolton. Name him.

Answers – see page 204

1 Which future United spearhead netted for Arsenal in their 3-2 triumph?
2 Which Republic of Ireland schemer created all of Arsenal's goals?
3 Who was the United boss at the time?
4 Who opened the scoring for the Gunners?
5 Who scored the first of the three goals which enlivened the last five minutes of an otherwise routine match?
6 Who equalised for the Red Devils after a mazy dribble?
7 Who became the first man of the 20th century to pocket FA Cup winners' medals with different clubs in successive seasons?
8 To whom fell the glory of poking home Arsenal's devastating late winner?
9 Who was the crestfallen rookie keeper between United's posts?
10 Why did the Gunners inspire the headline 'Terry's All Gold'?
11 At which club had the Arsenal boss and United assistant manager Tommy Cavanagh worked together?
12 Who did United conquer in a titanic semi-final replay at Goodison Park?
13 How many games did it take Arsenal to get past Sheffield Wednesday in the third round?
14 Which little Welshman worked himself to a standstill in United's number-11 shirt?
15 Who was the Arsenal captain?
16 Arsenal were in the middle of a sequence of three successive FA Cup Finals appearances. How many did they win?
17 Who led the United attack and enjoyed an epic confrontation with his countryman Willie Young?
18 United listened to a 'lucky' tape on their way to Wembley. Who provided the music?
19 The United boss had guided another club to FA Cup glory in 1970. Which club?
20 Arsenal replaced midfielder David Price with which defender as United pressed late on?

ANSWERS

Steve Bruce *(see page 204)*

1 Gillingham. 2 Yes. 3 Once. 4 Bobby Robson. 5 Sir Alex Ferguson. 6 Norwich City. 7 League Cup. 8 Second Division title medal. 9 His nose. 10 Kevin Moran. 11 Malta. 12 The 1992 League Cup. 13 Mark Hughes. 14 19 goals. 15 11 penalties. 16 Sheffield Wednesday. 17 The Republic of Ireland's Jack Charlton. 18 David May. 19 Birmingham City. 20 Sheffield United.

Answers – see page 209

1 In which county was the genial Sadler born?

2 What was David's first major senior honour as a Red Devil?

3 And what was his second?

4 In what season did David pocket an FA Youth Cup Winner's gong after scoring a hat-trick in the second leg of the final?

5 Who did United defeat in that final?

6 Against which opponents did Sadler make his First Division debut at Hillsborough in August 1963?

7 In what position did David play that day?

8 Who had been dropped, temporarily, to make way for the tall youngster?

9 In what position did David face Benfica in the 1968 European Cup Final?

10 In what role did the versatile Sadler eventually settle to play his finest football?

11 How many full England caps did David win?

12 David supplied the aggregate equaliser against which opposition in the 1968 European Cup semi-final?

13 Against which now-defunct nation did David make his final full England appearance in November 1970?

14 Sadler was an amateur international in his pre-United days. True or false?

15 Which United manager boss sold David in November 1973 when Sadler was still in his prime at 27?

16 Which club did David join?

17 Who was his new manager?

18 Alongside which future Liverpool star and current TV pundit did David play at his second club?

19 David's only League Cup goal as a Red Devil took United to victory over which club in September 1969?

20 With which United team-mate did the rookie Sadler share digs in the early 1960s?

ANSWERS

Jack Rowley *(see page 209)*

1 Bobby Charlton. 2 Six. 3 Wolverhampton Wanderers. 4 Bournemouth. 5 £3,000.
6 Outside-left. 7 Matt Busby. 8 Wolverhampton Wanderers. 9 The Gunner. 10 Two.
11 Stan Pearson. 12 30 goals. 13 True. 14 Five. 15 208. 16 Plymouth Argyle. 17 Arthur
Rowley. 18 Arthur. 19 1957. 20 Oldham Athletic.

Answers – see page 210

1 In what season was United's last senior meeting with Wolves during the 20th century?

2 What was the result of that encounter at Molineux?

3 Who scored twice for United in the Red Devils' 3-0 win over Wolves at Old Trafford that term?

4 Who was the Black Countrymen's manager during that relegation campaign?

5 Which ex-Red Devil had been Wolves boss prior to that manager?

6 Which former United boss took over the Molineux reins for the season following Wolves' most recent relegation from the top flight?

7 The escape of which Midlands-born Busby Babe to Old Trafford most upset the Molineux management during the early 1950s?

8 Who was the outraged Wolves boss at the time?

9 Which United full-back was sent off in an FA Cup tie at Molineux in January 1973?

10 What was the result of that game?

11 Which Irish Red notched a hat-trick at home to Wolves in October 1981?

12 United's first two hat-tricks in senior football were struck against Wolves in the same match, but during which season?

13 Who was the first to complete his threesome?

14 Who was the other hat-trick hero?

15 What was the result of the game?

16 Who was the lone scorer when the Red Devils triumphed at Molineux in February 1982?

17 Which pair of brothers both scored for the Red Devils in a victory at Molineux?

18 Who scored United's extra-time winner in an FA Cup quarter-final replay triumph at Molineux in March 1976?

19 Who scored two goals for United in each of two FA Cup victories at Molineux in successive seasons during the mid 1960s?

20 Decipher the anagram: NIBAR FREEFHONG.

ANSWERS

Jaap Stam *(see page 210)*

1 True. **2** PSV Eindhoven. **3** £10.75 million. **4** Gary Pallister. **5** The Premiership managers. **6** He was voted best defender in the Champions League. **7** Sheffield Wednesday. **8** Four. **9** Filbert Street. **10** United won 6-2 **11** The FA Cup Final against Newcastle. **12** 1997/98. **13** Brazil. **14** 1972. **15** Yes, with PSV. **16** False, he was a midfielder. **17** Goodison Park. **18** Arsenal's Dennis Bergkamp. **19** Filippo Inzaghi. **20** Five years.

Answers – see page 207.

1   Who was the only man to score more League goals for Manchester United than Jack Rowley?

2   Jack averaged a goal a game for England. How many times did he play for his country?

3   For which hometown club did Rowley sign on leaving school?

4   He failed to make the grade there, so stepped down to which Third Division (South) employers in 1937?

5   How much did Jack cost United when he signed later that year?

6   What was his specialist position at that stage?

7   Who converted Jack into a centre-forward after the war?

8   For which club did Rowley score eight goals in one game during the war?

9   What nickname was inspired by Jack's fearsome shot?

10 How many goals did Jack score in United's 1948 FA Cup Final triumph?

11 Rowley was United's top League scorer in five out of the first six campaigns after the war. Who pipped him in 1950/51, the odd season out?

12 Jack set what was then United's First Division scoring record in 1951/52. How many times did he strike?

13 That title-winning term Jack notched four League hat-tricks, including one each on the first and last days of the season. True or false?

14 How many goals did Rowley score when United annihilated Yeovil Town 8-0 in the FA Cup fifth round in 1948/49?

15 When he left United in 1955, Jack had played 422 League and Cup games for United. How many goals had he scored?

16 Rowley became player-boss of which club when he bowed out of Old Trafford?

17 Jack's younger brother was destined to become the highest scorer in English League history. Name him.

18 The Rowley brothers passed the milestone of 200 League goals on the same afternoon. Who got there first by 12 minutes?

19 In what year did Jack Rowley hang up his boots?

20 Which Lancashire club did Jack manage in two separate stints?

ANSWERS

David Sadler (see page 207)

1 Kent. 2 League title medal. 3 European Cup winner's medal. 4 1963/64. 5 Swindon Town. 6 Sheffield Wednesday. 7 Centre-forward. 8 David Herd. 9 Midfielder. 10 Central defender. 11 Four. 12 Real Madrid. 13 East Germany. 14 True. 15 Tommy Docherty. 16 Preston North End. 17 Bobby Charlton. 18 Mark Lawrenson. 19 Middlesbrough. 20 George Best.

Answers – see page 208

1   When Manchester United bought Jaap Stam, they made him the costliest defender in the world. True or false?

2   From which club was Jaap signed?

3   How much did the Red Devils pay for the Dutch colossus?

4   Which towering stopper did Jaap replace at the heart of United's rearguard?

5   In 1999, who nominated Stam as the player they coveted above all others?

6   What accolade did Jaap receive in both 1998/99 and 1999/2000?

7   Which English club gave Jaap a trial as a teenager but failed to sign him?

8   For how many senior Dutch clubs had Stam played before leaving his homeland?

9   On which ground did Jaap score the only goal of his first season as a Red Devil?

10   What was the result that day?

11   In which game did Jaap make his sole substitute appearance for United during 1998/99?

12   In what season was Stam voted Holland's Footballer of the Year?

13   Against which country did Jaap make his full international entrance?

14   In what year was Jaap Stam born?

15   Did Jaap ever win a Dutch Championship medal?

16   As a teenager Stam played regularly in goal. True or false?

17   Jaap scored an own goal in United's opening League fixture of 1999/2000 on which ground?

18   Stam deflected a shot from which Gunner past Peter Schmeichel in the 1999 FA Cup semi-final replay?

19   Jaap suffered similar misfortune following an effort from which Juventus marksman in that year's European Cup semi-final?

20   How long was the new contract signed by Jaap early in 2001?

EXTRA TIME

Answers - see page 215

1   In May 2001 United played out the so-called 'Battle of Britain' against which club?
2   Who was the beneficiary from that testimonial game?
3   Which infrequent scorer registered the first goal in the Reds' 2-0 victory?
4   Which Belgrade-born youngster, who had never played in a senior match at that point, contributed the second with an exquisite chip?
5   Which leading player from the past of United's opponents had died earlier that day?
6   Who became chairman of Manchester United in 1980?
7   Who was his predecessor in that high office?
8   Who did United play at Old Trafford in August 1978 to celebrate the centenary of Newton Heath's foundation?
9   What was the result?
10 United played in front of the highest attendance in Football League history. On what ground did that game take place?
11 In what season was the match played?
12 Who were the Reds' opponents?
13 What was the result?
14 To the nearest thousand, what was the attendance?
15 Again to the nearest thousand, what is the record attendance at Old Trafford?
16 What game was witnessed by that multitude of fans?
17 For which cricketer did the Red Devils play a testimonial at Scunthorpe in 1984?
18 In 1985 the Reds visited Hereford in a testimonial for the man who was managing Yeovil Town in 2000/2001. Name him.
19 Which great Scot was the beneficiary when United visited Celtic for a testimonial in August 1980?
20 Decipher the anagram: VIDAD DREH.

ANSWERS

Mark Hughes 2 *(see page 215)*
1 Clayton Blackmore. 2 Celtic. 3 Three. 4 1985. 5 It was his 100th League goal. 6 Gary Lineker. 7 Terry Venables. 8 Uli Hoeness. 9 Leicester City. 10 Spain. 11 False, he was third behind Zola and Juninho. 12 Eric Harrison. 13 Eric Cantona. 14 Mike England. 15 Violin. 16 Arsenal. 17 Ron Atkinson. 18 False, he scored once. 19 £1.5m. 20 £500,000.

Answers - see page 216

1 Who said of Jimmy Murphy: 'He was my first signing and my best'?

2 Jimmy Murphy was an Irishman. True or false?

3 Which team did Jimmy lead to the quarter-finals of the World Cup in 1958?

4 Which national FA failed in a bid to lure Murphy away from Old Trafford?

5 How many caps did Jimmy win for the country which he captained?

6 Which club did Jimmy serve throughout his League playing career?

7 What was Murphy's nickname?

8 When did Jimmy agree to become Matt Busby's number-two at Old Trafford?

9 In what year did Jimmy Murphy retire as assistant manager?

10 Which top London club sounded out Jimmy about taking over as manager in the summer of 1958?

11 Who eventually got the job at Highbury?

12 Which of Italy's leading clubs also was in the market for Murphy's inspirational services?

13 Why did Jimmy miss the fateful trip to Belgrade, which led to the Munich air disaster?

14 After visiting the Munich hospital, Jimmy journeyed home by train with two physically unscathed players. One was Bill Foulkes, who was the other?

15 What was Jimmy's great footballing achievement in the remainder of that season?

16 Over how many FA Cup games did Murphy preside during 1957/58?

17 To how many of United's League title successes did Jimmy contribute?

18 About which United man was Jimmy joking when he advised one of his own international charges, before facing England: 'Just keep out of his way, son'?

19 Jimmy's son made the United first team's substitutes' bench without ever getting a senior outing. Name him.

20 How old was Jimmy when he died in 1989?

Answers - see page 213

1. Which fellow Welsh international was best man at Mark's wedding?
2. Who were United's opponents for Hughes' Old Trafford testimonial match in May 1994?
3. How many goals did Sparky score in FA Cup Finals?
4. When was Mark voted the PFA's Young Player of the Year?
5. Apart from putting United on the road to a crucial victory, what was the significance of Hughes' goal at Crystal Palace in April 1993?
6. With which English marksman did Mark form a Nou Camp partnership?
7. Which manager took Sparky to Spain?
8. Which former West German international was Mark's Bundesliga boss?
9. Against which club did Hughes score on his full League debut?
10. A spectacular volley in a World Cup qualifier against which country cemented Mark's international reputation in April 1985?
11. Hughes was Footballer of the Year in 1997. True or false?
12. With what former United employee did Mark launch a soccer school?
13. Who was Sparky's new and inspirational front-running partner at Old Trafford as the Reds won the title in 1992/93?
14. Under which manager did Hughes make his debut for Wales?
15. What instrument did Mark play in his school orchestra?
16. Against whom did Sparky net his final senior goal for United?
17. Who was the United manager when Hughes broke into the first team?
18. Mark netted twice against Legia Warsaw in the European Cup semi-final of 1991. True or false?
19. How much did Chelsea pay United to sign Hughes in 1995?
20. What sum was involved when he moved on to The Dell three years later?

1 United's biggest home attendance of 2000/2001 (67,637) was recorded against which club?

2 Which Scottish club did United beat in the quarter-finals of the Coronation Cup in May 1953?

3 Which Scots eliminated the Reds in the semi-final three days later?

4 Who defeated the Red Devils in the final of the Watney Cup in August 1970?

5 A year later they lost in the quarter-final to which Yorkshiremen?

6 At which ground did that reverse take place?

7 United completed their Anglo-Italian Cup campaign of 1973 with victory over which opponents?

8 In 1985 who did the double over United in the short-lived Screen Sport Super Cup?

9 For which former Pittodrie favourite did United entertain Aberdeen for a testimonial match in 1983?

10 Who was the beneficiary when the Reds played an Eire X1 in a testimonial match at Dalymount Park in 1982?

11 Decipher the anagram: MIJ LOONTH.

12 Who were United's opponents at Bill Foulkes's testimonial in November 1970?

13 In what league did Newton Heath play before joining the Football League?

14 Which future West Ham boss scored an own goal when playing for Bournemouth against United in the League Cup in October 1982?

15 Which future Red Devil netted past his own keeper when turning out for Burnley against United in April 1969?

16 Which Gunner scored an own goal against United at Highbury in February 1968?

17 An own goal by an England full-back was enough for United to triumph in an FA Cup tie at Portman Road in January 1970. Who was the guilty party?

18 Who was the first Red Devil to become European Footballer of the Year?

19 Who was the second to receive that accolade two years later?

20 And who completed an Old Trafford hat-trick a further two years on?

Answers - see page 219

1 Which United chairman signed Alex Ferguson?
2 What was Fergie's first European match as United boss?
3 Who were the first European conquerors of Ferguson's Reds?
4 In what year did Fergie become Sir Alex?
5 With whom did Fergie have a well-publicised spat at Anfield in April 1988?
6 Which England stalwart did Brian Clough refuse to sell to Alex?
7 In one famous outburst, what did Fergie call Jimmy Hill?
8 Why is the racehorse of which Ferguson is part-owner named Queensland Star?
9 Where was Alex when he found out that United were champions in 1992/93?
10 Which three heroes did the United boss sell in the summer of 1995?
11 Who told the football world in general, and Fergie in particular, that 'you win nothing with kids', prior to United's double triumph of 1995/96?
12 Who would have 'loved it, really loved it' if Fergie's team had been beaten to the title by Newcastle in 1995/96?
13 Which Czech international did Alex sign from Slavia Prague in the summer of 1996?
14 When United lifted the League title in 2000, how many major trophies (excluding Super Cups, Charity Shields etc) had Fergie accumulated since arriving at Old Trafford?
15 Which Dutchman refused to respond to Ferguson's overtures in 1998?
16 For what trio of stars did Fergie fork out £28 million at the outset of the treble campaign?
17 Who did Sir Alex choose to replace Brian Kidd as his assistant?
18 Who took charge of United for their match against Middlesbrough in December 1998 when the manager was absent through a family bereavement?
19 Why was Sir Alex absent from the Manchester derby at Maine Road in November 2000?
20 Sir Alex is the father of how many sons?

Pot Luck - 69 (see page 219)
1 Jordi Cruyff. 2 Andrew Cole. 3 Ryan Giggs. 4 Walid Badir. 5 Massimo Taibi. 6 United won 5-1. 7 Neil Sullivan. 8 David Beckham's. 9 Chris Perry. 10 David Beckham. 11 Paul Scholes. 12 Robbie Earle. 13 Howard Gayle. 14 Eric Cantona. 15 Andrew Cole's. 16 Roy Keane. 17 Eric Cantona. 18 Steve Bruce. 19 Lawrie Sanchez. 20 Willie Morgan.

Answers - see page 220

1 Harry Gregg arrived at Old Trafford as the world's costliest goalkeeper. True or false?

2 What was the fee placed on the brilliant Irishman?

3 From what club did Matt Busby acquire Harry?

4 Who did Gregg replace as United's first-choice 'keeper?

5 How many title medals did Harry win as a Red Devil?

6 Harry was one of two Munich survivors who played in United's next match. Who was the other?

7 Which centre-forward barged Harry and the ball into the net for a controversial goal in the 1958 FA Cup Final?

8 Who replaced Harry, who had been absent through injury, between United's posts for the 1963 FA Cup semi-final and final?

9 Harry was voted the top goalkeeper of the 1958 World Cup Finals in Sweden. True or false?

10 At what stage of that tournament were the valiant Ulstermen knocked out?

11 Which was Harry's first major club in Irish football?

12 For which Ulster side was he playing immediately before crossing the Irish Sea to England?

13 Which great Irish footballer was Harry's first manager in the Football League?

14 How many full caps did Gregg win in his nine-year international career?

15 In what season did Harry make his full debut for Northern Ireland?

16 Who were Harry's first opponents as a Manchester United player?

17 Harry left the Red Devils in December 1966 to join which club?

18 In what year did the Irishman return to Old Trafford as a coach?

19 Harry became boss of four Football League clubs. Which was the first?

20 Who was employing Harry when he left management?

ANSWERS

Cream of Manchester - United v City - 3 *(see page 220)*
1 Bert Trautmann's Testimonial. **2** Brian Kidd. **3** Sammy McIlroy. **4** Peter Barnes. **5** Played eight, won eight. **6** Arthur Albiston's. **7** Gordon Strachan's. **8** Frank Stapleton. **9** Steve Coppell. **10** Joe Corrigan. **11** Gordon Hill. **12** 3-1. **13** Denis Law. **14** A pitch invasion. **15** Lou Macari. **16** Mike Doyle. **17** Clive Thomas. **18** Sammy McIlroy. **19** Mike Summerbee. **20** Wyn Davies.

Answers - see page 217

1 Who scored for United in both Premiership meetings with Wimbledon during 1999/2000?
2 Who popped up with United's late equaliser at Selhurst Park in February 2000?
3 Who ran almost the length of the pitch to create that goal?
4 Who put the Dons ahead against United at Old Trafford in September 1999?
5 Who was keeping goal for United that day?
6 What was the outcome when the Dons visited Old Trafford in October 1998?
7 Which keeper celebrated his Scotland call-up with a brilliant display that day?
8 Whose volley earned United a point when they travelled to meet Wimbledon while closing in on the Treble in April 1999?
9 Which future Tottenham central defender shone for the Dons that day?
10 Which substitute scored twice as United recorded a 5-2 away win over Wimbledon in November 1997?
11 Who put United in front with only a minute remaining of their FA Cup clash with Wimbledon at Old Trafford in January 1997?
12 Who grabbed the Dons' last-minute equaliser that day?
13 Who scored the only goal of the Selhurst Park replay?
14 On the day David Beckham scored his long-distance special at Selhurst Park, who opened the scoring for United in their 3-0 triumph over the Dons?
15 Whose winner claimed the Premiership points as United came from behind at home to Wimbledon in January 1997?
16 Who netted a pair as the Red Devils defeated the visiting Dons in August 1995?
17 Another double from which United star settled the return fixture at Selhurst Park in February 1996?
18 United claimed a scrappy away victory over Wimbledon in March 1995 thanks to a late goal from which defensive bulwark?
19 Which man who had once settled a Wembley FA Cup Final struck to earn Wimbedon an away win at Old Trafford in October 1992?
20 Decipher the anagram: LEILWI GROMNA.

Answers – see page 218

1 For which match did Bobby Charlton and Denis Law wear City shirts in 1964?
2 Which future United assistant manager top-scored for City in 1976/77 and 1977/78?
3 Which former Red lined up for City at Maine Road in September 1985?
4 Likewise, an ex-City man was wearing the red of United. Name him.
5 Before that game, United had played seven and won seven in the League. What was their record afterwards?
6 Whose late own goal gave City a draw at old Trafford in March 1986?
7 Whose penalty had given the Red Devils a two-goal lead in that game?
8 Who netted twice for United at Maine Road as defeat heightened City's justified relegation fears in March 1983?
9 Which England winger was on target twice for United as they coasted to a 3-0 victory at Maine Road in February 1979?
10 A future Liverpool coach was between City's posts that day. Name him.
11 Who scored two penalties as City drew 2-2 at Old Trafford in March 1978?
12 United did the League double over City with identical scores in 1976/77. Name that scoreline.
13 Who scored the only goal, for City, in the last Manchester derby before United were relegated in 1974?
14 The result stood, but why was that game abandoned a few minutes before the end?
15 Which United player, along with a City man, refused to leave the field after being sent off at Maine Road in March 1974?
16 Who was the City player who also stood his ground?
17 Who was the controversial referee who led the players off for a five-minute cooling-down period?
18 Which Irishman marked his senior debut for United with the opening goal of a 3-3 thriller with City?
19 Who snatched a City equaliser that day with only seconds remaining?
20 Which giant City target man did United enlist in September 1972?

ANSWERS

Harry Gregg *(see page 218)*
1 True. 2 £23,500. 3 Doncaster Rovers. 4 Ray Wood. 5 None. 6 Bill Foulkes. 7 Nat Lofthouse. 8 David Gaskell. 9 True. 10 The quarter-finals. 11 Linfield. 12 Coleraine. 13 Peter Doherty. 14 25. 15 1953/54. 16 Leicester City. 17 Stoke City. 18 1978. 19 Shrewsbury Town. 20 Carlisle United.

Answers - see page 223

1 Which former United favourite was the manager of Crystal Palace?
2 Who had Palace vanquished in a seven-goal semi-final at Villa Park?
3 What was the London club's nickname?
4 What was special about the crowd arrangements for the final?
5 Which goalkeeper was axed sensationally following United's 3-3 Wembley draw with Palace?
6 Who scored the first goal of that entertaining encounter?
7 Who headed an equaliser ten minutes before the break?
8 What was the score after 90 minutes?
9 Who put United in front, then supplied a late equaliser?
10 Who went on as a substitute and scored two for Palace?
11 Who did that player join after leaving Selhurst Park?
12 Britain's first £1 million keeper stood between Palace's posts. Who was he?
13 Which goalkeeper did Alex Ferguson call up for the replay?
14 Which hitherto unsung hero scored the only goal of the replay?
15 Who laid on that goal with a beautiful crossfield pass?
16 What record did United's victory equal?
17 In how many FA Cup Finals had they appeared previously?
18 This triumph meant a sole FA Cup medal for which former Southampton forward?
19 What colour shirts did United wear for the replay?
20 One player was substituted in both matches. Name him.

Answers - see page 224

1 Which German defender was sent off when United visited Pride Park in November 1999?

2 What was the result of the game?

3 Which substitute's late equaliser enabled the Red Devils to Derby with a point in October 1998?

4 A deft finish from which marksman fashioned victory for United when Derby came calling in February 1999?

5 Whose penalty sealed a 2-0 home victory for the Reds against the Rams in February 1998?

6 Four minutes after netting from the spot, the scorer was replaced by who?

7 To what ground did United pay their final visit in senior competition when they faced Derby County in September 1996?

8 Who netted the Rams third goal as they shocked the title-chasing Reds with a 3-2 victory at Old Trafford in April 1997?

9 Who played in goal for United when they beat Derby 3-1 at home in April 1991?

10 Who was sent off in the home defeat by Derby in January 1990?

11 Who netted United's only goal that day?

12 Who recorded his first United hat-trick, against the Rams, at Old Trafford in April 1988?

13 Which post-war United player netted two hat-tricks against Derby County?

14 In what season did United last meet Derby in senior knockout competition?

15 What was the outcome of that FA Cup encounter?

16 Who supplied the winning goal?

17 Which popular young marksman hit the target twice as Derby tumbled 3-1 at Old Trafford in December 1978?

18 Who scored twice against his future employers as United trounced Derby 4-0 at Old Trafford in January 1978?

19 Where did Manchester United beat Derby County in their FA Cup semi-final meeting in 1976?

20 Decipher the anagram: HONJ SONAT.

ANSWERS

Nobby Stiles (see page 224)

1 Norbert. 2 Nobby Lawton. 3 Bobby Moore. 4 Johnny Giles. 5 Eddie Colman's. 6 1959.
7 Bolton Wanderers. 8 True. 9 28. 10 Scotland. 11 One. 12 False. 13 Yes. 14 Eusebio.
15 Bill Foulkes. 16 Inside-forward. 17 Maurice Setters'. 18 Middlesbrough. 19 Preston
North End. 20 Youth coach.

Answers - see page 221

1 United's title in 1993/94 was the first leg of their first League and FA Cup double. True or false?

2 After which game did the Reds know they were champions?

3 The first match of the League campaign brought a 2-0 victory at which ground?

4 Ryan Giggs scored the first goal; who notched the second?

5 Who scored for Newcastle at Old Trafford as United dropped their first points of the season in a 1-1 draw?

6 A titanic August tussle at Villa Park was settled by a double from which United star?

7 Where did the Red Devils suffer their first League defeat?

8 Who netted twice in the 4-2 home victory over Swindon?

9 Which United full-back switched to centre-half to mark his old team-mate Les Ferdinand against QPR at Old Trafford?

10 Bookmakers refused to take more bets on United after they moved 15 points clear in early December. True or false?

11 Who were the Reds' opponents at Old Trafford in December as three goals were scored in the final three minutes?

12 Whose late equaliser at Upton Park ruined the home fans' afternoon?

13 Who scored both Blackburn goals as Rovers beat United to move within three points at the top of the table in April?

14 Which recruit from Cambridge helped steady the Reds' nerves by scoring in a narrow home victory over Oldham?

15 Who capitalised on a rare Schmeichel fumble as United lost to Wimbledon at Selhurst Park?

16 What was the Reds' final points margin over runners-up Blackburn?

17 Who made his sole senior appearance for United at home to Coventry on the last day of the League season?

18 How many previous League Championships had United won?

19 Who was United's only Premiership ever-present during 1993/94?

20 Who was the club's top scorer with 18 League goals?

FA Cup Final 1990 (see page 221)

ANSWERS

1 Steve Coppell. 2 Liverpool. 3 The Eagles. 4 It was the first all-seater FA Cup Final.
5 Jim Leighton. 6 Gary O'Reilly. 7 Bryan Robson. 8 2-2. 9 Mark Hughes. 10 Ian Wright.
11 Arsenal. 12 Nigel Martyn. 13 Les Sealey. 14 Lee Martin. 15 Neil Webb. 16 Highest
number of FA Cup victories (seven, shared by Spurs and Aston Villa). 17 Ten. 18 Danny
Wallace. 19 Red. 20 Palace's Phil Barber.

1 Nobby is short for what name?
2 In the early 1960s there was another Nobby in and out of the United side. Name him.
3 Who was Nobby Stiles's captain when England won the World Cup in 1966?
4 Which United team-mate was Nobby's brother-in-law?
5 As a teenage amateur, Nobby used to clean the stars' boots. For which of his United heroes' footwear did he reserve an extra rub?
6 During the summer of which year did Stiles turn professional with United?
7 Against which Lancashire rivals did he impress on debut in November 1960?
8 Nobby wore contact lenses on the pitch throughout his footballing prime. True or false?
9 How many full England caps did Nobby accumulate?
10 He faced the same opponents at both ends of his five-year international career. Name them.
11 How many times did Nobby score for his country?
12 The Mancunian's first major club honour was an FA Cup winner's medal in 1963. True or false?
13 United won the title in 1964/65 and 1966/67. Did Nobby earn a medal in both those seasons?
14 Which 'Black Panther' was successfully caged by Nobby in the 1968 European Cup Final?
15 With which central defensive partner did Stiles excel for United during the 1960s?
16 Before switching into the back four, Nobby alternated between wing-half and which other position?
17 Whose place did he take before settling into Matt Busby's side as a regular?
18 To which club was Nobby transferred in May 1971?
19 Which club did he manage from 1977 to 1981?
20 In what role did Nobby return to Old Trafford for a four-year stint in 1989?

Answers - see page 227

1 Whose scorching long-distance howitzer gave United a 3-1 lead at the Riverside as they closed in on the 1999/2000 Premiership title?

2 Which former Red bundled home a cross to make it 3-2?

3 Whose contentious strike put the game beyond Boro's reach?

4 Earlier in the season, United had beaten Boro at Old Trafford thanks to a soft late goal from which England star?

5 In that Old Trafford encounter, which Middlesbrough man was sent off?

6 Who missed a penalty in the same match?

7 Who was the referee confronted by a controversially zealous posse of United protesters after he had awarded the spot-kick?

8 Who put Boro three up at Old Trafford in December 1998, during United's last defeat of their Treble-winning campaign?

9 Some two weeks later, the Reds ejected Boro from the FA Cup on the same ground. Who put the visitors ahead that day?

10 Soon after that, who netted the penalty which gave United the upper hand?

11 United strengthened their title credentials with a single-goal victory at the Riverside in May 1999. Who supplied that crucial strike?

12 Who headed United into the lead in the second half at The Riverside in 1996?

13 Whose subsequent penalty tied up a 2-2 draw for the north-easterners?

14 Two Brazilians netted against the Reds at Old Trafford on Easter Monday 1997. One was Juninho; name the other.

15 Whose headed equaliser secured United a point in that six-goal thriller?

16 Who put the Red Devils ahead against his former club as United triumphed 2-0 over Middlesbrough at Old Trafford in October 1995?

17 Which substitute's adroit, over-the-shoulder dink put the Reds two up on their way to clinching the title at the Riverside in May 1996?

18 Who put the Reds in front in the second leg of their 1992 League Cup semi-final against Boro at Old Trafford?

19 Who popped up with United's extra-time winner in that tie?

20 Decipher the anagram: RONDOG NEMUQEC.

Answers – see page 228

1 United's left-winger had the game of his life in the last League match before Munich in 1958. Name him.

2 Which tiny striker, who would go on to FA Cup glory with Wimbledon, netted for United at home to Arsenal in January 1987?

3 What was the result of that game, United's first against Arsenal with Alex Ferguson in charge?

4 Who missed a penalty as United went out of the FA Cup at Highbury in 1988?

5 Which Arsenal man ostentatiously mocked the spot-kick culprit?

6 Which winger made his full United debut at home to Arsenal in April 1989?

7 To whom were United indebted for the own goal which salvaged a point that day?

8 Who scored on his United debut against Arsenal on the first day of 1989/90?

9 That day a certain businessman did tricks in front of the Stretford End. Name him.

10 Which Scottish stopper was bought from Arsenal to shore up United's shaky defence in August 1969?

11 In what season did Andrew Cole make a senior appearance for Arsenal?

12 Who was the Arsenal boss who allowed him to leave Highbury?

13 Tommy Docherty played for Arsenal, but did he ever manage them?

14 Which striker who spent two matches on loan at Old Trafford in 1974/75 started his career as a Gunner?

15 Whose fabulous hat-trick was the centre-piece of United's 6-2 League Cup victory at Highbury in November 1990?

16 Who put the Red Devils ahead in the second minute of that game?

17 United were fined a point following a fracas between the two sets of players at Old Trafford in October 1990. What penalty did Arsenal pay?

18 Who scored the only goal of that ill-tempered contest?

19 Which Gunner scored a hat-trick against United on the day that Arsenal sealed the 1990/91 title?

20 Which former United marksman was coaching at Highbury in 2001?

Answers - see page 225

1 Where did United face Barcelona in the Cup Winners' Cup Final?
2 Following whose header was the Red Devils' opening goal forced over the line?
3 After some debate, who was credited with United's first goal?
4 What was the half-time score?
5 Who scored United's second with a spectacular acute-angled drive?
6 Who scored from a 79th-minute free-kick to set up a tense finish?
7 Who cleared off United's line in the dying stages?
8 Who recovered from an injury suffered at Wembley to keep goal for the Red Devils?
9 Which Danish marksman was the focal point of Barcelona's attack?
10 United were not allowed to wear their red shirts. To what colour did they switch?
11 Who skippered United to glory?
12 Who was manager of Barcelona?
13 The Catalans had just clinched the Spanish title. True or false?
14 What Bulgarian star was missing from the Barcelona side through injury.
15 Which Old Trafford player was facing his former employers?
16 Who did Alex Ferguson detail to mark Dutch danger-man Ronald Koeman?
17 United took the field with only one recognised winger? Who was he?
18 Who was the Barcelona keeper in the absence of the injured Zubizarreta?
19 This was the second time a side managed by Alex Ferguson had lifted the Cup Winners' Cup. True or false?
20 Did United's win complete a clean sweep of all three major European trophies?

Answers - see page 226

1　Who was substituted when one short of a hat-trick at the City Ground, Nottingham, in February 1999?

2　Who replaced the scorer and made an impression in the final minutes?

3　How many League goals did the Reds total against Nottingham Forest during that Treble-winning campaign?

4　How many times did United score against Forest on the way to the title in 1996/97?

5　Which midfielder, no friend of Roy Keane's, mustered Forest's only reply?

6　Who was the only man to score in both meetings with Forest that term?

7　Which ex-Red, who never played a senior game for United, faced them as a Forest substitute at Nottingham in 1995?

8　Who scored two of United's five goals against Forest at Old Trafford as they romped towards the Championship in the spring of 1997?

9　Who scored Forest's equaliser as they took a point from the Red Devils at the City Ground in August 1994, then netted again in the Old Trafford return?

10　Who grabbed the decisive goal as Forest visited United during Christmas 1994?

11　Who netted in both United's 2-0 victories over Nottingham Forest during their first victorious title campaign under Alex Ferguson?

12　Who was the Forest boss during that term?

13　What was the last occasion on which United met Forest in senior knockout competition?

14　As United strove to land the Championship in 1991/92, they lost two springtime encounters with Forest. True or false?

15　Who made the pass for Mark Robins to score the FA Cup goal at the City Ground in 1989 which might or might not have saved his manager's job?

16　Who scored United's first in their Boxing Day win over Forest in 1988?

17　Whose goal sunk United in their 1988/89 FA Cup quarter-final clash with Forest?

18　Which Red was dismissed in a First Division encounter with Nottingham Forest at the City Ground in April 1980?

19　Which England player scored twice as United lost 4-0 to Forest in 1977/78?

20　Decipher the anagram: EERPT VANDROPET.

Answers - see page 231

1 What is the title of Paul McGrath's autobiography?
2 From which Dublin club did United sign Paul in April 1982?
3 Who was the manager who took him to Old Trafford?
4 What was the transfer fee?
5 Paul was an outstanding central defender, but in which other position did he also operate successfully during his early seasons as a Red Devil?
6 Where was Paul McGrath born?
7 Paul pocketed one senior medal with United. What was it?
8 How many full international caps did Paul accumulate for the Republic of Ireland?
9 For whom was Paul playing when he faced Diego Maradona in 1987?
10 What was the reason for that match?
11 Injuries plagued Paul's career. What part of his anatomy gave him the most trouble?
12 Off-the-field problems led to his departure from Old Trafford during what summer?
13 In 1985 a McGrath own goal put which opponents in front against United in an FA Cup semi-final replay?
14 Earlier that season Paul scored in successive FA Cup ties. The first was against Coventry, but who were his second victims?
15 To which club was the Irish star sold by United?
16 What were they paid for his services?
17 Under what boss did Paul's new club push United in the 1992/93 title race?
18 What personal accolade did Paul receive in 1993?
19 Which was Paul's penultimate League club?
20 For what club did Paul McGrath complete his League career during 1997/98?

Answers - see page 232

1   In what position did Billy Meredith star for Manchester United?
2   What was the tall, gaunt Welshman's most-used nickname?
3   What was his trademark accessory, frequently depicted by cartoonists?
4   What record total of Welsh caps did Billy set?
5   Who finally exceeded that total in 1962?
6   How long was Meredith's career in top-class football?
7   In what year was Billy born?
8   In what Welsh border town was he born?
9   What job outside football was Billy doing from the age of 12?
10 With which club did Meredith make his Football League debut?
11 Billy scored the winning goal for Manchester City in which FA Cup Final?
12 In one week of 1895 Billy played internationals against Ireland, England and Scotland and spent three days as a farm labourer. True or false?
13 Of what modern footballing organisation was Billy Meredith a crusading pioneer?
14 Throughout which season was he suspended for alleged financial irregularities by the greedy and hypocritical authorities of the day?
15 On which New Year's Day did he play his first game for Manchester United?
16 In which term did he inspire the Reds to lift their first League title?
17 Against which opponents did Billy excel as United enjoyed their initial FA Cup Final triumph in 1909?
18 How old was Billy when he picked up his second title gong with United in 1911?
19 To what club was he transferred in 1921?
20 At what age did Billy Meredith play in his last FA Cup semi-final?

ANSWERS

Young Devils (see page 232)
1 Arsenal. **2** Royal Antwerp. **3** The Belgian Second Division title. **4** Luxembourg. **5** Aston Villa. **6** Villa won 3-0. **7** John O'Shea. **8** Atletico Madrid. **9** £2 million. **10** Cape Town. **11** 1977. **12** True. **13** Newcastle United. **14** Bradford City. **15** The Riverside. **16** Tottenham Hotspur. **17** Brazil. **18** Newton Heath. **19** Royal Antwerp. **20** Stockport County.

Answers - see page 229

1   United's last senior encounter with Burnley was in the League Cup, but in what season?
2   What was the aggregate score in that tie?
3   Who score a hat-trick in the first leg at Old Trafford?
4   Who scored twice at Turf Moor?
5   Who scored in both games as United completed the double over Burnley in 1975/76, the last season in which they occupied the same division?
6   Which substitute netted against his former employers as United beat Burnley 3-2 in a League Cup meeting in November 1974?
7   Why might United have been seen as underdogs that night?
8   In what season did United last experience senior action against Preston North End?
9   In what competition did that match take place?
10 It was played at Preston's ground. Name it.
11 What was the result?
12 Who hit the target twice for the winners?
13 Two World Cup-winning Red Devils went on to manage Preston. One was Bobby Charlton, who was the other?
14 During what campaign did United and Blackpool last contest a game at senior level?
15 In what competition did that occur?
16 On what ground did that meeting between the Reds and the Seasiders take place?
17 Who was the last United player to be sent off against Blackpool?
18 Who was the last Red Devil to receive his marching orders against Burnley?
19 Which United man scored two hat-tricks against Burnley during 1960/61?
20 Who was the last Red Devil to score three goals in a game against Blackpool?

Answers - see page 230

1 With which club was Luke Chadwick affiliated until he was 14?

2 Luke went on loan to which European club during 1999/2000?

3 Which honour did Chadwick help that club to attain?

4 Luke scored on his debut for England under-21s, a 5-0 victory over which opponents?

5 Against which Midlanders did Luke make his senior debut for United in a League Cup tie in October 1999?

6 What was the result of that match?

7 Which central defender made his United debut on the same night?

8 From which club did the Red Devils sign Quinton Fortune in August 1999?

9 How much did he cost?

10 In which city was the South African international born?

11 In what year was Quinton born?

12 There is a club named after Fortune in his homeland. True or false?

13 Against which United did Quinton play his first senior game for the Reds in August 1999?

14 It was Boxing Day 1999 when Quinton made his first Premiership start for United and contributed his first goal. Who provided the opposition?

15 Quinton poached the sixth goal in a seven-goal thriller at which ground in April 2000?

16 With which club was Quinton associated as a schoolboy, only to find he could not obtain a work permit?

17 Quinton scored against which South Americans in the 2000 Olympics?

18 In what area of Manchester was Ronnie Wallwork born and raised?

19 For which club was Ronnie on loan when he was threatened with a life ban following an incident with a referee?

20 In 1997/98 Ronnie was loaned to two English clubs. The first was Carlisle United, which was the other?

Answers - see page 235

1   In which season did George Best score 32 times in major club competitions?

2   George topped United's League scoring charts in five consecutive campaigns between 1967/68 and 1971/72. True or false?

3   Who were the opponents when Best grabbed his first senior hat-trick for the Red Devils, at Old Trafford in May 1968?

4   Who was West Ham's expensive Scottish international keeper when George plundered a spectacular hat-trick at Old Trafford in September 1971?

5   In which season did George help United to lift the FA Youth Cup?

6   With which future United player did George share the honour of topping the First Division's scoring chart in 1967/68?

7   For which Southern League club did George Best turn out in August 1974?

8   Which chat-show host collaborated with George on a controversial biography in 1975?

9   For which Fourth Division club did George make three League appearances during 1975/76?

10 He scored a hat-trick on his Fourth Division debut. True or false?

11 For which League of Ireland club did George play during that same season?

12 Who were his first employers in the North American Soccer league?

13 For which London club did George sign in the autumn 1976?

14 With which former Manchester City star did he link up at his new club?

15 How long did it take Best to score his first goal for the Londoners in his debut against Bristol Rovers?

16 For which Scottish club did George sign for in 1979?

17 Which former United colleague was George's coach when he signed for San Jose Earthquakes in 1980?

18 George made a Football League comeback with a south-coast club in 1982/83. Name that club.

19 George scored the only goal in the Old Trafford first leg of the European Cup semi-final of 1968. Who provided the opposition?

20 Did George Best ever figure in a World Cup Finals tournament?

Answers – see page 236

1 Who was dismissed as the Reds ejected Sheffield United from the FA Cup in a roaring gale at Bramall Lane in January 1995?

2 Who was involving in the sending-off incident, then contributed United's clinching goal with an exquisite finish near the end?

3 Who was the Sheffield boss who had no sympathy following his player's loss of discipline?

4 Who started and finished the delicious move which resulted in the only goal of United's FA Cup clash at Bramall Lane in January 1994?

5 Who was sent off three minutes from the end of that tumultuous contest?

6 Who was the victim of the assault which provoked the dismissal?

7 Whose superb goal put the Reds in front in yet another FA Cup encounter at Bramall Lane in February 1993?

8 Whose penalty miss condemned Alex Ferguson's men to an unexpected exit from the competition?

9 What was the score by which United beat the Blades in both League meetings during 1993/94?

10 Who scored twice for the Mancunians when the two Uniteds met in the August?

11 How did bookmakers greet the second of those triumphs in the December?

12 Manchester United opened their triumphant title campaign of 1992/93 at Bramall Lane. What was the result?

13 What was special about the opening goal, five minutes into that contest?

14 Who scored it?

15 Which substitute contributed a late winner as the Reds came from behind to win at Bramall Lane in March 1992?

16 Who was the first Red Devil to notch a senior hat-trick against Sheffield United?

17 Whose goal at Bramall Lane saw the Manchester United through to the 1990 FA Cup semi-finals?

18 Who scored twice in both the 1975/76 encounters with Sheffield United?

19 A different Manchester marksman hit the target in both games. Name him.

20 Decipher the anagram: REGYR ADYL.

FA Cup Final 1963 *(see page 236)*

ANSWERS

1 It had been the winter of the Big Freeze. **2** Fourth. **3** Three. **4** Denis Law. **5** Paddy Crerand. **6** Ken Keyworth. **7** David Herd. **8** Gordon Banks. **9** Albert Quixall. **10** Johnny Giles. **11** Coventry City. **12** Colin Appleton. **13** Frank McLintock. **14** Tottenham Hotspur. **15** Matt Gillies. **16** Shay Brennan. **17** Harry Gregg. **18** Nobby Stiles. **19** Graham Cross. **20** United captain Noel Cantwell.

1 Johnny Morris, the 'baby' of the 1948 FA Cup-winning team, played in what position?

2 That day at Wembley, Johnny created United's first equaliser for which colleague?

3 What was the British record fee for which United sold Johnny in March 1949 following a disagreement with the Reds' boss?

4 Who was that United manager?

5 Which club did Johnny join when he left Manchester United?

6 Morris won three full England caps. How many goals did he score for his country?

7 Johnny made all his England appearances while a United player. True or false?

8 Morris scored twice for England against which opposition?

9 How many times did Johnny pocket a League title medal?

10 With which club did Johnny win two Second Division championship gongs during the 1950s?

11 Jimmy Delaney was born and died in the same Lanarkshire community. Name it.

12 From which Scottish giants did Matt Busby recruit Jimmy in February 1946?

13 How old was the balding veteran when he arrived at Old Trafford.

14 In which position did he operate?

15 What was the fee?

16 What was Delaney's only major club honour as a Red Devil?

17 What unique cup treble did Jimmy achieve?

18 Jimmy won nine pre-war caps with his Scottish club. Did he add to his total after joining United?

19 Name the home of the club Delaney joined after leaving United in November 1950.

20 How old was Jimmy Delaney when he retired as a professional footballer in April 1957?

George Best - 3 *(see page 233)*

ANSWERS

1 1967/68. 2 True. 3 Newcastle United. 4 Bobby Ferguson. 5 1963/64. 6 Ron Davies of Southampton. 7 Dunstable Town. 8 Michael Parkinson. 9 Stockport County. 10 False, he scored twice. 11 Cork Celtic. 12 Los Angeles. 13 Fulham. 14 Rodney Marsh. 15 71 seconds. 16 Hibernian. 17 Bill Foulkes. 18 Bournemouth. 19 Real Madrid. 20 No.

Answers - see page 234

1 The game was played on May 25. Why so late?

2 Where had United's opponents, Leicester City, finished in that term's League table.

3 By how many points had United outstripped relegated Manchester City?

4 Who swivelled on the spot to net a glorious opener for United?

5 Whose precision pass created that goal, which set United on their way to a 3-1 triumph?

6 With his side 2-0 down, who put Leicester back in contention with a diving header?

7 Which Scottish international centre-forward scored twice for Matt Busby's men?

8 Who was the goalkeeper whose fumble led to United's clincher?

9 Which former 'Golden Boy' of English football wore the Reds' number-eight shirt?

10 Which Irishman, who would go on to find fame with Leeds, was playing on the United's right flank?

11 Which Third Division club had United removed from their Wembley path at the quarter-final stage?

12 Who was Leicester's skipper?

13 Which Foxes star would one day lead Arsenal to the League and FA Cup double?

14 This was Leicester's second FA Cup Final defeat in three seasons. Who had beaten them in 1961?

15 Who was the Midlanders' boss?

16 Who missed a Wembley appearance after playing 41 League and Cup games for United that season?

17 Which injury-plagued keeper failed to regain his place from young David Gaskell in time for the big day?

18 Which future World Cup hero was another unlucky near-regular?

19 Which Leicester player was looking forward to a summer's county cricket?

20 Who proved to have a safe pair of hands when the FA Cup was hurled high in the air in celebration?

Answers - see page 239

1 Whose own goal assisted United's 2-0 home victory over Crystal Palace in October 1997?

2 Who scored his first Premiership goal at Old Trafford that same afternoon?

3 Who took over United's captaincy from the injured Roy Keane that day?

4 What was settled by United's 3-0 victory at Selhurst Park in April 1998?

5 Which United keeper made his senior debut as a substitute for Peter Schmeichel in the 3-0 home victory over Crystal Palace in November 1994?

6 Whose glorious free-kick produced a United equaliser in the Reds' FA Cup semi-final meeting with Crystal Palace in 1995?

7 The crowd for United's replay against Palace in the last four of the FA Cup in 1995 was the lowest ever for an FA Cup semi-final. True or false?

8 Which United striker received a serious injury at home to Crystal Palace in September 1992?

9 Whose 88th-minute goal won the match?

10 Whose two goals sealed the points for United against Palace in February 1992?

11 Which soon-to-be-capped England winger scored twice as Palace tanned the Reds 3-0 at Selhurst Park in May 1991?

12 Which flankman on the other side made his League entrance that day?

13 Who struck twice to dump Crystal Palace out of the League Cup at Old Trafford in October 1987, soon after his arrival from Celtic?

14 In 1985/86 United beat Palace 1-0 in both legs of a League Cup clash. Which England winger netted in the Selhurst park leg?

15 Which League Cup-winner with Swindon starred and scored twice in Palace's 5-0 humbling of United at Selhurst Park in December 1972?

16 Who scored a hat-trick as United won 5-3 at Palace in April 1971?

17 Which United forward struck a hat-trick at home to Millwall in September 1989?

18 Who scored in three out of United's four League meetings with Millwall during the Londoners' two seasons in the top flight between 1988 and 1990?

19 What is Millwall's nickname?

20 Decipher the anagram: NARKF TENSTOLPA.

Answers - see page 240

1 Bryan made his United debut in a League Cup encounter on which ground?

2 In what year did Robbo end his playing days?

3 Robbo scored a hat-trick for England against which opponents in 1984?

4 Bryan notched the last goal of United's 1992/93 title-winning campaign against which opposition?

5 How many goals did Bryan score in FA Cup Finals?

6 Was Robbo already a full international when he was signed by United?

7 Against which nation did he make his full England debut?

8 Which England boss awarded that first cap?

9 How many times did Robbo find the net in his first Charity Shield appearance?

10 Bryan signed for United on the pitch before a First Division clash with which Midlanders?

11 Who were the opponents when Robson played his first League game for United?

12 What was the result of that encounter?

13 What shirt number became Robbo's private property from the outset of his Old Trafford stay?

14 How many times did Bryan hit the target when Barcelona came calling at Old Trafford in March 1984?

15 Against which Lancashire club did Bryan make his final FA Cup appearance for the Red Devils?

16 Who were the Hungarian opponents when Robson made his debut in Europe's premier club competition?

17 Against which club did he register his first and last European Cup goal?

18 Including Charity Shield efforts, how many times did Bryan score in senior competition for the Red Devils?

19 As a manager, how many times has Robbo led his club into the Premiership?

20 Who did that club enlist to assist Bryan with coaching duties during a difficult 2000/2001 season?

Pot Luck - 76 *(see page 240)*

ANSWERS

1 Dwight Yorke. 2 Ole Gunnar Solskjaer. 3 Andrei Kanchelskis. 4 Peter Schmeichel had been sent off. 5 True. 6 Bobby Charlton's. 7 Eric Cantona's. 8 Ray Wilkins. 9 Paul Scholes. 10 Les Ferdinand. 11 2-0 to United. 12 Ryan Giggs. 13 Paul Parker. 14 Paul Parker. 15 Willie Morgan. 16 1968/69. 17 8-1 to United. 18 United lost 1-4. 19 300 minutes. 20 Arnold Muhren.

Answers - see page 237

1   In what summer did the relatively unknown Ole Gunnar Solskjaer arrive at Old Trafford?
2   What was the fee?
3   Which was his previous club?
4   What is his nationality?
5   Against which opponents was he first plunged into the Premiership fray?
6   Who was the first 'keeper in English football to retrieve the ball from the net after a Solskjaer goal?
7   Ole made 25 Premiership starts in his first season as a Red Devil. How many League goals did he score that term?
8   In how many subsequent campaigns has he made more Premiership starts?
9   Which club made a substantial bid to sign Ole in August 1998?
10 Against which club did Ole score four times in 11 minutes in February 1999?
11 Who did he replace on that memorable afternoon?
12 Who were the victims of Solskjaer's next four-goal extravaganza, in December 1999?
13 Ole's father was a champion in what sport?
14 On what Midlands ground did Ole contribute an Easter Saturday double to earn a draw after United had gone two down during the 1996/97 title run-in?
15 On which London ground were two early Solskjaer strikes cancelled out by two headers from an England centre-half in December 1998?
16 Against which opponents was Ole credited with a goal after smashing home a rebound from a Scholes shot which had already crossed the line in May 1997?
17 In United's Treble-winning campaign, did Ole make more starts or substitute appearances?
18 Did he start in the FA Cup Final against Newcastle, or did he rise from the bench?
19 Who was the last player to touch the ball before he scored the most crucial goal of his career?
20 In what year was Ole Gunnar Solskjaer born?

Answers – see page 238

1 Who netted twice in three minutes for United either side of the interval at home to Charlton in September 1998?

2 Which other Red Devil contributed two goals in that match?

3 Who netted twice for ten-man United in an FA Cup quarter-final against Charlton at Old Trafford in March 1994?

4 Why were the Reds down to ten men?

5 United failed to complete a League double over Charlton during the Addicks' top-flight spell between 1986 and 1990. True or false?

6 Whose 1957 hat-trick against Charlton helped to end Athletic's 21-year sojourn in the top flight?

7 Whose last-gasp header salvaged a point for the Red Devils when they visited QPR in March 1996?

8 Which former Red was managing Rangers at the time?

9 Who netted twice as the Reds triumphed by the odd goal in five at Loftus Road in December 1994?

10 That day who replied with a brace for QPR?

11 What was the result of United's FA Cup quarter-final clash with Rangers in March 1995?

12 Who scored the Reds' final goal following a breathtaking dribble in the 3-2 victory at Loftus Road in February 1994?

13 Which Red Devil was facing his former club that day?

14 Which United man was sent off in the home clash with QPR in August 1994?

15 Who is the only Red Devil to score a senior hat-trick against QPR since the war?

16 In what season was that feat accomplished?

17 What was the result of the match?

18 What was the outcome when Rangers met title-hunting United at Old Trafford on New Year's Day 1992?

19 How many minutes did it take for United to see off the challenge of QPR when the clubs met in the third round of the FA Cup in January 1989?

20 Decipher the anagram: LANDRO REMHUN.

Answers - see page 243

1   Who is Darren's dad?
2   During his time as a Red Devil, Darren earned one senior honour on merit. What was it?
3   In what position did Ferguson operate for United?
4   To what level did he rise in the international ranks?
5   In his 30 senior outings for United, how many goals did Darren score?
6   Darren has a twin brother. True or false?
7   Against which club did Darren make his senior debut for the Red Devils?
8   To which Midlanders was Ferguson sold in January 1994?
9   By how much did the deal swell the Old Trafford coffers?
10 For which club was Darren excelling during 2000/2001?
11 In how many major cup finals did Les Sealey guard United's net?
12 Alex Ferguson signed him for United on two occasions. What was the combined total of his fees?
13 From which club was he acquired by the Red Devils, at first on loan, in December 1989?
14 Who were Sealey's employers prior to his return to Old Trafford in January 1993?
15 Who was axed to make way for Les in a Wembley replay in 1990?
16 In another final, Sealey's knee was cut to the bone. Who were the opponents that day?
17 Les saved a penalty in the 1991 European Cup Winners' Cup Final. True or false?
18 With which club did Les begin his professional career?
19 On what occasion did Sealey make his farewell senior appearance for United?
20 Apart from the Reds, with which club did Les contest a Wembley final?

Pot Luck - 77 *(see page 243)*
1 Norwegian. 2 French. 3 Danish. 4 Dutch. 5 Swedish. 6 Czech. 7 Italian. 8 Yugoslavian.
9 Dutch. 10 Australian. 11 Ukrainian. 12 Dutch. 13 Norwegian. 14 Dutch. 15 Tobagan.
16 Danish. 17 Norwegian. 18 Dutch. 19 French. 20 Norwegian.

ANSWERS

Answers – see page 244

1 Against which Greeks did United begin their defence of the Cup Winners' Cup in September 1991?

2 Who made his European debut between the Reds' posts in the Apostolos Nikaidis Stadium?

3 Which slim Lancastrian midfielder wore United's number-11 shirt?

4 Two goals in two extra-time minutes at Old Trafford settled the tie. Brian McClair got the second, but who notched the first?

5 Which future West Ham forward scored twice as United crashed 3-0 in Spain to Atletico Madrid in the second round?

6 Back in Manchester, whose strike gave the Reds early hope before the game petered out in a 1-1 draw?

7 United and Torpedo Moscow failed to score a goal in 210 minutes of open play over two legs the 1992/93 UEFA Cup. True or false?

8 By what score did United lose the penalty shoot-out?

9 In which Hungarian city did the Reds kick their first ball in the Europe's main club competition when they re-entered in September 1993?

10 Which feisty new signing struck twice as United beat Honved 3-2?

11 Who had scored United's previous goal in European Champions Cup football?

12 Which Frenchman, who became one of the Reds' most famous number sevens, was wearing the number-nine shirt in Hungary?

13 Whose two goals emphasised United's superiority over Honved in the second leg?

14 The Reds played host to which Turks in the first leg of the second round in October 1994?

15 Who scored what was to prove his last goal in European football to give United an early lead?

16 What was the score with only ten minutes of that match remaining?

17 Who scored the final goal of that dramatic encounter?

18 What record did that preserve?

19 What did banners proclaim as United arrived at Istanbul airport for the second leg?

20 What was the score in Istanbul as United went out on the away-goals rule?

Answers - see page 241

Name the nationalities of these Red Devils past and present:

1   Ole Gunnar Solskjaer.
2   William Prunier.
3   Johnny Sivebaek.
4   Jaap Stam.
5   Jesper Blomqvist.
6   Karel Poborsky
7   Massimo Taibi.
8   Nikola Jovanovic.
9   Jordi Cruyff.
10 Mark Bosnich.
11 Andrei Kanchelskis.
12 Ruud van Nistelrooy.
13 Henning Berg.
14 Arnold Muhren.
15 Dwight Yorke.
16 Jesper Olsen.
17 Erik Nevland.
18 Raimond van der Gouw.
19 Mikael Silvestre.
20 Ronny Johnsen.

Answers - see page 242

1   When did Matt Busby become one of the first winners of the Manager of the Year award?

2   Which Italian club once attempted to woo Matt away from Old Trafford?

3   Which world-class striker did Matt make repeated attempts to sign in 1967 and 1968?

4   Which international centre-half was targeted by Busby in the summer of 1966?

5   What prevented Matt from emigrating to the United States as a teenager?

6   How many times did Busby's United finish as Championship runners-up?

7   What was the Reds' lowest finishing position during Sir Matt's reign?

8   Which chum of Matt Busby's managed the Manchester City side which pipped United to the title in 1967/68?

9   Who did Matt Busby persuade not to resign, soon after his fellow manager had started work for a rival club?

10 Who was the famous scout who first put Matt Busby in touch with Manchester United towards the end of the Second World War?

11 Who was United's club secretary when Matt Busby became manager?

12 Who said: 'Matt will seek the board's advice, ponder over it, then go away and do precisely as he wants.'?

13 Who was known as Matt's first and most important recruit?

14 Which former boxer and prominent Manchester nightclub proprietor was a close friend of Busby?

15 What was the name of the Manchester nightclub which was a favourite haunt of Matt and his players in the 1950s and 1960s?

16 Matt Busby was once approached with an offer to manage Manchester City. True or false?

17 Who was Matt's friend and rival in charge of Wolverhampton Wanderers, the club with whom United vied for supremacy in the 1950s?

18 Which club tried and failed to lure Matt Busby to Spain in the mid 1950s?

19 What's the name of the road which runs past Old Trafford?

20 How many times did Matt lead United to FA Cup final victory?

Answers - see page 247

1 Paul enlisted with United during which close season?
2 Which might-have-been pig farmer joined that same summer?
3 For which club would Paul have played had he remained in his birthplace?
4 As it was, Parker began his professional career with which employers?
5 What ground was his home base before Old Trafford?
6 How much did United pay to sign the versatile defender?
7 For what club was Paul operating when he made his England debut?
8 How many full appearances did he make for his country?
9 In which position did Parker play the majority of his outings as a Red Devil?
10 Against which opponents did Paul score his only goal in 105 League games for United?
11 He managed one in the FA Cup, too. Who were his victims?
12 Paul won three title medals at Old Trafford. True or false?
13 Which Brazilian did Paul man-mark when the Reds faced Barcelona at Old Trafford in October 1994?
14 Paul helped England to what stage of the 1990 World Cup tournament?
15 Past 'keeper was beaten by Paul's deflection at a crucial free-kick as England were knocked out?
16 How many full international caps did Parker earn after joining United?
17 Who was Paul Parker freed to join in the summer of 1996?
18 For how many clubs did Paul make League appearances during 1996/97?
19 One of them was in Yorkshire. Name it.
20 With which club did Paul bow out of League football?

Season 2000/2001 - 3 *(see page 247)*

ANSWERS

1 Ole Gunnar Solskjaer. 2 Ole Gunnar Solskjaer. 3 In 1989, to Aston Villa. 4 Stuart Pearce. 5 Teddy Sheringham. 6 Gary Walsh. 7 Luke Chadwick. 8 Gary Neville. 9 Juan Pablo Angel. 10 100-1 on. 11 Paolo di Canio's. 12 Andrew Cole. 13 Andrew Cole. 14 Everton's Steve Watson. 15 Jimmy Floyd Hasselbaink. 16 Gianfranco Zola. 17 Aimar. 18 Dwight Yorke. 19 5-1 to United. 20 Roy Keane.

Answers - see page 248

1   Where is United's matchday park-and-ride scheme based?
2   Decipher the anagram: RAIDEN LAKESHICKNS.
3   Which United keeper conceded a goal after 60 seconds of his League debut without having touched the ball?
4   In what season did that game take place?
5   Where was that game played?
6   Who won?
7   What nationality was the unfortunate goalkeeper?
8   How many times was he capped by his country?
9   Who took over in goal for the injured Alex Stepney at Birmingham in August 1975?
10 Which man who scored against Gary Bailey in 1978 had netted against Bailey's dad, Ipswich's Roy, some 15 years earlier?
11 For which club was that man playing on both occasions?
12 Who preceded Raimond van der Gouw as United's oldest post-war goalkeeper?
13 What is the name of the television channel dedicated to the Red Devils?
14 To what part of the world did United jet for their summer tour in 2001?
15 Who was United's Football In The Community Officer during 2000/2001?
16 Who was heading the Manchester United Radio team during that same campaign?
17 What is the name of United's themed video restaurant?
18 In what year was the Manchester United Development Association launched?
19 Whose autobiography was entitled 'Matt, United and Me'?
20 Who was the first black player to win a regular place in the United team?

1 Who scored twice as United overcame the challenge of ever-improving Ipswich at Old Trafford?

2 Who broke the deadlock of a tight Boxing Day contest at Villa Park?

3 When was the last time United lost on Boxing Day?

4 Who deflected a Phil Neville cross into West Ham's goal on New Year's Day?

5 Luke Chadwick set up the winner for which fellow substitute in United's first FA Cup tie since the 1999 final?

6 Which former Red Devil made Teddy Sheringham's breakthrough goal at Valley Parade?

7 Who scored his first senior goal for United that day?

8 Whose deft backheel nudged the Reds in front at home to Villa in January?

9 Which expensive South American was making his Villa entrance that day?

10 After that match what odds were major bookies quoting for United's title chances?

11 Whose slickly taken goal at Old Trafford dumped United out of the FA Cup?

12 Three men were sent off when the Reds met the Black Cats on Wearside. Who was the dismissed Red Devil?

13 Who was the only man to score in that stormy encounter at the Stadium of Light?

14 A scrappy Old Trafford meeting with Everton was settled by one goal. Who got the final touch?

15 At Stamford Bridge in February, who made it three goals in three matches against United during the season?

16 Which Chelsea man netted brilliantly from near the touchline, only for the referee to give a throw-in?

17 Which newly-signed Argentinian was outstanding for Valencia against United at the Mestalla Stadium?

18 Who grabbed a hat-trick as United annihilated Arsenal 6-1 at Old Trafford?

19 What was the score at the interval?

20 Who did the hat-trick hero set up to volley United's fourth?

ANSWERS

Paul Parker *(see page 245)*

1 1991. **2** Peter Schmeichel. **3** West Ham United. **4** Fulham. **5** Loftus Road. **6** £1.7 million. **7** QPR. **8** 19 appearances. **9** Right-back. **10** Tottenham Hotspur. **11** Reading. **12** False, he won two. **13** Romario. **14** Semi-finals. **15** Peter Shilton. **16** Three. **17** Derby County. **18** Four. **19** Sheffield United. **20** Chelsea.

Answers - see page 246

1   Who nodded the game's only goal for Everton?
2   Whose shot against the Reds' crossbar set up the chance?
3   Which Welsh warrior was playing his last game for United?
4   Who replaced hamstrung Steve Bruce at half-time?
5   Who switched into Bruce's central defensive role?
6   Who was Everton's unused substitute?
7   Which Swedish ex-Gunner starred for the Toffees?
8   This was Paul Ince's last senior game for the Red Devils. True or false?
9   Who was the Everton manager?
10 Which Everton substitute would rise from the bench again to face United at Wembley four years later?
11 Which United star was unable to play because he was cup-tied?
12 Which Red Devil was banned at the time of the final?
13 Who did Everton defeat in their semi-final?
14 What disappointment had United suffered six days earlier?
15 Who was the veteran Welshman between the Everton posts?
16 Who did that 'keeper deny with a brilliant double save late in the game?
17 What United man saw his header turned on to the Everton bar?
18 What tag did the Goodison boss attach to his combative midfield?
19 Defeat meant that United had not lifted a major trophy for the first time since which season?
20 Who were Everton's shirt sponsors?

Answers - see page 251

1 With which club did Lee Sharpe narrowly escape relegation in 2000/2001?
2 Which former team-mate of Lee's was not so lucky, his team going down on the day that Sharpe's survived?
3 Which former United marksman scored a quarter of a century of League goals during 2000/2001?
4 Which side did those goals help to rise from the Second Division?
5 Which former United keeper accepted the challenge of competing for a place with Cudicini and De Goey at a Premiership club in the spring of 2001?
6 Decipher the anagram: TRIMNA HACBUN.
7 With which club did Michael Appleton make the 2000/2001 Division One play-offs?
8 How much did United bank when they sold Northern Ireland international stopper Pat McGibbon in March 1997?
9 Who bought him?
10 Which former United stalwart was guiding the fortunes of a club in the 2000/2001 Second Division play-offs?
11 Where was he in charge?
12 Which older ex-Red suffered the trauma of relegation that season?
13 Who famously mentioned prawn sandwiches and United supporters in the same breath during 2000/2001?
14 Who was the last major purchase made by Ron Atkinson as United boss?
15 Ron made three major overseas signing during his term as Reds manager. Name the first, from Holland?
16 The second was a fleet-footed Danish winger blessed with a scorching shot. Who was he?
17 Who was the last of the trio, a cultured utility man who failed to adjust to the English game?
18 Who was Alex Ferguson's first major acquisition from overseas?
19 And who was his second?
20 Who was the sole foreigner introduced during the Dave Sexton years?

Reds in Europe 57/8 - Part 2 *(see page 251)*
1 Dennis Viollet. 2 Ernie Taylor. 3 Cesare Maldini. 4 AC Milan won 4-0. 5 Pepe Schiaffino. 6 Ronnie Cope. 7 Real Madrid. 8 True. 9 Captain James Thain. 10 Stan Crowther. 11 Walter Crickmer. 12 Bert Whalley. 13 Trainer Tom Curry. 14 23. 15 Frank Swift. 16 Jack Crompton. 17 Les Olive. 18 Harold Hardman. 19 True. 20 He was on England duty.

ANSWERS

Answers - see page 252

1   Against which country did Duncan Edwards make his full international entrance?
2   In what year did he win his first full cap?
3   Who were the opponents when he scored a 17-minute hat-trick after switching to centre-forward for England under-23s?
4   What twin memorials to Duncan Edwards exist in a church in his home town?
5   Duncan lived for two weeks after the Munich crash. How many players had died before him?
6   How old was Duncan when he first enlisted with the Reds as an amateur?
7   Against which champion club did Duncan make his European Cup entrance?
8   On which ground did that game take place?
9   Against which club did Duncan score the only goal of an FA Cup fifth round clash in February 1957?
10 That was Edwards' only FA Cup goal. True or false.
11 Against which country did Duncan score twice and hit a post while playing for England in 1956?
12 How many goals did Duncan score for his country?
13 Who did he face in his final full international, in November 1957?
14 What cousin of Duncan's excelled for Bolton Wanderers and later won a title medal with Everton?
15 Which future Manchester City boss tipped off Matt Busby about the schoolboy prodigy Duncan Edwards?
16 Under which skipper did Duncan play nearly all his games for Manchester United?
17 Who was his captain when on England duty?
18 Against which seaside club did Duncan score his first senior goal for United, on New Year's Day 1955?
19 In which position did the versatile teenager play ten games towards the end of 1954/55?
20 In April 1955, Duncan became the first full international to do what?

Pot Luck - 80 *(see page 252)*

ANSWERS

1 Gavin McCann's. 2 Roy Keane's. 3 Henning Berg. 4 Ole Gunnar Solskjaer. 5 They lost 2-1. 6 Peter Reid. 7 Division One. 8 Eric Cantona's. 9 Phil Gray's. 10 Paul Scholes. 11 Andrew Cole. 12 Kevin Moran. 13 Frank Stapleton. 14 Nikola Jovanovic. 15 Dave Sexton. 16 Manchester City. 17 George Best. 18 Denis Law. 19 Charlie Hurley's. 20 Pat Crerand.

Answers - see page 249

1 Against all odds, United beat AC Milan 2-1 in the first leg of the semi-final. Who levelled for the Reds after the visitors had gone ahead?

2 Who scored United's late winner from the spot?

3 Which future manager of Italy conceded the penalty?

4 What was the outcome of the second leg in Milan?

5 Who was Milan's star Uruguayan centre-forward?

6 Which centre-half toiled valiantly against Milan's sharpshooter in both legs?

7 Who went on to win the final between AC Milan and Real Madrid?

8 United would not play another game in the European Cup until 1965. True or false?

9 What was the name of the pilot of the plane which crashed at Munich?

10 Who was the first inheritor of the late, great Duncan Edwards' number-six shirt?

11 Among the Munich victims was the United club secretary. Who was he?

12 United lost their coach, too, a former Old Trafford player. Name him.

13 Who was the third United official to perish in the crash?

14 In all, how many people lost their lives in the tragedy?

15 Among the victims was which former England goalkeeper?

16 In the wake of the accident, which former Reds keeper was appointed club trainer?

17 Another one-time goalkeeper became the club secretary, then later a member of the board. Name him.

18 Who was the Old Trafford club chairman at the time of the disaster?

19 United were offered a place in the 1958/59 European Cup but were forbidden to enter by the English football authorities. True or false?

20 Why did Bobby Charlton miss both legs of the 1958 European Cup semi-final?

Answers - see page 250

1 Whose second-minute goal put Sunderland in front at the Stadium of Light in December 1999?

2 Whose shot set United on the road to recovery after Sunderland had doubled their lead?

3 A rare goal from which defender capped the Reds' 4-0 hammering of Sunderland at Old Trafford in April 2000?

4 Two men netted twice as United sunk Sunderland 5-0 at Old Trafford in December 1996. One was Eric Cantona, who was the other?

5 How did United fare on their last senior visit to Roker Park in the spring of 1997?

6 Who was the Sunderland manager?

7 What division were Sunderland in when United met them in the FA Cup on their way to the 'double double' in 1995/96?

8 Whose late equaliser enabled the Reds to escape with a draw in the cup meeting at Old Trafford?

9 Whose goal gave Sunderland a half-time lead in the Roker replay?

10 Which player equalised for United?

11 Who kept United on course for Wembley with a majestic 90th-minute header?

12 Which Irishman scored twice as United beat Sunderland 2-1 at Old Trafford in February 1984?

13 Another Irishman registered his first League double for United in their 5-1 defeat of the Wearsiders in November 1981. Name him.

14 Which Yugoslavian scored his first senior goal in English football against Sunderland at Old Trafford in August 1980?

15 Who was the United manager at that time?

16 United lost to Sunderland on the last day of 1967/68 and conceded the Championship to which club?

17 Who scored for the Red Devils in that 2-1 reverse at Old Trafford?

18 Which United player netted a hat-trick at home to Sunderland during 1968/69?

19 Whose own goal gave United a point at Roker Park earlier in that season?

20 Decipher the anagram: APT REDNARC.

Answers - see page 255

1 How many FA Cup semi-final games did United contest with Oldham Athletic in the 1990s?

2 What was the venue for the 3-3 draw between the two clubs in April 1990?

3 Who scored an early goal for the Latics?

4 Who equalised with his fourth goal in FA Cup semi-finals?

5 An England international midfielder put United in front with 18 minutes left. Name him.

6 Who was the Oldham player whose goal ensured extra time?

7 United regained the lead early in added time through which costly signing?

8 Whose goal earned a replay?

9 Who put the Reds ahead in the replay?

10 Which former Old Trafford favourite tied the scores after 81 minutes?

11 Which son of a policeman supplied United's extra-time winner?

12 Who remained manager of Oldham when the two clubs met at the same stage of the competition four years later?

13 Where did the Lancashire rivals fight out their 1-1 draw in 1994?

14 After a barren 90 minutes, whose goal broke the deadlock?

15 Who netted one of the most famous goals in United history to secure a replay?

16 Which teenaged substitute played a vital part in the build-up to that explosive equaliser?

17 Whose early goal settled United's nerves in the replay?

18 Who added a spectacular second after a quarter of an hour?

19 Who was the only man to score two goals in the tie?

20 What was the final margin of United's victory?

Answers - see page 256

1 What is Ronny Johnsen's nationality?
2 From which Turkish club was he recruited in the summer of 1996?
3 How much did United pay to sign him?
4 Ronny's first goal for United came in the 1997 Charity Shield against which opponents?
5 Which Londoners were on the receiving end of his first League goal for United in March 1998?
6 Johnsen scored twice against Nottingham Forest on Boxing Day 1998. Who was the Forest 'keeper that day?
7 Ronny has played senior football in central defence, at full-back, in midfield and as a centre-forward. True or false?
8 David May and Henning Berg were signed from the same club. Which one?
9 What was David's fee?
10 And Henning's?
11 Which of the pair has scored for United in a Championship clincher?
12 Who were the opponents on that afternoon at the Riverside?
13 Who won a title medal in 1994/95, May or Berg?
14 From how many FA Cup Finals has David May emerged victorious?
15 Henning has captained which Scandinavian country's football team?
16 To which club was Berg loaned, then sold, during 2000/2001?
17 To which manager was David May bidding farewell when he signed for United?
18 How many Premiership medals has Henning earned?
19 David's sole goal in European competition opened the scoring in a Champions League quarter-final against which opponents?
20 Which former United colleague took David on loan during 1999/2000, only for May's ongoing injury jinx to halt his progress with the borrowing club?

Early Days - 3 *(see page 256)*

ANSWERS

1 Three. 2 1921/22. 3 John Chapman. 4 Sacked for unspecified improper conduct.
5 Clarence Hilditch. 6 Leicester City. 7 Leeds United. 8 True. 9 Middlesbrough.
10 James Gibson. 11 1950. 12 Walter Crickmer. 13 One. 14 Millwall. 15 Matt Busby.
16 Scott Duncan. 17 Gigg Lane, Bury. 18 George Mutch. 19 Walter Winterbottom.
20 United were relegated.

Answers - see page 253

Name the clubs with which these players, Red Devils all, won League title or FA Cup medals, or both, away from Old Trafford:

1 Mark Hughes
2 George Graham
3 Jeff Whitefoot
4 Henning Berg
5 John Connelly
6 Garth Crooks
7 Stan Crowther
8 Colin Gibson
9 Johnny Giles
10 Viv Anderson
11 Ernie Taylor
12 Joe Jordan
13 Terry Gibson
14 Jim McCalliog
15 Gordon Strachan
16 Stuart Pearson
17 Frank Stapleton
18 Tommy Jackson
19 Peter Beardsley
20 Gordon McQueen

Answers - see page 254

1 Between the wars, United were relegated from the top flight on how many occasions?

2 In which term did the first of these demotions take place?

3 Which manager presided over this crushing setback?

4 What was his ultimate Old Trafford fate?

5 Who became player-manager in October 1926?

6 United returned to the top flight as Second Division runners-up in 1924/25. Who topped the table?

7 United finished nine points adrift of which club at the bottom of the First Division in 1930/31?

8 The gate at Old Trafford for the final game of that calamitous term was below 4,000. True or false?

9 Ironically, the fans witnessed a thrilling 4-4 draw against which opponents?

10 Who was the benefactor who saved the club from oblivion when the cash ran out in December 1931?

11 When did that generous man step down as United's chairman?

12 Which club secretary was placed in charge of team affairs for 1931/32?

13 By how many points did United avoid slipping into the Third Division in 1933/34?

14 Who did the Reds condemn to go down instead of them by beating them in the final game of that season?

15 Who captained Manchester City to FA Cup glory in the same term that United reached that lowest ebb?

16 Who guided the Reds to the Second Division crown in 1935/36?

17 On what ground did they clinch that trophy?

18 Who was United's top scorer in that uplifting campaign?

19 Which future England manager made his England debut for United in November 1936?

20 What happened at season's end?

1 Who was Manchester United's assistant manager when they lifted the European Cup?
2 In how many previous European finals had the Red Devils played?
3 Which United hero skipped the homecoming to Manchester to fulfil a golfing obligation?
4 Who pocketed a medal as United's non-playing substitute?
5 Which Portuguese marksman wasted a late match-winning opportunity by blasting the ball instead of placing it?
6 Who was the goalkeeper who pulled off the save of the match to keep United in contention?
7 Manchester United were the first British club to lift the European Cup. True or false?
8 Which full-back played in the first leg of the semi-final but missed the final?
9 Which BBC commentator covered United's European Cup games all season, but gave way to Kenneth Wolstenholme for the final?
10 Who was the right-back tormented all evening by United's on-form left winger?
11 Who refereed the final?
12 Which player's father was a member of United's coaching staff?
13 Which horse won the Derby on the same day as United's triumph?
14 Which creative Scottish midfielder ran himself into the ground in United's cause?
15 Who was Benfica's diminutive international left-winger?
16 Who was the keeper who had to pick the ball out of his net four times?
17 Who was United's trainer on the big night?
18 Which United and England hero was dubbed 'The Bad One' by Benfica fans?
19 What did Matt Busby sing at the after-match banquet?
20 Who took the corner which led to United's third goal?

Eric Cantona - 3 (see page 259)
ANSWERS
1 United's unbeaten home record in Europe. 2 David Ginola. 3 The 1993 League Cup Final against Aston Villa. 4 1994. 5 1996. 6 Inter Milan. 7 Liverpool. 8 None. 9 Leeds United in December 1996. 10 Ewood Park in April 1997. 11 Derby County in April 1997. 12 Wimbledon. 13 1987. 14 For insulting the national coach. 15 West Ham United. 16 St James' Park. 17 Arsenal. 18 Loftus Road. 19 False. 20 Once.

Answers - see page 260

1 Which Norwegian marksman made his senior entrance for the Red Devils in a League Cup visit to Ipswich in October 1997?
2 Which blond defender, who captained his country at a succession of junior levels, enjoyed his first senior outing for United on the same night?
3 The Reds' third senior debutant in that Portman Road tie was already a full international midfielder. Name him.
4 Which future England keeper was in goal for Ipswich that night?
5 What was the result of the game?
6 Who scored on his League debut at Ipswich in September 1994, only three days after netting on his senior entrance in the League Cup?
7 What was the outcome of the League encounter?
8 Who scored twice for Ipswich that day?
9 Which relatively recent arrival scored five times against Ipswich at Old Trafford in March 1995?
10 Who added an almost unremarked-upon double for the Red Devils that day?
11 What was the result of the match?
12 Ipswich were relegated at the end of that season. True or false?
13 Who was the Ipswich boss at that time?
14 What award did that same fellow win in the spring of 2001?
15 United's 2-1 victory at Portman Road on Mayday 1994 took them to the verge of a second successive League title, but who put Ipswich in front?
16 Who grabbed United's winner just after the interval?
17 Which former Liverpool and Scotland midfielder was enjoying his second lengthy successful spell with Ipswich at the time?
18 Which motor racing icon died in an accident on that same Mayday?
19 What was the result when United visited Portman Road in the January before their first title triumph under Alex Ferguson?
20 Decipher the anagram: SOMANIS BITIA.

Answers - see page 257

1 What record did Eric preserve with a late goal against Galatasaray at Old Trafford in October 1993?

2 Who did Cantona blame for the mistake which meant France did not qualify for the 1994 World Cup Finals?

3 What was the only cup final in which Eric finished on the losing side for United?

4 In what year was Eric Cantona voted player of the year by his fellow professionals?

5 When did he receive the writers' Footballer of the Year accolade?

6 Which Italian giants attempted to sign Cantona in 1995?

7 In the autumn of 1995, against which bitter rivals did Eric score on his return from lengthy suspension?

8 How many hat-tricks did Eric score for United in senior competition?

9 Against which opponents did Eric score his last penalty for United?

10 His last League goal for the Red Devils was netted on which ground?

11 Eric's final League goal at Old Trafford could not avert defeat against which team?

12 Who were the victims of Cantona's spectacular FA Cup volley in February 1994?

13 In what year did Eric win his first full cap?

14 Why was Cantona once banned from the French team for a year?

15 Who were the visitors to Old Trafford when Eric made his farewell Premiership appearance?

16 In March 1996 Eric transformed the title race with a goal against the League leaders at which ground?

17 That month the Frenchman supplied the only goal in two more crucial 1-0 victories. One was against Spurs, but who were the other victims?

18 During that March, too, he equalised with a last-minute header at which London ground?

19 Eric won a European Cup winner's medal with Marseille. True or false?

20 How many times did Alex Ferguson bring on Eric Cantona from the substitutes' bench?

ANSWERS

European Cup Final 1968 - Part Two (see page 257)
1 Jimmy Murphy. 2 None. 3 Bill Foulkes. 4 Jimmy Rimmer. 5 Eusebio. 6 Alex Stepney. 7 False, it was Celtic. 8 Francis Burns. 9 David Coleman. 10 Adolfo. 11 Concetto Lo Bello. 12 John Aston's. 13 Sir Ivor. 14 Pat Crerand. 15 Antonio Simoes. 16 Henrique. 17 Jack Crompton. 18 Nobby Stiles. 19 What A Wonderful World. 20 Bobby Charlton.

Answers - see page 258

1 Against which Maltese part-timers did United start their most glorious European campaign?

2 Denis Law netted twice in a 4-0 home victory. Who chipped in with another brace?

3 What was the result of the return leg in the Gzira Stadium?

4 Which full-back shone in midfield when United beat Sarajevo 2-1 at home?

5 George Best scored one of United's goals that night, but who supplied the other?

6 Sarajevo finished with ten men after Prljaca was sent off for a tackle on which player?

7 Who replaced the injured Denis Law for the home leg of the quarter-final against Gornik Zabrze?

8 Whose narrow-angled shot caused the Florenski own goal which gave United the lead?

9 Whose cute backheel gave the Reds an invaluable late second goal?

10 Who was the brilliant Pole whose goal gave his side a 1-0 victory in Katowice?

11 Which Scot was called in to play a defensive midfield role in Poland?

12 United triumphed by a single goal in the first leg of the semi-final against Real Madrid at Old Trafford. Who scored it?

13 Which great Scot was playing his last game of the European campaign because of a knee injury?

14 Another Scot, who had played in every European match that season, would not be selected for the next two matches. Name him.

15 Which Real Madrid veteran put the Spaniards 2-0 up in the second leg?

16 Whose own goal restored overall parity for United, albeit briefly?

17 Who gave Real what looked likely to be a decisive 3-1 lead by the interval?

18 Who nudged United level on aggregate with 19 minutes to go?

19 Whose inspired dash down the right flank set up the winning goal?

20 Who side-footed the most important goal of his career to make it 3-3 on the night and book the Reds' final place?

Answers - see page 263

1 Whose goal secured United's most recent home League victory over Norwich?
2 The Reds most recent visit to Carrow Road produced what outcome?
3 Which TV pundit incurred the wrath of Alex Ferguson for his remarks about Eric Cantona following United's FA Cup win at Carrow Road in January 1994?
4 Who netted the Reds' opener in that 2-0 victory?
5 Who scored the first goal of United's 1993 season against Norwich?
6 Who played for the Reds that day because of injury to Eric Cantona – and scored?
7 What was the result when United met the Canaries at Old Trafford in December 1993?
8 Whose goal against Norwich in December 1992 was his fourth straight in the league?
9 Had Norwich beaten United at Carrow Road in April 1993, the Canaries would have moved to the Premiership summit with five games to play. True or false?
10 What was the result of that match?
11 Who was top after the Norwich-United encounter?
12 Three goals in eight first-half minutes gave the Reds control at home to Norwich in September 1991. Who supplied the opener?
13 A double by which player secured United's 3-1 away victory the following spring?
14 What was the score when Norwich and United met in the fifth round of the FA Cup in February 1991?
15 Who scored the winning goal?
16 Who netted twice against his former employers as the Reds left Carrow Road with three points in March 1991?
17 Which England international made his United entrance at home to Norwich in August 1989?
18 The result was not a happy one for the Old Trafford faithful. What was it?
19 Between March 1988 and January 1990, United lost five successive League games to Norwich. True or false?
20 Decipher the anagram: NADMORI WEGNURVADO.

ANSWERS

Ray Wilkins *(see page 263)*
1 84 caps. 2 38 caps. 3 19 years old. 4 1986/87. 5 Chelsea. 6 None. 7 Dave Sexton.
8 £825,000. 9 The FA Cup in 1983. 10 Bryan Robson. 11 A fractured cheekbone.
12 The Crab. 13 Because he made so many square passes. 14 Ten times. 15 2-1 to United. 16 AC Milan. 17 £1.5 million. 18 Graeme Souness. 19 QPR. 20 Leyton Orient.

Answers – see page 264

1 Who scored twice in United's opener, a 2-2 home draw with Birmingham City?
2 Which youngster made two appearances at centre-half?
3 Which future Old Trafford boss showed promise as Duncan Edwards' deputy?
4 Which goalkeeper made his sole senior appearance for United, at Blackpool in October?
5 How far ahead of the nearest opposition did United finish?
6 Who was manager of the runners-up?
7 Who was the side's top scorer in League games?
8 Nobody was ever-present but one man played 40 times. Who was he?
9 A reserve full-back who would die at Munich made half a dozen appearances. What was his name?
10 Which Lancashire cricketer played six times at right-half?
11 Which goalkeeper who would go on to serve the club as chief scout enjoyed his only two senior outings?
12 Which teenager stood in for the injured Tommy Taylor in the last three games of the League campaign?
13 That rookie centre-forward scored in each of those three matches. True or false?
14 How many League games did United go without losing at the start of the season?
15 How many times had the Reds been beaten by the end of term?
16 Who made his senior debut during 1956/57 and went on to win more than 100 England caps?
17 United were involved in no 0-0 draws. True or false?
18 At which ground did the Reds attract their lowest League gate?
19 Who did United beat twice over Easter?
20 How many previous titles had Matt Busby won at Old Trafford?

Answers - see page 261

1 Ray Wilkins rides high in the list of England cap-winners. How many does he have in his collection?

2 How many of those were garnered in his Red Devil days?

3 How old was Ray when he made his full international debut?

4 In what season did his England career end?

5 With what club did Ray play his first League game?

6 What major domestic honours did he lift with that club?

7 With which former club boss was he reunited when he arrived at Old Trafford?

8 How much did United pay for this sweet-passing midfielder?

9 Ray helped United to secure which trophy?

10 Who succeeded Ray as both United and England skipper?

11 What serious injury caused Wilkins to lose those jobs?

12 With what uncharitable nickname was Ray saddled by Ron Atkinson?

13 What inspired the United manager to choose that tag?

14 How many times did Wilkins captain his country?

15 What was the score against Brighton after Wilkins netted a sublime 25-yard curler in the 1983 FA Cup Final?

16 To which team was Ray sold in June 1984?

17 How much money did his transfer net for the Reds?

18 Who was his boss when he entered Scottish football in 1978?

19 Which Londoners did he play for in two spells, before going on to manage them?

20 For which League club did Ray make his final appearance during his 41st year?

Answers - see page 262

Name the clubs who signed these Welshmen after they left Old Trafford:

1 Colin Webster
2 Mark Hughes
3 Caesar Jenkyns
4 Jack Warner
5 Deiniol Graham
6 Kenny Morgans
7 Billy Meredith
8 Clayton Blackmore
9 Reg Hunter
10 Graham Moore
11 Mickey Thomas
12 Tom Jones
13 Wyn Davies
14 Tommy Bamford
15 Clive Griffiths
16 Ron Davies
17 Ray Bennion
18 Jonathan Clark
19 Alan Davies
20 Roy John

Title Trail 1956/57 *(see page 262)*
1 Dennis Viollet. 2 Ronnie Cope. 3 Wilf McGuinness. 4 Tony Hawksworth. 5 Eight points. 6 Jimmy Anderson of Spurs. 7 Liam Whelan. 8 Johnny Berry. 9 Geoff Bent. 10 Freddie Goodwin. 11 Gordon Clayton. 12 Alex Dawson. 13 True. 14 Twelve. 15 Six. 16 Bobby Charlton. 17 False, they drew 0-0 at home to Spurs. 18 The Valley (16,308). 19 Burnley. 20 Two.

Answers - see page 267

1 Who scored the only goal of the match as the Saints went marching in?
2 Which former Red Devil delivered the pass which created that crucial strike?
3 Who was the United keeper who dived unavailingly to repel the shot?
4 Which division were Southampton in at the time?
5 Who was the Saints' high-profile manager?
6 United's boss was no shrinking violet, either. Who was he?
7 Who would have received the trophy if United had won?
8 Which international full-back lifted the pot for Southampton?
9 Which sometimes controversial Welsh referee was in charge of proceedings?
10 Which reigning League champions did United overcome in the semi-final?
11 Which United marksman nodded against the Wembley woodwork when the scoresheet was blank?
12 Which Southampton star had served under the United manager at Stamford Bridge?
13 Who was the multi-capped West Countryman wearing the Saints' number eight shirt?
14 Who became United's first substitute in an FA Cup Final?
15 Who left the pitch to make way for that number-12?
16 What time-honoured promise did the United manager make after the match?
17 Where had the Reds finished in that campaign's title race?
18 Which London side finished one place above them?
19 Southampton wore a change strip. What colour were their shirts?
20 Which United star would pocket two FA Cup winner's medals over the course of the next four seasons with different clubs?

Answers - see page 268

1 Who ran from halfway before netting with a thunderbolt to help eject Liverpool from the League Cup in October 1990?

2 Which feisty Scot netted against United at Old Trafford on his debut for Liverpool in February 1991?

3 Who had replaced Kenny Dalglish as Liverpool boss by the time the sides met in 1991/92?

4 Which 19-year-old future England full-back made his debut for the Merseysiders in a goalless Old Trafford affair in October 1991?

5 Who netted his first goal for Liverpool in 24 matches against United as the Red Devils' title hopes died at Anfield in April 1992?

6 Who netted twice in the last 12 minutes to wipe out a Liverpool lead at Old Trafford in October 1992?

7 Whose header clinched a 2-1 victory at Anfield which lifted United to the top of the table in March 1993?

8 Whose free-kick put United 3-0 up at Anfield in January 1994?

9 Who scored two to pull Liverpool back to 3-2 at the interval?

10 Who completed the comeback by equalising for Liverpool with a header?

11 What were United's colours on that unforgettable night?

12 Whose glancing header claimed the points for United at Old Trafford on a tense night at Old Trafford in March 1994?

13 Who persisted in turning up Eric Cantona's collar to goad the Frenchman at Old Trafford in September 1994?

14 Whose own goal capped a Liverpool victory at Anfield in March 1995?

15 Who returned from exile to face Liverpool on 1 October 1995?

16 Who opened the scoring in the second minute?

17 Which Scouser rocked United with two high-quality finishes?

18 Who was felled by Jamie Redknapp to bring about the climactic penalty?

19 Whose two goals sunk United at Anfield in December 1995?

20 Which Liverpool marksman was credited with 13 goal-attempts in that match, but could do no better than hit the woodwork?

Answers - see page 265

1   Who scored twice on United's most recent League visit to the Hawthorns in the autumn of 1985?

2   What was the outcome of that contest?

3   Which Dane scored a hat-trick for United in the Old Trafford return in the following February?

4   Who scored against his former club when United won 2-1 at West Bromwich in September 1984?

5   Who scored three times in United's two League victories over WBA that term?

6   Which of West Bromwich Albion's so-called 'Three Degrees' was later to play for Manchester United?

7   What was the scoreline when United and Albion combined for eight goals at Old Trafford in December 1978?

8   A replay was needed when United and Albion last met in senior knockout competition. Which team prevailed?

9   In which season did those encounters take place?

10 Which former Red scored in Albion's 4-0 demolition of United in October 1976?

11 A former Villan scored United's winner when Birmingham City visited Old Trafford on New Year's Day 1986. Name him.

12 Who was the last man (a Scot) to score for United in both League meetings with Birmingham City?

13 In what season did that occur?

14 That term the Reds lost 5-1 at St Andrews and the Brummies were relegated at season's end. True or false?

15 Who scored a hat-trick for United on the opening day of 1977/78?

16 Which Irishman earned United the points at Birmingham in August 1975?

17 Who was the sole scorer when Birmingham visited Old Trafford in October 1973?

18 Who made a much-heralded comeback for the Red Devils that day?

19 Which Scot, who had cost a record fee for a Third Division player, opened his United account at home to Birmingham in October 1972?

20 Decipher the anagram: ORN NINTOKAS.

Answers - see page 266

1 Which United keeper started and finished an FA Cup Final between the posts and didn't let in a goal, yet went home with a loser's medal?

2 In what year did that bizarre occurrence take place?

3 Which 16-year-old goalkeeper was called from the crowd to be a United substitute during the 1956 FA Charity Shield game?

4 Who were the Red Devils' opponents that day?

5 Which England Schoolboys and Youth international keeper joined United on the same day as his young chum, Duncan Edwards?

6 Which future long-term secretary of the club had two First Division outings between United's posts during 1952/53?

7 Another England Youth international 'keeper made his only First Division appearance for the Reds at Blackpool in October 1956. Name him.

8 From which club did Matt Busby recruit Ray Wood in December 1949?

9 Eighteen-year-old Ray made an immediate senior debut against a club for which he had played as an amateur. Name that club.

10 In which season did Ray establish himself as United's first-choice keeper?

11 Ray made his England debut during the 1954 World Cup Finals. True or false?

12 Did Wood lose his place to Harry Gregg before or after he survived the Munich crash?

13 Ray departed to which Yorkshire club in December 1958?

14 In which season did David Gaskell earn an FA Cup winner's medal?

15 For which club did David play Rugby Union during a dispute with United in the mid 1960s?

16 Gaskell spent a loan stint with which non-League club while he was still a Red Devil?

17 With which Welsh club did David make a successful comeback from serial injuries in 1969/70?

18 Ray Wood finished his playing career with which club?

19 Which national team did Ray coach successfully between 1969 and 1972?

20 Who earned more title medals, Ray Wood or David Gaskell?

Answers - see page 271

1 Which of the Neville brothers was an unused substitute?
2 Who was switched unexpectedly from United's left flank to the right?
3 Injury deprived Bayern of which French World Cup-winner?
4 The Germans were missing a Brazilian marksman through a fitness problem. Name him.
5 Who was the Italian referee?
6 Who returned to the United side after missing the FA Cup Final through suspension?
7 Who was the big blond between Bayern's posts?
8 With whom did the Germans replace Alexander Zickler in the 71st minute?
9 Whose sublime chip bounced off a post and into Schmeichel's arms late in the second half?
10 With six minutes remaining on the clock, who rattled United's bar with an overhead kick?
11 Who was the only player on the pitch to receive a yellow card?
12 Had the game moved into extra-time, would the golden goal rule have operated?
13 Who glanced on the corner which set up the decisive goal?
14 Who pounded the ground, consumed with anguish, when the winner went in?
15 Which future Liverpool player finished on the losing side?
16 Who had Bayern beaten in their semi-final?
17 The final was played on the 90th anniversary of whose birth?
18 The attendance topped the 100,000 mark. True or false?
19 Who presented the massive hunk of silverware?
20 Who was the United captain on the club's most glorious night for 31 years?

Answers - see page 272

These Red Devils were all born blond. But can you say where they were born?

1 Jimmy Greenhoff

2 Ian Ure

3 Teddy Sheringham

4 Gary Bailey

5 Denis Law

6 Peter Schmeichel

7 Mark Robins

8 Peter Barnes

9 Albert Quixall

10 Jordi Cruyff

11 Jesper Olsen

12 Gordon McQueen

13 David May

14 John Curtis

15 Ashley Grimes

16 Alan Brazil

17 Henning Berg

18 Scott McGarvey

19 Arthur Graham

20 Luke Chadwick

ANSWERS

Bobby Charlton - 3 (see page 272)

1 Preston North End. 2 1974/75. 3 Wigan Athletic. 4 True. 5 Tom Finney. 6 Nat Lofthouse.
7 Jim Langley. 8 1984. 9 Three. 10 Tommy Taylor. 11 Four. 12 Steve Bloomer.
13 Stamford Bridge. 14 Sheffield United. 15 Celtic. 16 Verona. 17 Colombia. 18 The
Valley. 19 No. 20 2006.

270

Answers - see page 269

1 What tragic incident overshadowed the football when United faced Crystal Palace in the 1995 FA Cup semi-final?
2 United needed two games to win. Where were they played?
3 What unwanted record did the second clash create?
4 What was the half-time score in the first match?
5 Iain Dowie put Palace ahead. Who equalised with a free-kick?
6 Which future Spurs marksman regained the lead for Palace early in extra time?
7 Whose header saved the day for United?
8 Who was the Palace keeper who played 120 minutes with a severe hand injury?
9 Who was his replacement for the replay?
10 In the second match, which United man was sent off for stamping?
11 Which Palace player was given his marching orders for retaliating?
12 Who nodded the Red Devils into the lead?
13 Whose towering header clinched their place at Wembley?
14 In 1996, who set up Chelsea's opener for Ruud Gullit?
15 Who headed United's equaliser?
16 Four minutes later and Alex Ferguson's men were in front, courtesy of a clinical finish by which midfielder?
17 Which Chelsea man committed the error which led to the winning goal?
18 Who was United's unlikely saviour with a header off his own line?
19 United played with only one recognised central defender. Who was he?
20 Who was the losing Chelsea manager?

ANSWERS

European Cup Final 1999 - Part Two (see page 269)

1 Phil. 2 Ryan Giggs. 3 Bixente Lizarazu. 4 Giovane Elber. 5 Pierlugi Collina. 6 Denis Irwin. 7 Oliver Kahn. 8 Mehmet Scholl. 9 Mehmet Scholl's. 10 Carsten Jancker. 11 Stefan Effenberg. 12 Yes. 13 Teddy Sheringham. 14 Samuel Kuffour. 15 Markus Babbel. 16 Dynamo Kiev. 17 Sir Matt Busby's. 18 False, it was 91,000. 19 UEFA president Lennart Johanssen. 20 Peter Schmeichel.

1 Of which Lancashire club did Bobby become manager after leaving Manchester United?

2 During which season did Bobby come out of retirement to play for that club?

3 Bobby became acting manager of another Lancashire club in 1983. Which one?

4 Bobby spent four seasons in the early 1960s as a left-winger. True or false?

5 When Bobby became England's record scorer he succeeded two players who had netted 30 goals each. Name the one who hailed from Preston?

6 Who was the other England marksman whose tally was overhauled by Bobby?

7 Which Fulham full-back made his England debut in the same game as Bobby Charlton?

8 In what year did Bobby Charlton become a director of Manchester United?

9 In how many games did Bobby captain his country at full international level?

10 For which centre-forward, absent on England duty, did Bobby stand in when he made his League debut for United?

11 How many hat-tricks did Bobby score for England?

12 Before Bobby Charlton, only one player held simultaneous England scoring and appearance records. Name him.

13 On what ground did Bobby make his final League appearance for United?

14 Who beat the Red Devils 2-1 in Charlton's farewell League outing at Old Trafford?

15 Who were the opponents for Bobby's testimonial match at Old Trafford in September 1972?

16 Bobby's last first-team match as a Red Devil yielded a goal against which opponents in the Anglo-Italian Cup?

17 Against which country did Bobby score his final international goal?

18 On which ground did Bobby bag his first senior hat-trick for United, in 1957?

19 Did Bobby Charlton ever play in a League Cup Final?

20 Sir Bobby campaigned tirelessly, but unsuccessfully, for England to host the World Cup Finals in which year?

Answers - see page 275

1 In what season did United pay their final senior visit to the Victoria Ground before Stoke City relocated to the Britannia Stadium?

2 Who scored twice in that first leg of a League Cup encounter?

3 Who contributed a late aggregate winner in the second leg at Old Trafford?

4 Two men scored twice on Stoke's most recent League visit to Old Trafford. One was Mark Hughes; who was the other?

5 What was the result of that game in April 1985?

6 Who was the Stoke manager at that time?

7 Which Red Devil scored on his full League debut when United played host to Stoke on the last day of 1981/82?

8 Two future bosses of Stoke netted for United in both League meetings with the Potters during 1980/81. Who was the tall (ish) Scottish one?

9 And who was the short Scottish one?

10 A United centre-half struck twice against newly-promoted Stoke in a 4-0 home victory in September 1979. Name him.

11 Which future United player scored twice for Stoke against the Reds in a 3-3 draw at the Victoria Ground in May 1977?

12 United lost 4-0 at Stoke in their last game before being relegated to the Second Division in April 1974. True or false?

13 A future Old Trafford idol netted for Stoke during the 2-2 draw in the Potteries in April 1973. What's his name?

14 In what season, approximately three-quarters of the way through the 20th century, did Stoke meet United in an FA Cup quarter-final?

15 Who moved into the semi-finals following extra time in a replay?

16 Why did United play their 1971 home league game with WBA at Stoke?

17 Where had the Reds played their previous home fixture, against Arsenal?

18 Which future Stoke player scored FA Cup goals for United against the Potters as the Reds made FA Cup progress in both 1964/65 and 1966/67?

19 Who netted for the Red Devils on his senior debut at Stoke in March 1968?

20 Decipher the anagram: RALEK RYKPOSOB.

Answers - see page 276

1 Against which club did Roy Keane score his first European Cup goal for United?

2 Who had contributed United's previous goal in that competition?

3 In how many FA Cup Finals has Roy Keane competed?

4 How many times has he finished on the losing side?

5 Against which 'Old Lady' did Roy score with an inspirational header when the Reds were two goals down in their 1999 European Cup semi-final?

6 Why did Keane miss the final?

7 Which Leeds midfielder was Roy tackling when he received the injury which put him out for most of 1997/98?

8 What was the nature of that injury?

9 Who did Roy succeed as United's captain?

10 What was the first major trophy lifted by Keane as the Red Devils' skipper?

11 How long did Roy's appearance in the 1999 FA Cup Final last?

12 Who made the challenge which forced Roy to limp off early?

13 He was in too much pain to mount Wembley's 39 steps to receive the trophy. True or false?

14 The departure of which England star made Keane assume new responsibility and scale new heights of excellence in 1995/96?

15 In which campaign did Roy receive both major Player of the Year awards?

16 Against which Brazilian club did Roy net the winner in the 1999 World Club Championship?

17 What international landmark did Roy reach when the Republic met Cyprus in March 2001?

18 How did he celebrate during that World Cup qualifier?

19 Who was Roy's first full international manager?

20 In which season did Roy play for a club which was relegated?

Answers - see page 273

1 In which summer did Raimond van der Gouw join Manchester United?
2 What is his nationality?
3 From which club was he signed?
4 In which season did Rai play enough games to qualify for a title medal?
5 With what part-time occupation did he combine his football before joining United?
6 In what year was Van der Gouw born?
7 Rai is the oldest man to play senior soccer for the Red Devils since the war. True or false?
8 Who were the Reds' opponents when he performed brilliantly as a last-minute deputy for Peter Schmeichel in a European Cup semi-final?
9 In what season did Mark Bosnich make his senior debut for Manchester United?
10 For whom was he standing in on that occasion in April 1990?
11 Why did Mark leave Old Trafford in 1991?
12 With which club did he make a successful comeback in English football?
13 Under which manager did Bosnich finish as a title runner-up with that club?
14 What fee was involved when Mark returned to Old Trafford in 1999?
15 Bosnich starred in the first leg of a European Cup quarter-final against which opponents?
16 For which country has he won full international caps?
17 Which club was Bosnich freed to join in January 2001?
18 Massimo Taibi was signed from which Italian club in August 1999?
19 He excelled on his debut against Liverpool, but allowed a soft shot from which England forward to squirm agonisingly through his grasp in a later game?
20 Massimo returned to Italy, rebuilding his reputation with which club?

Answers - see page 274

Name the senior clubs for which these Irishmen first played after leaving Old Trafford:

1 Harry Gregg
2 Liam O'Brien
3 Johnny Giles
4 Frank Stapleton
5 Joe Carolan
6 George Best
7 Sammy McMillan
8 Don Givens
9 Pat McGibbon
10 Pat Dunne
11 Phil Mulryne
12 Mick Martin
13 Norman Whiteside
14 Ashley Grimes
15 Tom Sloan
16 Kevin Moran
17 Mal Donaghy
18 Tony Dunne
19 Trevor Anderson
20 David McCreery

Roy Keane - 2 *(see page 274)*

ANSWERS

1 Kispest-Honved. 2 Bobby Charlton. 3 Five. 4 Twice. 5 Juventus. 6 He was suspended. 7 Alf-Inge Haaland. 8 Cruciate ligament (knee). 9 Eric Cantona. 10 The 1998/99 Premiership. 11 Nine minutes. 12 Gary Speed. 13 False. 14 Paul Ince. 15 1999/2000. 16 Palmeiras. 17 His 50th cap. 18 By scoring twice. 19 Jack Charlton. 20 1992/93 (Nottingham Forest).

Answers - see page 279

1   Who scored the only goal of United's victory over Liverpool?
2   Who took the corner from which the decisive goal ensued?
3   Whose mistimed punch fell at the feet of the scorer?
4   Who might have scrambled a late equaliser?
5   What unique achievement did United's triumph complete?
6   Who was the winning skipper?
7   To what indignity was he subjected by Liverpool fans as he climbed Wembley's 39 steps to collect the trophy?
8   Who led the losers to collect their medals?
9   Who was United's second-half substitute for Andrew Cole?
10 Who played up front for Liverpool alongside Robbie Fowler?
11 Which Welsh veteran rose from the bench to make his farewell appearance for the Merseysiders?
12 Who was Liverpool's only non-playing substitute?
13 What colour suited Liverpool on the day before the final?
14 What colour were Liverpool's shirts for the match?
15 Who was United's non-playing club captain?
16 Which United midfielder was voted man of the match?
17 Who managed the Merseysiders on their progress to Wembley?
18 Who replaced his friend to join his brother on the pitch for the last minute?
19 Who was the referee?
20 Who was wearing United's number-12 shirt?

Answers - see page 280

1 Who supplied United's equaliser in the 1-1 Premiership draw at Old Trafford in January 2000?

2 Who scored for Arsenal, thus having netted in each of his three League outings against United to that point?

3 Who was sent off during United's 3-0 Highbury defeat in September 1998?

4 Which Arsenal and England midfielder scored in two 1-1 draws against United in 1991/92?

5 Before 2000/2001, had United ever faced Arsenal in European competition?

6 Which new signing watched from the stand as United won 1-0 at Highbury in November 1992?

7 Who scored the winner that day?

8 Whose wrist was in plaster as he rifled home a sensational winner at home to Arsenal in September 1993?

9 Which England winger twice put United in front in the 2-2 draw in March 1994?

10 Who was sent off during that passionate contest?

11 Which winger with a Presidential name lined up for Arsenal against United at Highbury in November 1994?

12 Whose uncharacteristic error allowed Dennis Bergkamp to score the only goal of the game at Highbury in November 1995?

13 Whose sublime volley earned United the win at home to Arsenal in March 1996?

14 Who was Arsenal's top League goalscorer in 1974/75 and 1975/76?

15 Which United boss never managed Arsenal but was a Highbury coach?

16 Whose own goal at Old Trafford in November 1996 ended United's run of three successive League defeats?

17 Who scored one and created another against his old team as United won at Highbury in February 1997?

18 David Platt was on United's books as a youngster. True or false?

19 Who started on United's left wing at home to the Gunners in March 1998?

20 Who tore a hamstring after charging upfield in the final minute of that 1-0 defeat?

Denis Law - *(see page 280)*

1 A hospital bed. **2** No. **3** Yes, with Huddersfield Town. **4** Norwich City. **5** 1964/65. **6** Four. **7** 41. **8** Ian Rush, 44. **9** 1940. **10** 28. **11** No. **12** False. **13** First. **14** Five. **15** Waterford. **16** Tony Book. **17** David Herd. **18** Ipswich Town. **19** Yes, for Manchester City in the 2-1 defeat by Wolves in 1974. **20** Number ten.

ANSWERS

1 Who was Fulham's chief operating officer when they met United in the fifth round of the FA Cup at Old Trafford in February 1999?

2 What was his next job?

3 Who scored the only goal of that FA Cup clash?

4 Where had the Fulham chief and the scorer worked together before?

5 Which popular marksman made his final senior appearance for United when they drew with Fulham in an FA Cup clash at Craven Cottage in January 1979?

6 Who scored for the Reds in that game, and settled the replay in United's favour?

7 Prior to 2001/2002, in what season did United last meet Fulham in League competition?

8 In what division was that?

9 Who netted twice as United forced a fine win at Craven Cottage that season?

10 Which future Fulham player scored three League goals for the Reds against the Cottagers during 1967/68?

11 Which Red Devil, and not an obvious candidate, netted against Fulham on two consecutive days in the title-hunting spring of 1967?

12 Fulham conceded a hat-trick to which United striker at Old Trafford in October 1965?

13 A future Fulham player contributed a goal to the Reds' 5-0 rout of the Londoners at Craven Cottage in March 1960. Name him.

14 A man destined for a high-profile move to Manchester scored for Fulham in their 4-1 defeat by United at Old Trafford in March 1965. Who was he?

15 Who was the Scottish international who struck a hat-trick against United in Fulham's 3-3 draw at Old Trafford in November 1959?

16 Two men scored for United against Fulham on both Christmas Day and Boxing Day 1951. Name the prolific spearhead who did so.

17 Now name the winger who equalled that feat.

18 Which Fulham star was Bobby Charlton's England captain during the late 1950s?

19 Which former United man was made manager of Fulham in 1997?

20 Decipher the anagram: RICHLEA TREORBS.

Answers - see page 278

1 From what vantage point did Denis watch the 1968 European Cup Final?
2 Did Denis Law ever suffer relegation with a Football League club?
3 Did he ever play in the Second Division?
4 Who were the opponents when Denis played his final League game for United in April 1973?
5 In which title-winning campaign did Law score in eight out of the opening nine matches?
6 In how many seasons was Denis United's leading scorer in League games?
7 How many FA Cup goals made Denis the competition's record scorer?
8 Who eventually passed Law's FA Cup tally?
9 During what Second World War year was Denis born?
10 Denis played 33 European games for United. How many goals did he score?
11 Has any Red Devil outstripped his record in continental competition?
12 Denis netted against Estudiantes in the 1968 World Club Championship. True or false?
13 Did Denis score United's first, second or third goal in the 1963 FA Cup Final?
14 How many hat-tricks did the Lawman notch in European competition?
15 His biggest European haul was four goals, at Old Trafford in September 1968. Who were the opposition?
16 Who was Denis Law's manager at the time of his retirement as a player?
17 With what fellow Scottish international did Denis form a potent dual spearhead at Old Trafford in the mid 1960s?
18 When Denis scored his first hat-trick as a Red Devil, he went on to bag four goals. Who were his victims in November 1962?
19 Did Denis ever play in a League Cup Final?
20 What number was on Denis Law's back in the 1963 FA Cup Final?

ANSWERS

All Guns Blazing - United v Arsenal - 4 *(see page 278)*
1 Teddy Sheringham. 2 Freddie Ljungberg. 3 Nicky Butt. 4 David Rocastle. 5 No. 6 Eric Cantona. 7 Mark Hughes. 8 Eric Cantona. 9 Lee Sharpe. 10 Eric Cantona. 11 Jimmy Carter. 12 Denis Irwin's. 13 Eric Cantona's. 14 Brian Kidd. 15 Dave Sexton. 16 Nigel Winterburn's. 17 Andrew Cole. 18 True. 19 Ben Thornley. 20 Peter Schmeichel.

Answers - see page 283

1 When had United last won the League Cup?
2 Who scored the only goal of their victory over Nottingham Forest?
3 Who supplied the pass?
4 What was the score at the interval?
5 What was the predominant colour of United's Wembley kit?
6 What did derisive rival fans call the shirts?
7 Who was wearing the number six for Nottingham Forest?
8 Who did Alex Ferguson send on to replace Andrei Kanchelskis after 75 minutes?
9 Which United substitute was not required to join the action?
10 The Forest manager's son figured in the Midlanders' attack. Name him.
11 Steve Bruce was one of two former Canaries who pocketed winner's medals. Who was the other?
12 Who was expected to provide Forest's principal goal threat?
13 Which international, whose son would play Premiership football, was at the heart of the Nottingham midfield?
14 Who was missing from United's midfield through injury?
15 Which Red Devil was presented with the trophy?
16 Who handed the silverware to the United captain?
17 Which future manager of a League club was used as a Forest substitute?
18 Who did United overcome in the two-legged semi-final?
19 Who were Forest's victims in the last four?
20 Two Red Devils were ever-present during the League Cup campaign. One was Brian McClair; who was the other?

ANSWERS

Alex Stepney (see page 283)
1 No. 2 Millwall. 3 Chelsea. 4 One. 5 £55,000. 6 Tommy Docherty. 7 Title medal.
8 Eusebio. 9 Jimmy Rimmer. 10 Paddy Roche. 11 Five. 12 Pat Jennings. 13 False.
14 Birmingham City. 15 Two. 16 One. 17 Sweden. 18 Two. 19 1977/78. 20 Manchester City.

Answers - see page 284

Name the Lancashire clubs to which these players moved after exiting Old Trafford. NOTE: traditional Lancashire boundaries apply.

1 David Healy
2 Andrei Kanchelskis
3 Denis Law
4 Alex Dawson
5 Norman Whiteside
6 John Curtis
7 Willie Morgan
8 Henning Berg
9 Terry Cooke
10 Phil Chisnall
11 Tony Dunne
12 Martin Buchan
13 Ian Moir
14 Mickey Thomas
15 Michael Appleton
16 John Connelly
17 John O'Kane
18 Pat McGibbon
19 Stan Pearson
20 David Sadler

ANSWERS

Title Trail 1966/67 (see page 284)
1 Upton Park. 2 Four points. 3 Nottingham Forest. 4 Denis Law. 5 West Bromwich Albion.
6 George Best. 7 David Gaskell. 8 John Connelly. 9 John Fitzpatrick's. 10 Bobby Noble.
11 Roker Park. 12 True. 13 It was their last of the season. 14 None. 15 Willie Anderson.
16 Noel Cantwell. 17 Denis Law. 18 Fifteen. 19 Liverpool. 20 Alan Ball.

282

Answers – see page 281

1   Has any 'keeper played more games for United than Alex Stepney?
2   Which was Alex's first League club?
3   From which Londoners' did United acquire Alex in September 1966?
4   How many League games did he play for that club?
5   What was the fee which secured his signature?
6   Who was the manager who sold Stepney to United?
7   What medal did Alex pocket at the end of his first season as a Red Devil?
8   Who did Alex prevent from scoring what must surely have been the winning goal near the end of normal time of the 1968 European Cup Final?
9   Which keeper ousted Alex for half of season 1970/71?
10 Which Irishman was handed Stepney's jersey for a brief spell in December 1975?
11 Under how many managers did Alex play during his time at Old Trafford?
12 Which famous opposition keeper once scored against Alex?
13 Stepney was United's joint top-scorer at the end of the 1973/74 relegation season. True or false?
14 Against which Midlands opponents did he score the winner from the spot in October 1973?
15 How many penalties did Alex convert in senior games for the Red Devils?
16 How many full England caps were awarded to Alex Stepney?
17 Against which country did he make his international debut?
18 In how many FA Cup Finals did Alex guard United's net?
19 Which was Alex's last season as a Red Devil?
20 Which club was employing Alex as a coach in 2000/2001?

Answers - see page 282

1 United clinched the Championship at which London ground?
2 By what margin did they top the table?
3 Who were runners-up in the title race?
4 Who scored 12 goals in his first 11 League appearances of the campaign?
5 Against whom did the Reds score five goals in the first 22 minutes of the season?
6 United had two ever-presents during the League campaign. One was Bobby Charlton; who was the other?
7 Who began the season between United's posts?
8 Which England winger left the club unexpectedly in early autumn?
9 Which youngster's splendid form kept Paddy Crerand sidelined for the first three games?
10 Which hugely promising full-back never played again after being injured in a road accident?
11 From which ground was the victim returning when the accident happened?
12 United lost four of their first away games. True or false?
13 What was the significance of the Reds' Boxing Day defeat by Sheffield United?
14 How many times were United beaten at Old Trafford in the League season?
15 Which young winger made his sole appearance of the term as a substitute before joining Aston Villa?
16 Who was the club captain?
17 Who usually skippered the team?
18 How many years had passed since Matt Busby first led United to the title?
19 Who did United replace as champions?
20 Which England redhead was a rumoured transfer target before the season began?

Answers - see page 287

1 Five players scored once in United's seven-goal thriller at Oldham in December 1993, but who netted twice?

2 Who grabbed United's third goal in a 3-2 win over Oldham in April 1994?

3 Two strikes from which ex-Celt helped United to a three-goal advantage after half an hour of their home clash with Oldham in November 1992?

4 A goal from which Latic inflicted on the Red Devils their last defeat of their triumphant 1992/93 title campaign?

5 What is the name of Oldham's ground, where that goal was scored?

6 Which ex-Oldham defender struck twice for United in a nine-goal thriller on Boxing Day 1991?

7 What was the result of that encounter?

8 Which former Manchester star managed Oldham during their Premiership years?

9 Which ex-United hero managed the Latics during two stints in the 1960s?

10 Another of United's all-time greats occupied the Oldham hot seat for a spell between the wars. Name him.

11 Who equalised against rivals Blackburn at Old Trafford on Boxing Day 1993?

12 Whose forward charge had created the mayhem and led to the goal?

13 Who had given Rovers a first-half lead in that enthralling contest?

14 Whose shot hit a Blackburn post during the 2-0 win by Rovers at Ewood in April 1994 which threw the title race wide open?

15 Who put Blackburn ahead at Old Trafford in May 1993 on the delirious night that the Reds celebrated their first title under Alex Ferguson?

16 Who contributed the second strike in United's three-goal response?

17 Gordon Strachan scored one of United's two goals in an FA Cup triumph at Ewood Park in February 1985 on the way to Wembley. Who netted the other?

18 Which future Blackburn winger netted in both the Reds' victories over Rovers during their successful 1964/65 title campaign?

19 Which extrovert centre-forward scored a hat-trick for Blackburn against United at Old Trafford on the opening day of season 1960/61?

20 Decipher the anagram: AYR KILSNIW

Answers - see page 288

1   Who scored the winner in United and City's final clash of the 20th century?

2   Who opened the scoring in that evenly-fought contest?

3   Who committed the foul which led to United's equaliser from the penalty spot?

4   How many times have City and United (including their predecessor clubs Newton Heath and Ardwick) met in the FA Cup?

5   Who scored the only goal when the two were paired in the third round at Old Trafford in January 1987?

6   That game was Alex Ferguson's first cup tie as United boss. True or false?

7   Who scored City's late winner in their epic 4-3 aggregate League Cup semi-final in 1969/70?

8   Which keeper had clutched needlessly at an indirect free-kick, thus setting up that crucial shot?

9   Whose typically alert tap-in had levelled the scores at 3-3?

10 Which United full-back netted with a 20-yarder in the second leg?

11 Who netted from the spot with two minutes remaining of the first leg at Maine Road?

12 Who conceded that penalty?

13 Who scored twice as United gained revenge with an FA Cup triumph less than six weeks later?

14 Which future Leeds boss netted for City against United on the way to the FA Cup Final in 1955?

15 Whose penalty took United to victory when the Reds saw off the Blues in the League Cup at Old Trafford in October 1974?

16 City thrashed United at Maine Road on their way to lifting the League Cup in 1975/76. Who struck twice in their 4-0 victory?

17 United and City met in the 1926 FA Cup semi-final. What was the outcome?

18 Where did Newton Heath and Ardwick contest the first senior game between the future Manchester giants?

19 In what year did that historic confrontation take place?

20 What was the result?

Answers – see page 285

1 When United embarked on the 1990/91 Cup Winners' Cup campaign, how many years had they been absent from European competition?
2 Which manager was leading the Reds into Europe for the first time?
3 Who was United's skipper that season?
4 The Reds' first opponents were Pecsi Munkas. From which country?
5 Who scored United's first European goal of the 1990s, against Pecsi at Old Trafford?
6 The second opponents came from a lot nearer home. Who were they?
7 United triumphed by an aggregate of 5-0 in that second round. Which player scored in each leg?
8 Who gave the Reds a first-minute lead in the Old Trafford leg of the quarter-final encounter with Montpellier?
9 Who gave the Frenchmen an equaliser with an own goal a few minutes later?
10 Which United man was involved in a butting incident which resulted in a Montpellier player being sent off controversially?
11 Whose second-minute free-kick at La Mosson Stadium put the Red Devils on their way to the last four?
12 Whose penalty clinched that coveted semi-final berth?
13 Which big-haired Colombian was appearing for Montpellier?
14 United were paired with Legia Warsaw in the last four, thus avoiding Barcelona and which Italian giants?
15 Which much-fancied Italians had Legia beaten to reach the semi?
16 The Reds went a goal down in Warsaw but levelled a minute later through which Scot?
17 Mark Hughes made it 2-1, then a defender put United in the driving seat at 3-1. Name him.
18 What was the result of the second leg in Warsaw?
19 Who scored United's only goal in Poland?
20 Who announced his intention of leaving Old Trafford two days before the second leg against Legia?

Answers - see page 286

Name the senior clubs to which these north-easterners switched after leaving
Manchester United:

1. Allenby Chilton
2. Peter Beardsley
3. Bobby Charlton
4. Paul Wratten
5. Billy Bryant
6. Steve Pears
7. Ray Wood
8. Jack Wilson
9. Alan Foggon
10. Billy Chapman
11. Charlie Roberts
12. Peter Coyne
13. Ernie Taylor
14. Joe Spence
15. George Wall
16. Paul Bielby
17. Beresford Brown
18. Bryan Robson
19. Tom Smith
20. Steve Bruce

ANSWERS

Sudden Death Derbies - United v City in Cups *(see page 286)*
1 Lee Sharpe. **2** Uwe Rosler. **3** Michael Frontzeck. **4** Six. **5** Norman Whiteside. **6** True.
7 Mike Summerbee. **8** Alex Stepney. **9** Denis Law's. **10** Paul Edwards. **11** Francis Lee.
12 Ian Ure. **13** Brian Kidd. **14** Don Revie. **15** Gerry Daly's. **16** Dennis Tueart. **17** City won
3-0. **18** North Road. **19** 1891. **20** Newton Heath won 5-1.

Answers - see page 291

1   By what name was Liam Whelan known to team-mates?
2   From which club did Matt Busby recruit the massively talented Dubliner in May 1953?
3   Liam's first game in United colours was a cup final. Which one?
4   Which injured inside-right was Whelan called in to replace for both legs of that final?
5   Liam netted in both legs against which opponents?
6   How many Republic of Ireland caps had Liam gained by the time he died at Munich?
7   How old was the softly-spoken Dubliner at the time of the calamity?
8   Though not a spearhead, Liam scored more than half a century of senior goals for United in fewer than 100 appearances. True or false?
9   Against which Spaniards did he run half the length of a muddy pitch before slamming a crucial goal in a European Cup quarter-final in 1956/57?
10 In what season did Liam top United's League scoring charts?
11 On which Lancashire ground did he bag his only hat-trick of that title-winning campaign?
12 What was the longest run of consecutive games in which Liam scored that term?
13 Liam had what would have been a late equaliser rightly disallowed for offside in the 1957 FA Cup Final. Who was the opposing keeper?
14 Like Liam, John Doherty was a Dubliner. True or false?
15 Doherty earned a Championship medal on merit in which season?
16 To which club was John transferred in October 1957?
17 What finished John's first-class career prematurely?
18 Why was utility forward Colin Webster withdrawn from the European expedition which ended disastrously at Munich?
19 For which injured Welsh legend did Colin deputise in his country's 1958 World Cup quarter-final clash with Brazil?
20 Colin left the Red Devils to join which club in October 1958?

Answers - see page 292

1   In which position did Gary specialise?

2   In which county was he born?

3   Pallister rose to prominence with which League club?

4   During 1985/86 Gary completed a loan stint with which Third Division north-easterners?

5   While on loan, what was Pallister's home ground?

6   When did Gary join United?

7   After protracted negotiations, how much did the Reds fork out for his signature?

8   What was Gary's first major honour with Manchester United?

9   Gary won half a century of England caps. True or false?

10 How many League title medals can be found in the Pallister collection?

11 In how many League and FA Cup doubles did Gary play an integral part?

12 Who were the opponents when Gary made his First Division debut for the Red Devils at Old Trafford?

13 What was the result of the match?

14 Gary was the last of United's regular outfielders to score a League goal when they lifted the title in 1992/93. Against which club did he finally do it?

15 Who were the opponents when Pallister netted in both installments of United's FA Cup semi-final in 1995?

16 Two thunderous Pallister headers on a spring morning at which ground had a massive influence on the destination of the 1997 Championship?

17 What personal accolade went Gary's way in 1992?

18 The purchase of which Dutch colossus signalled the end for Gary at Old Trafford?

19 Which former United team-mate took Gary back to his first club in the summer of 1998?

20 How much were United paid to relinquish the stalwart Pally's services?

Tottenham Teasers - United v Spurs - 3 *(see page 292)*

ANSWERS

1 1995/96. **2** Teddy Sheringham. **3** Kevin Pilkington. **4** William Prunier. **5** Eric Cantona. **6** Nick Barmby. **7** Steve Bruce. **8** Jimmy Greaves'. **9** Dave Mackay. **10** Dave Mackay's. **11** Noel Cantwell. **12** Bobby Charlton. **13** Garth Crooks. **14** Denis Law's. **15** Gary Lineker. **16** Jimmy Robertson. **17** Martin Peters. **18** Andy Ritchie. **19** Brian McClair. **20** Paul Stewart.

1   Which future Stamford Bridge hero put United in front against Chelsea at Old Trafford as the Reds romped towards the title in the spring of 1993?

2   Who was the Chelsea keeper who, it is fair to say, was not at his best that day?

3   Which Chelsea defender contributed an own goal to United's 3-0 triumph as they consolidated their position at the top of the table?

4   Another man who would one day join Chelsea put the Blues in front with the softest of own goals at Old Trafford in February 1992. Name him.

5   Whose Old Trafford penalty sunk the Reds after they had recovered from a two-goal deficit against Chelsea in November 1990?

6   Which United keeper registered an own goal at Stamford Bridge in August 1987?

7   Which Irish international scored as United won at the Bridge in February 1988?

8   Which Dane scored in both United's league clashes with Chelsea during 1985/86?

9   Which Scottish Red was sent off at Stamford Bridge in October 1985?

10 Which Irish Red received his marching orders at the Bridge in August 1971?

11 Which United man struck a Boxing Day hat-trick against Chelsea in 1960?

12 Which Irish international wing-half hit the target twice in the same match?

13 Which former Red netted against United in a 1-1 away draw for Chelsea in September 1984?

14 A Chelsea skipper scored against his future employers when the Red Devils visited the Bridge in February 1978. Name him.

15 Who scored all of Chelsea's goals in their league wins over United during 1969/70?

16 Who netted twice for Chelsea as they won 4-0 at Old Trafford in 1968/69?

17 Which winger, who would star on the greatest of all club stages, registered twice for United in their 3-1 victory at Chelsea in 1966/67?

18 Who scored in both Chelsea's league games with United in 1959/60?

19 Which future assistant boss of United helped Chelsea to lift the League title in 1954/55?

20 Decipher the anagram: RAKM NOSEJ.

Answers - see page 290

1 In which of their three League/FA Cup double-winning campaigns did United lose 4-1 at Tottenham on New Year's Day?
2 Who gave Spurs a first-half lead in that game?
3 Which goalkeeper replaced the injured Peter Schmeichel at half-time?
4 Which Frenchman played his last match for the Reds that day at White Hart Lane?
5 Who ran from midway inside his own half to score the only goal of the game when Spurs visited Old Trafford in March 1996?
6 Klinsmann, Sheringham, Dumitrescu and Anderton: who was the final member of Spurs' 'Famous Five' forwards who were at home to United in August 1994?
7 Who grabbed the only goal of that contest?
8 Whose hat-trick contributed to United's 6-2 defeat at White Hart Lane in October 1962?
9 Who scored Spurs' first goal as they beat United 2-0 in the first leg of a European Cup Winners' Cup tie in December 1963?
10 Whose leg was shattered in the match at Old Trafford a week later?
11 With whom did the accident victim collide in that fateful challenge?
12 Who netted twice as United triumphed 4-3 on aggregate?
13 Which popular Spurs marksman, now working for the BBC, spent a brief spell on loan with United in 1983/84?
14 Whose hat-trick scuppered Spurs at Old Trafford in November 1963?
15 Who scored his last goal in English football, against United in May 1992, two minutes from the end of his final game?
16 An extra-time winner from which Spurs winger put United out of the FA Cup in a 1968 replay?
17 Who scored all four goals as Tottenham tanned the Reds at Old Trafford in October 1972?
18 Who was the teenage hat-trick hero of United's 4-1 home hammering of Spurs in April 1980?
19 Who scored in his first four League games against Tottenham?
20 Who missed a penalty against United on his Spurs debut in 1988?

ANSWERS

Gary Pallister (see page 290)
1 Central defence. 2 Kent. 3 Middlesbrough. 4 Darlington. 5 Feethams. 6 August 1989. 7 £2.3 million. 8 The FA Cup in 1990. 9 False, he won 22. 10 Four. 11 Two. 12 Norwich City. 13 United lost 0-2. 14 Blackburn Rovers. 15 Crystal Palace. 16 Anfield. 17 Players' Player of the Year. 18 Jaap Stam. 19 Bryan Robson. 20 £2 million.

Answers - see page 295

1   Who became the first footballer to be sent off in an FA Cup Final?
2   Who was the victim of the offence for which he was dismissed?
3   Who was the referee who made the fateful decision?
4   Was the dismissed player allowed to climb the 39 steps to collect his medal?
5   Who scored the only goal of the game with an exquisite curling shot?
6   Who set it up with an equally delicious raking pass?
7   Which Everton striker would go on to become a top TV soccer pundit?
8   What two trophies already had been won by Everton when they faced United at Wembley?
9   Only one Everton player was not a full international. Who was he?
10   Which Everton star had just been voted Footballer of the Year?
11   And which Goodison hero was Players' Player of the Year?
12   Which United defender missed the final after appearing in most of the previous rounds?
13   Which former Toffee was turning out against his old club?
14   Which former Everton manager had died at Goodison following the quarter-final draw with Ipswich?
15   Who led out the Red Devils at Wembley?
16   Who was the Everton boss, that season's manager of the year?
17   Early in the game, which Evertonian's volley was deflected against a United upright?
18   How many from the 1983 Wembley win remained in the United team?
19   Who was the Everton captain?
20   Which TV commentator, situated behind Everton's net, kicked his heels in the air when United scored?

ANSWERS

Pennine Jumpers - Joe Jordan & Gordon McQueen (see page 295)
1 Leeds United. **2** Dave Sexton. **3** Joe Jordan. **4** £500,000. **5** £350,000. **6** True. **7** Morton. **8** St Mirren. **9** Against Arsenal in 1979. **10** Gordon McQueen. **11** Two. **12** AC Milan. **13** £175,000. **14** Yes, for Leeds in 1973/74. **15** FA Cup medal in 1983. **16** 30 times. **17** 52 caps. **18** Bristol City. **19** Airdrieonians. **20** Heart of Midlothian.

Answers - see page 296

Name the Yorkshire clubs to which these men moved after leaving Manchester United. NOTE: traditional Yorkshire boundaries apply.

1   Ben Thornley
2   Lee Sharpe
3   Ray Wood
4   Stewart Houston
5   Gary Walsh
6   Mark Dempsey
7   Clayton Blackmore
8   Brian Greenhoff
9   Jimmy Nicholson
10 Johnny Giles
11 Mark Pearson
12 Arnold Sidebottom
13 Steve James
14 Viv Anderson
15 Alan Gowling
16 Gary Pallister
17 Deiniol Graham
18 Freddie Goodwin
19 John Connaughton
20 Chris Turner

Answers - see page 293

1 From which club did United acquire Joe Jordan and Gordon McQueen?
2 Who was the manager who bought the two Scottish stars?
3 Which of the two was the first to arrive at Old Trafford in January 1978?
4 What was the record fee placed on Gordon's blond head?
5 How much did the Reds pay for Jordan?
6 Before starting for United, Joe had to serve a suspension for misdeeds at his previous club. True or false?
7 What was Joe's first senior club?
8 With which club did Gordon kick off his career in the Scottish league?
9 The two chums played together for Manchester United in which FA Cup Final?
10 Which of the two scored a goal that day at Wembley?
11 In how many seasons was Joe United's top scorer?
12 To what club was he transferred in July 1981?
13 How much were the Reds paid for his services?
14 Did Jordan ever win a title medal?
15 Which major club honour did Gordon win during his Old Trafford sojourn?
16 How many times did the giant centre-half play for Scotland?
17 How many international caps are in the Jordan collection?
18 Of which English club has Joe Jordan been the manager for two spells?
19 Gordon McQueen was boss of which Scottish club?
20 Joe also had a spell as a manager north of the border. With which club?

Answers - see page 294

1 Eddie Coleman hailed from which United heartland?
2 In which position did precocious little Eddie forge an increasingly colossal reputation?
3 What was Eddie's nickname?
4 Against which fierce Lancashire rivals did Coleman make his League entrance in November 1955?
5 How many full international caps had this brilliant young Red Devil won by the time of his death at Munich?
6 One of Eddie's rare goals came in the home leg of the 1956/57 European Cup quarter-final against which opposition?
7 How many times was Eddie part of United sides which lifted the FA Youth Cup?
8 How many League Championship medals did he win?
9 Who did Eddie replace in Matt Busby's First Division line-up?
10 Was Coleman part of the side which lost the FA Cup Final to Aston Villa in 1957?
11 Mark Jones was a Geordie. True or false?
12 What was Mark's position in the United team?
13 With whom did he wage constant battle for a regular place in the side?
14 Who was in possession at the time Mark was killed at Munich?
15 Did big, blond Jones face Aston Villa in the 1957 FA Cup Final?
16 How old was Mark when he lost his life?
17 Was he a full international?
18 Mark made his senior debut in October 1950 against opponents from his home county. Name that club.
19 From which stalwart Red Devil did Mark take over on a regular basis in February 1955?
20 Mark was United's only ever-present as they romped away with the League Championship in 1955/56. True or false?

Answers - see page 299

1   Which Hammer netted with a rebound from a knee to derail United's title challenge at Upton Park in April 1992?

2   In what position did West Ham finish in that season's First Division table?

3   Who was dismissed when West Ham met United in Manchester in January 1996?

4   At Upton Park in October 1982 a bubble-haired Irishman received his marching orders? Name him.

5   Whose hat-trick dumped West Ham out of the FA Cup in March 1985?

6   A season later the Hammers took their revenge in a fifth-round replay. Which Scottish full-back, known as Tonka, contributed a goal?

7   Which soccer pundit scored for the Hammers in a 2-1 home win in 1977?

8   Which future Old Trafford coach chipped in with two goals for West Ham as the Reds went down 4-2 at Upton Park in May 1977?

9   Whose hat-trick against West Ham kept United top in September 1971?

10 That man's namesake registered for the Hammers when they took their revenge on New Year's Day. Name him.

11 Which winger's hat-trick put the Hammers to the sword at Old Trafford in September 1958?

12 Which Red was sent off at home to Newcastle as United's title challenge petered out in April 1998?

13 That dismissal was caused by a foul on which England international?

14 Which six-foot-two stopper was ordered off when the Reds played host to the Magpies in March 1973?

15 Whose hat-trick knocked Newcastle out of the League Cup in October 1976?

16 What was the score that evening?

17 Less than four months later, another United marksman scored a hat-trick against the Tynesiders, this time in the League. Name him.

18 Which future Magpie scored the winner in a 2-0 home victory in October 1994?

19 Whose leg was sliced open in a collision while scoring United's goal at St James' Park in January 1995?

20 Decipher the anagram: RAGY LABYIE.

ANSWERS

Fergie in Scotland (see page 299)
1 Govan. 2 Apprentice toolmaker. 3 Martin Ferguson. 4 Queen's Park. 5 Hampden Park. 6 Scottish Second Division title medal with St Johnstone in 1962/63. 7 Dunfermline Athletic. 8 Rangers. 9 No. 10 Second Division Championship medal with Falkirk in 1969/70. 11 East Stirlingshire. 12 Three months. 13 St Mirren. 14 1978. 15 Pittodrie. 16 Three. 17 1981/82 to 1983/84. 18 Real Madrid. 19 Because Jock Stein died. 20 Alan Hansen.

Answers - see page 300

1 United and Arsenal met twice at which ground as they both chased the League and FA Cup double in 1999?

2 The first game was goalless, but which United player had a goal disallowed controversially for offside?

3 Which Arsenal man was sent off for elbowing Nicky Butt in extra time?

4 What colour were United's shirts in the second match?

5 Who scored the first goal of the tie with a 20-yard bender?

6 Who set up that breathtaking effort with an exquisite lay-off?

7 Who netted an extremely fortunate equaliser?

8 Who was the unlucky defender whose deflection proved crucial to that goal?

9 Who netted for Arsenal shortly afterwards, only to see his effort ruled out for offside?

10 Who was sent off after 73 minutes?

11 Who was the victim of the second bookable offence which resulted in the dismissal?

12 Who gave away the late penalty which seemed certain to hand Arsenal victory?

13 Who was fouled inside the United penalty box?

14 Who took the resulting spot kick?

15 Was the penalty driven wide or did Peter Schmeichel save it?

16 Who won the match with a goal hailed as one of the greatest of all time?

17 Who made the misplaced pass which led to that unforgettable shot?

18 How many challenges did United's inspired dribbler evade on his sensational run?

19 Who was the Arsenal keeper who failed to repel the climactic shot?

20 The match-winner was a 61st-minute substitute for which player?

Answers - see page 297

1   In which district of Glasgow was Alex Ferguson born and raised?

2   What was Fergie's first job on leaving school?

3   What is the name of Ferguson's brother, who went on to become a scout with United?

4   With what famous old club did Alex begin his senior football career?

5   Name the home ground of Fergie's first club.

6   What was Alex Ferguson's first senior club honour?

7   For whom was Alex playing when he was Scottish football's top scorer in 1965/66?

8   Who did Fergie join for £65,000, a record between two Scottish clubs, in the summer of 1967?

9   Did Alex win any full Scottish caps?

10   What was Ferguson's second senior club honour?

11   With which club did Alex enter management?

12   How long did Fergie remain in his first hot seat before moving on to greater things?

13   With which club did Alex lift the Scottish First Division crown in 1976/77?

14   When did Fergie move to Aberdeen?

15   Where do The Dons play?

16   How many Scottish League titles did Aberdeen win under Ferguson?

17   In what consecutive seasons did Fergie's Dons complete a hat-trick of Scottish Cup successes?

18   Who did Aberdeen vanquish to lift the European Cup Winners' Cup in 1983?

19   Why did Alex become Scotland's caretaker boss in 1985?

20   Whom did he omit controversially from the 1986 World Cup squad?

1 Which of Bryan Robson's brothers played for West Bromwich Albion and Bradford City?

2 Which United centre-half's father played for Crewe and was nicknamed 'Killer'?

3 Who is Joe Jordan's Scottish under-21 international son?

4 With which club did Nobby Stiles' son, John, spend five years as a midfielder before joining Doncaster Rovers?

5 Whose son was on the books of Manchester City while dad was managing United?

6 Former Red Devil Mark Dempsey's cousin Chris Makin led which team out at Old Trafford in April 2000?

7 Which Irish club had Alex Ferguson, father of Sir Alex, among its playing staff?

8 Sir Alex's grandad turned out for which Scottish League outfit?

9 Which former United trainee, whose father Steve excelled for Chelsea and QPR, helped Brighton to become Third Division champions in 2000/2001?

10 For which League club did Lee Sharpe's brother, John, make more than 30 appearances in the mid 1990s?

11 The son of which ex-United boss captained the British Universities soccer team before working up to a top job with the Reds' youth coaching academy?

12 Harvey Cunningham, who was playing for Doncaster Rovers when they dropped out of the Football League, is the stepbrother of which former Red?

13 Name the son of Gordon Strachan who has won under-21 honours for Scotland?

14 With which club did Strachan Jnr break through in the late 1990s?

15 Ray Wilkins' father, George, finished his English League career with which club?

16 Ray's older bother, full-back Graham. made more than 130 League appearances for which London club?

17 Another brother, Dean, enjoyed a lengthy career with which south-coast club?

18 Les Sealey helped United win the European Cup Winners' Cup in 1991. His uncle, Alan Sealey, scored twice as which club lifted the same trophy in 1965?

19 For which League club did David Herd, one of United's finest marksmen, play alongside his father, Alec Herd?

ANSWERS

FA Cup Semi-Final - Arsenal Epic *(see page 298)*
1 Villa Park. 2 Roy Keane. 3 Nelson Vivas. 4 White. 5 David Beckham. 6 Teddy Sheringham. 7 Dennis Bergkamp. 8 Jaap Stam. 9 Nicolas Anelka. 10 Roy Keane. 11 Marc Overmars. 12 Phil Neville. 13 Ray Parlour. 14 Dennis Bergkamp. 15 Schmeichel saved it. 16 Ryan Giggs. 17 Patrick Vieira. 18 Five. 19 David Seaman. 20 Jesper Blomqvist.

Answers - see page 303

1 What might Peter Schmeichel have become, according to a Reebok commercial?

2 From which Gunner did Peter save a penalty in the 1999 FA Cup semi-final replay?

3 With which Bayern Munich defender did Peter contest a header when he went forward in the dying seconds of the 1999 European Cup Final?

4 For how many senior games did United go unbeaten after Schmeichel made his entrance?

5 Which was the first team to defeat the Reds with Peter guarding their net?

6 Only one team scored six against Peter during his United career. Which one?

7 Six days earlier Peter had let in five. Who had been his tormentors that day?

8 How many times did Schmeichel have to be replaced by a substitute during his United career?

9 Who replaced Peter at half-time in the 4-1 defeat by Spurs at White Hart Lane on New Year's Day 1996?

10 What was the most consecutive clean sheets Peter had during any season?

11 How many times did he achieve that feat?

12 How many senior games (all competitions) did Peter play for United?

13 With which Arsenal forward did Peter have a long-running disagreement, beginning in November 1996?

14 Against which Londoners did Peter make his final Premiership appearance?

15 Which Oldham player benefited from a rare Schmeichel fumble to put the Latics ahead in the 1994 FA Cup semi-final?

16 Who were the first European Cup opposition Peter faced as a United man?

17 Peter thought he had equalised with a last-minute swivel kick but it was disallowed for offside against which FA Cup opponents in February 1997?

18 Against which Spaniards was Peter omitted when there were European restrictions on the number of overseas players?

19 Which club did Schmeichel join after leaving United?

20 How did his new employers fare in their national league in the first season with Peter between their posts?

1   Who have won most Manchester derbies, City or United?

2   Who played in most Manchester derbies for United?

3   Who played in most Manchester derbies for City?

4   Who played in most Manchester derbies in total?

5   In a tackle with which United star did City full-back Glyn Pardoe suffer a broken leg at Old Trafford in December 1970?

6   Which City hero hammered a hat-trick in front of United's fans that same day?

7   What did Eamon Andrews say to Sir Matt Busby before the Maine Road derby on the last day of 1970/71?

8   Sir Matt's opposite number at Maine Road told the crowd that Busby was 'the greatest manager Britain had ever known'. Name that City boss.

9   Colin Bell never fully recovered following an accidental collision with which United defender in the League Cup clash at Maine Road in November 1975?

10 Who was the first player to receive his marching orders in a Manchester derby?

11 Who was the first substitute to go on in a Manchester derby?

12 Two City players share the honour of being top scorer in Manchester derbies with ten goals each. One is Francis Lee, who is the other?

13 Who is United's most prolific marksman, with nine goals against City?

14 When did City become the only club to score six in a Manchester derby?

15 Who wore the number-four shirt for City against United at Old Trafford in February 1931?

16 Who scored twice against his former club in the Old Trafford derby in September 1962?

17 Which 20-year-old scored a hat-trick at home to City in December 1960?

18 The father of a winger who would play for both City and United scored in the derby of August 1957 at Maine Road. Name that dad.

19 When was the first League meeting between the two clubs?

20 What was the result?

Answers - see page 301

Name the clubs from which the Red Devils recruited these great Scots:

1   Pat Crerand
2   Ralph Milne
3   Jim Holton
4   Denis Law
5   Jimmy Delaney
6   Ted MacDougall
7   David Herd
8   Lou Macari
9   Alan Brazil
10 Arthur Graham
11 Brian McClair
12 Stewart Houston
13 John Downie
14 Gordon Strachan
15 Ian Ure
16 Harry McShane
17 Martin Buchan
18 George Graham
19 Alex Forsyth
20 Willie Morgan

Answers - see page 302

1 United's first Champions League opponents were Kosice. From which country?

2 The Reds kicked off with a 3-0 away win. Who opened their scoring account?

3 Who gave Juventus the lead after 19 seconds at Old Trafford?

4 Who nodded in the equaliser shortly before the interval?

5 Who waltzed past the Italian keeper to put the Reds in front?

6 Who cut in from his left-flank beat to smash home United's third and underline his claim to be man of the match?

7 Whose late curling free-kick reduced Juve's deficit to a single goal?

8 The opening goal at home to Feyenoord was steered home by Salford's favourite redhead. Who?

9 Whose hat-trick in Holland completed the United double over the Dutchmen?

10 Which United full-back was seriously injured by a sickening challenge from Paul Bosvelt?

11 By what margin did United beat Kosice at Old Trafford?

12 On whose ground did the Reds suffer their first defeat of the 1997/98 European campaign?

13 Whose scored the vital late goal which signalled that reverse?

14 Who was the goalkeeper for Monaco, whom the Reds met at the quarter-final stage?

15 Which future Arsenal marksman did United encounter in France?

16 What was the score at the Stade Louis II?

17 Which future Everton and Fulham midfielder excelled in midfield for Monaco?

18 The man whose goal would clinch Euro 2000 for France scored what proved to be the decisive away goal at Old Trafford. Name him.

19 Who registered for the Red Devils in a 1-1 draw?

20 How far did Monaco get in the 1997/98 Champions League?

Answers - see page 307

1 By what record margin did United win the Premiership title?
2 Where did they clinch the crown?
3 In that match, who opened the scoring in spectacular fashion?
4 On the day the Championship was claimed, which opposition player scored an own-goal?
5 Before which home fixture was the trophy presented?
6 Who started the Premiership campaign between United's posts?
7 Who headed past his own keeper in the opening game against Everton?
8 Who left the bench and equalised at home to Wimbledon?
9 United thrashed Newcastle 5-1 at Old Trafford. Who scored for the Magpies?
10 Which Latvian nutmegged Jaap Stam on the way to scoring at Old Trafford?
11 Against which club did the Reds claim a Boxing Day victory with four goals in the last 15 minutes?
12 Who snatched United's late equaliser at the Stadium of Light?
13 A Belgian netted twice at Old Trafford in February. Name him.
14 United suffered their final defeat of the season on February 12. Who beat them?
15 Whose quickfire double put the Reds two up in their 4-0 victory at Valley Parade?
16 Who scored a brilliant individual late goal for Middlesbrough at the Riverside?
17 United needed a late winner at Vicarage Road. Who supplied it?
18 Who scored United's last League goal of the campaign at Villa Park?
19 By how many did United miss out on a century of League goals?
20 How many times were the Reds defeated during the League season?

ANSWERS

Tommy Taylor - 2 (see page 307)
1 True. 2 Anderlecht. 3 Real Madrid. 4 A header. 5 Aston Villa. 6 No. 7 Bill Foulkes.
8 The Republic of Ireland. 9 Johnny Berry. 10 Maine Road. 11 Cardiff City. 12 True.
13 Liam Whelan. 14 Arsenal. 15 Tommy Docherty. 16 Walter Winterbottom. 17 Jackie
Blanchflower. 18 Dickie Bird. 19 The Smiling Executioner. 20 Jack Rowley.

Answers - see page 308

These Mancunians were parted from their home city (Greater Manchester, in some cases, to be precise) when they checked out of Old Trafford. But where were their first ports of call after ceasing to be Red Devils?

1   Harold Hardman
2   Tony Young
3   Danny Higginbotham
4   Albert Scanlon
5   Nobby Stiles
6   Michael Appleton
7   Don Gibson
8   Brian Kidd
9   Billy Redman
10 Dennis Viollet
11 Phil Chisnall
12 Tom McNulty
13 Nobby Lawton
14 John Hanlon
15 Walter Whitehurst
16 Michael Twiss
17 John Doherty
18 Peter Fletcher
19 Laurie Cassidy
20 John Anderson

Answers - see page 305

1 During 1956/57 Tommy averaged a goal a game in European. True or false?

2 Against which opposition did Tommy grab his only European Cup hat-trick?

3 Taylor netted in each leg of the 1957 European Cup semi-finals. Who provided the illustrious opposition?

4 Tommy scored United's consolation goal in the 1957 FA Cup Final. Was it with a shot or a header?

5 Who were United's opponents on that disappointing afternoon at Wembley?

6 Did Tommy score against Red Star Belgrade in United's final game before the Munich crash?

7 Tommy and Roger Byrne were two of United's three ever-presents from the start of their first European campaign until Munich. Who was the third?

8 The second of two consecutive Taylor hat-tricks in World Cup qualifiers for England was scored against which opponents at Wembley in May 1957?

9 Tommy laid on United's winning goal for which England winger in the gripping quarter-final clash with Athletic Bilbao in February 1957?

10 What was the venue for that unforgettable encounter?

11 Tommy clipped the Bluebirds' wings with four goals at Old Trafford in October 1954? The opponents were?

12 Tommy netted 25 times in 1955/56 without notching a hat-trick. True or false?

13 Tommy was outscored in the League in 1956/57 by which Irishman?

14 Against which club did Tommy score his last League goal?

15 Which United boss of the 1970s, who had faced Tommy while playing for Preston, described Taylor as 'the greatest centre-forward of all time'?

16 Who was the England manager during Tommy's international days?

17 Tommy was best man at the wedding of which Irish team-mate?

18 Which famous cricket umpire was Tommy's schooldays friend?

19 The sub-title of the book 'The Tommy Taylor Story', written in 1996 by Brian Hughes, summed him up perfectly. What was it?

20 For which free-scoring centre-forward was Tommy signed as the long-term replacement at Old Trafford?

Answers – see page 306

1 What nationality is Andrei Kanchelskis?

2 What was his first senior club in his homeland?

3 From what club was he transferred to the Red Devils?

4 What was the fee?

5 When did Andrei sign on at Old Trafford?

6 Why was Andrei sent of in the last minute of the 1994 League Cup Final?

7 Did Andrei compile a complete set of major domestic honours as a Red?

8 Against which United did Kanchelskis score his first senior goal for the Red Devils, in November 1991 at Old Trafford?

9 Andrei netted twice in an FA Cup quarter-final against which opposition at Old Trafford in March 1994?

10 He also contributed a stunning left-foot curler in the semi-final replay. Who were his victims that day?

11 Andrei scored one senior hat-trick for United. Who suffered on that memorable Old Trafford night?

12 At the end of which season did Kanchelskis top the club's League scoring chart?

13 How many times did he hit the target during that Premiership campaign?

14 To what club was Andrei sold, after a protracted transfer saga, in August 1995?

15 Who was the buying manager?

16 How much were United paid for the flying flankman's services?

17 Soon after joining his new club, Kanchelskis received a serious shoulder injury in an accidental collision with which former United colleague?

18 Later Andrei was employed by which Italian club?

19 Which club brought Kanchelskis back to British football?

20 Which was Andrei's home ground in the spring of 2001?

Answers - see page 311

1 Of which club did Steve Coppell become manager in the spring of 2001?

2 Which towering Welsh marksman scored on his United debut against Derby County in 1972?

3 Who made his senior entrance as a Red Devil at White Hart Lane in May 2001?

4 That afternoon, who clinched his title medal by making his tenth League appearance of the season?

5 Which Dutchman scored twice in Spurs' 3-1 victory that day?

6 Who mustered United's sole reply?

7 On 18 May 2001 who announced that he would sever all ties with the Red Devils at the end of the following season?

8 Which centre-half was United's inspirational skipper during the mid 1920s?

9 From which club did they sign him in August 1922?

10 To which club did he depart in May 1928?

11 Away from football, what was this tough, barrel-chested, controversial fellow's trade?

12 What is Peter Schmeichel's middle name?

13 Jim Ryan won two title medals during the 1960s. True or false?

14 Which Welsh international Red Devil died, aged 68, in March 2001?

15 Which six-foot Dubliner made only one senior appearance for the Reds, as a substitute defender at home to Southampton in November 1980?

16 Nobby Stiles' after-dinner speaking schedule includes appearing alongside two other celebrated 'hard men'. One is Norman Hunter; who is the other?

17 Name the son of a former United stopper who made his Test cricket debut for England against Pakistan in May 2001.

18 Which club did marksman Eddie Lewis join when he left the Red Devils in December 1955?

19 For which club did he make the most senior appearances, but as a defender?

20 Decipher this anagram: ILBLY RIMDEHET

Answers - see page 312

1 Whose goal doomed table-topping Liverpool to defeat at Old Trafford on a sunny Saturday morning in October 1996?

2 When Karel Poborsky was substituted in that game, the whole United line-up cost less than the price of Stan Collymore. True or false?

3 Soon after that game, who said: 'I am playing some of the worst football of my career. I will try to do better'?

4 Who netted with two bullet headers in the so-called Championship decider at Anfield in April 1997?

5 Who was the much vilified Liverpool goalkeeper?

6 Who threw his boots into the Kop on the way to the dressing room?

7 Whose high-velocity free-kick entered Liverpool's net via the crossbar at Anfield in December 1997?

8 Who scored twice for the rampant visitors that day?

9 Who nodded United ahead at Old Trafford on Good Friday 1998?

10 Who equalised, then was sent off after fouling United's scorer?

11 Which former technical director of the French World Cup winners was in joint charge of Liverpool when they visited United in September 1998?

12 Who conceded the penalty from which the Red Devils took the lead that night?

13 Who doubled the margin with a fabulous shot near the end?

14 Which Liverpool striker scored, only for the 'goal' to be disallowed?

15 To whom did United fans address the chant: 'Charlie, Charlie, what's the score?'

16 Who grabbed the late, late winner when United ejected Liverpool from the FA Cup in January 1999?

17 Which United stalwart was dismissed when United visited Anfield in May 1999?

18 Who contributed two own goals to United's victory at Anfield in September 1999?

19 Two United men made their debuts that day. One was Mikael Silvestre; who was the other?

20 Who contributed the Red Devils' deft equaliser against Liverpool shortly before the interval at Old Trafford in March 2000?

Answers - see page 309

1 Who put United in front against Leeds at Elland Road in March?
2 Who conceded the penalty which Ian Harte failed to convert that Saturday morning?
3 Who headed Leeds' late equaliser?
4 Whose stoppage-time scorcher spared the Reds' blushes against Panathanaikos in Greece?
5 Who put United ahead against Sturm Graz in the match which qualified them for the Champions League quarter-finals?
6 Who opened the scoring at home to Leicester with a fortunate deflection?
7 Who scored his first goal for United in that home victory over the Foxes in March?
8 Who received his League baptism against Leicester that day?
9 What brought about that unexpected debut?
10 On March 31, Liverpool completed their first League double over United for more than 20 years. True or false?
11 Who notched Liverpool's opening goal with a stunning 30-yard drive?
12 Whose smart finish sealed the result for the Merseysiders?
13 Who was sent off that day at Anfield?
14 Who shocked the Reds with a late winner for Bayern Munich at Old Trafford?
15 A booking in that match kept which Red Devil out of the second leg?
16 Who grabbed United's winner at home to Charlton in April?
17 Who ruffled the Reds' feathers by scoring twice for Coventry at Old Trafford on Easter Saturday?
18 Who replied with a brace for United?
19 Who put the Reds in front with a fabulous 17-yard header?
20 What is the nationality of the two own-goal scorers who made United champions by teatime on Easter Saturday?

ANSWERS

Pot Luck - 99 (see page 309)
1 Brentford. 2 Wyn Davies. 3 Bojan Djordic. 4 Raimond van der Gouw. 5 Willem Korsten.
6 Paul Scholes. 7 Sir Alex Ferguson. 8 Frank Barson. 9 Aston Villa. 10 Watford.
11 Blacksmith. 12 Boleslaw. 13 False, he didn't win any. 14 Colin Webster. 15 Anto Whelan. 16 Tommy Smith. 17 Ryan Sidebottom. 18 Preston North End. 19 Leyton Orient. 20 Billy Meredith.

1   Eric Cantona celebrated his 35th birthday on the same day, 24 May 2001, that which rock music icon marked his 60th?

2   His band is Simply Red and he supports Manchester United. Name him.

3   Which multiple world champion motorbike racer is a loyal United fan?

4   Which former England cricket captain, based just down the road, will be a United follower until the day he dies?

5   Which cricketing clubmate, nicknamed 'Creepy', marches beneath the same soccer banner?

6   A famous female athlete, who rose through Sale Harriers and has known her share of controversy, is an avid United fan. Name her.

7   Which former world snooker champion watches the Red Devils whenever he has the opportunity?

8   Another member of the snooker fraternity, born in Salford and a workmate of Jim Davidson, is also a Red. What's his name?

9   He's played Jesus Christ, he's been a sidekick of Jasper Carrott and he loves the Red Devils. Who is he?

10 Which morning TV presenter, a Belfast boy, is a well-known United fan?

11 Who was the first England captain to sport a Mohican haircut?

12 Against which opponents did he first lead his country with his hair thus styled?

13 On what ground did that game take place?

14 What future Scotland manager scored for Blackburn against United in two successive seasons, 1959/60 and 1960/61?

15 How many players were ever-present in United's title-winning campaign of 2000/2001?

16 Who was the only Red Devil to be sent off twice during that season?

17 How many League hat-tricks were hit by Red Devils during 2000/2001?

18 Which London club offered Steve McClaren the management chair in May 2001?

19 Which club did he join instead?

20 Decipher the anagram: KULE WACKDICH.

ANSWERS

1 _____

2 _____

3 _____

4 _____

5 _____

6 _____

7 _____

8 _____

9 _____

10 _____

11 _____

12 _____

13 _____

14 _____

15 _____

16 _____

17 _____

18 _____

19 _____

20 _____

ANSWERS   SECOND HALF

1 _____   11 _____

2 _____   12 _____

3 _____   13 _____

4 _____   14 _____

5 _____   15 _____

6 _____   16 _____

7 _____   17 _____

8 _____   18 _____

9 _____   19 _____

10 _____   20 _____

ANSWERS

1 _____

2 _____

3 _____

4 _____

5 _____

6 _____

7 _____

8 _____

9 _____

10 _____

11 _____

12 _____

13 _____

14 _____

15 _____

16 _____

17 _____

18 _____

19 _____

20 _____

ALSO AVAILABLE:

THE OFFICIAL
MANCHESTER UNITED
100 GREATEST PLAYERS

Selected by the fans themselves this book
focuses on the 100 finest players to pull
on a United shirt. Featuring over 150
colour and black and white photographs.

ISBN 0-233-99963-9
£14.99

Available from all good bookshops

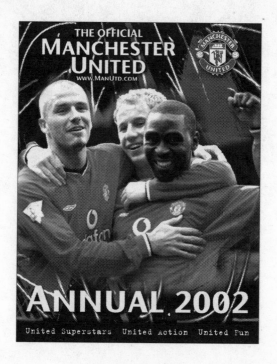

THE OFFICIAL
MANCHESTER UNITED
ANNUAL 2002

Containing player profiles, puzzles and
quizzes and a guided tour behind the
scenes at Old Trafford all accompanied by
stunning action images from United's
official photographer.

ISBN 0-233-99953-1
£6.99

Available from all good bookshops

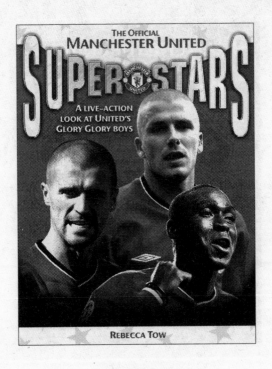

THE OFFICIAL
MANCHESTER UNITED
SUPERSTARS

No young United fan will want to be
without this book. Contains photo portraits
of 28 "Heroes of the Shirt" including David
Beckham, Ryan Giggs and Andrew Cole.

ISBN 0-23305-004-3
£4.99

Available from all good bookshops

MANCHESTER UNITED
OFFICIAL YEARBOOK 2001

Features a fully illustrated match report on
every single game played in the 2000-
2001 season. Also includes statistics,
monthly reports and a season timeline.

ISBN 0-233-99952-3
£9.99

Available from all good bookshops